Forces of Compassion

Publication of the Advanced Seminar Series is made possible by generous support from The Brown Foundation, Inc., of Houston, Texas.

School for Advanced Research
Advanced Seminar Series

James F. Brooks
General Editor

Forces of Compassion

Contributors

Jonathan Benthall
Department of Anthropology, University College London

Erica Bornstein
Department of Anthropology, University of Wisconsin, Milwaukee

Harri Englund
Department of Social Anthropology, Cambridge University

Didier Fassin
School of Social Science, Institute for Advanced Study

Ilana Feldman
Anthropology Department, George Washington University

Sandra Teresa Hyde
Department of Anthropology, McGill University

Mariella Pandolfi
Université de Montréal Département d'anthropologie

Peter Redfield
Department of Anthropology, University of North Carolina, Chapel Hill

Miriam Ticktin
Department of Anthropology, New School for Social Research

Forces of Compassion

Humanitarianism Between Ethics and Politics

Edited by Erica Bornstein and Peter Redfield

School for Advanced Research Press

Santa Fe

School for Advanced Research Press

Post Office Box 2188
Santa Fe, New Mexico 87504-2188
www.sarpress.sarweb.org

Managing Editor: Lisa Pacheco
Editorial Assistant: Ellen Goldberg
Designer and Production Manager: Cynthia Dyer
Manuscript Editor: Cecile Kaufman
Proofreader: Sarah Soliz
Indexer: Catherine Fox
Printer: Cushing Malloy, Inc.

Library of Congress Cataloging-in-Publication Data

Forces of compassion : humanitarianism between ethics and politics / edited by Erica Bornstein and Peter Redfield.
　　p. cm. — (School for advanced research advanced seminar series)
　Includes bibliographical references and index.
　ISBN 978-1-934691-40-3 (alk. paper)
　1. Humanitarian assistance. 2. Humanitarian assistance—Political aspects.
3. Humanitarianism. 4. International relief. I. Bornstein, Erica, 1963–
II. Redfield, Peter, 1965–
　HV553.F59 2010
　361.2'5—dc22
　　　　　　　　　　　　2010045212

♻ This book was printed on paper containing 30% PCR.

Cover illustration: Maxan Jean Louis, *Médecins sans Frontières* (Doctors Without Borders). Acrylic on canvas, 26 x 31 inches. Reproduced by permission from Men Nou Galerie (www.mennouhaiti.com).

Contents

Figures

Tables

Acknowledgments

As volume coeditors, we first salute the seminar participants, who combined intense critical engagement with a remarkable spirit of conviviality. Together we all owe thanks to the School for Advanced Research and its marvelous staff: James Brooks, John Kantner, and Nancy Owen Lewis steered our proposal into reality, while Leslie Shipman and Carla Tozcano kept us fully cosseted and magnificently fed. At SAR, Rebecca Allahyari and Omri Elisha both attended parts of the seminar and contributed to our discussions. In addition, Erica Bornstein would acknowledge the SAR Resident Fellows of 2006–07, and Peter Redfield those of 2007–08, all of whom contributed to the longer conversations surrounding our individual research projects and the collaborative work of this endeavor. We likewise collectively thank the many colleagues and students who read drafts of our evolving introduction and gave us exceedingly helpful responses. At SAR Press, Catherine Cocks saw us through the initial stages of assemblage (and provided an insightful early reading), and Lynn Baca and Lisa Pacheco patiently and cheerfully championed the manuscript to its completion. Two reviewers offered generously detailed and perceptive comments. One of our anonymous reviewers read our manuscript immediately following the Haitian earthquake, inspiring us to add an afterword, assisted by Lawrence Cohen's commentary and reports from Haiti by Laura Wagner. Finally, we express our gratitude to A. Aneesh and Silvia Tomášková, who have endured our obsession with this project during its many years in the making.

Forces of Compassion

1

An Introduction to the Anthropology of Humanitarianism

Peter Redfield and Erica Bornstein

Imagine, for a moment, that during the Spanish sack of Tenochtitlan a team of medics had arrived to treat the wounded, pleading with combatants to spare civilians. Or that television cameras had relentlessly broadcast the aftermath of the great Chinese earthquake of 1556 to concerned audiences worldwide, or that sympathetic peasants in fourteenth-century Japan had launched a campaign to sponsor Italian orphans in the wake of the Black Death. The surrealism of imagining contemporary humanitarian techniques applied to historical events indicates more than dramatic technological transformation; it also suggests limits to contemporary assumptions about common human feeling and associated action. We highlight the temporal specificity of phenomena that now appear "humanitarian" in order to underscore their current moral fervor. What is it about the present, we might wonder, that casts the care of strangers in such a leading role?

Suffering and charity both have long histories. The sorrows of human experience and efforts to alleviate them were amply familiar to previous generations, as world literatures and religious traditions attest. Nonetheless, the final decades of the twentieth century witnessed an emergence of reconfigured forms and norms of both on an international scale. Natural disasters and civilian casualties in war now feature as "humanitarian crises," recurring dramas presented by international media, while an extensive complex of interstate entities and nongovernmental organizations (NGOs) seeks to supply aid to victims. Alongside development and human rights, the humanitarian impulse to alleviate suffering constitutes a central element in international moral discourse, referenced by advocacy groups, states, and military forces alike. The mediated experience of "distant suffering" (Boltanski 1999) features prominently in the discursive production of global sentiment (Tsing 2000). At the same time, efforts to intervene produce both extensive connections and local effects (for example, Leopold 2005; Nordstrom 2004), fueling an aid industry that effectively promotes and reproduces itself (De Waal 1997; Terry 2002).

Although anthropology can claim a long and tormented engagement with development, and similar association with discourses and practices of human rights and environmentalism, the humanitarian sector of the aid world has only recently registered on the disciplinary horizon (see, for example, Fassin and Pandolfi 2010; Feldman and Ticktin 2010; Minn 2007; Saillant 2007; Wilson and Brown 2008). Anthropologists may now be aware of the dynamics of displacement and the significant role that NGOs and advocacy groups play in international governance, particularly amid states of emergency. Nonetheless, they do not always distinguish between humanitarianism and human rights, on the one hand, and humanitarianism and development on the other, conflating what at times may be conflicting claims, allegiances, and temporal assumptions regarding resolutions.[1] Nor do they recognize the comparative range between different sorts of aid organizations, their ideological commitments, and infrastructural practice. In order to clarify such categorical distinctions—as assumed in official reports, or asserted and contested in specific projects—we first differentiate humanitarianism as understood by its professional adherents from other related efforts to "do good" in the world. We then offer several possible genealogies for the present moment, noting both religious and secular traditions of aid and charity. Finally, we review anthropology's engagement with humanitarianism and survey some recent literature relevant to the topic. Throughout, the term "humanitarianism" itself will remain a matter of some contest. Whereas actors in the aid world and most political scientists might stabilize it in their accounts of international affairs, anthropologists cast a wider net through geography and history, remaining attuned to differences in how people claim and define the value of humanity. We ourselves will therefore deploy the term in several ways, seeking both to situate its dominant usage in international aid and to suggest the limitations and tensions of that understanding.

HUMANITARIANISM IN THE AID WORLD

Advocates of humanitarianism, development, and human rights all broadly seek to ameliorate and improve aspects of the human condition. However, amid the contemporary aid world each key term suggests a different emphasis, temporality, and potential mechanism for doing so. Although some organizations embrace multiple mandates, or migrate from one mandate (such as relief) to another (such as development) over time, they also recognize these distinctions when advocating a course of action, planning its execution, and justifying its approach. Even efforts to blend approaches such as "rights-based development" only underscore the assumed divides and failings they seek to overcome. For the larger public on both donating and receiving ends of the aid equation, however, definitional lines generally remain less clear. In addition, political actors can and do appropriate these terms at every level, deploying them in multiple ways. Indeed, as a number of the essays in this volume suggest (for example, Bornstein, Feldman, Pandolfi, Redfield), the expansion or delimitation of categories like humanitarianism can precisely serve instrumental and political ends in given settings. Nonetheless, general distinctions between aid "sectors" remain significant in discourse and practice, and hence are helpful points of reference for analysis. To that end we offer brief capsule descriptions.

Although full of additional connotations, development focuses on the economic end of political economy. The contemporary conception grew out of the era of European colonial empire and crystallized in its Cold War aftermath; once established as a staple of international relations it has refused to fade despite copious criticism. Whether derived from top-down planning or grassroots empowerment, the official language of development commonly filters through statistical and technocratic measures, in which livelihood defines well-being. At its core, development seeks to confront poverty, which is usually identified through material lack. In temporal terms, development discourse is inherently and resolutely progressive; conditions *should* improve, with the promise of an open and potentially infinite future.

By contrast, human rights claims emphasize the political end of political economy, in legal form if not always specific content. Although rights discourse has several lineages (most classically that of European liberal political theory), the founding of the United Nations following the Second World War and its adoption of the Universal Declaration of Human Rights in 1948 marks a nominal watershed. Whether conceived strictly as political liberties, or more inclusively to encompass social and economic concerns, the language of rights is fundamentally legalistic and philosophical: justice defines well-being. At its core, human rights advocacy seeks to confront general wrongs usually identified through specific violations. Where development frames human good through an imagined future, human rights discourse defines its version through past failure.

Humanitarianism, by contrast yet again, emphasizes the physical (and increasingly the psychological) condition of suffering people above all else. Although it has several lineages in charity and beyond, as we shall outline below, its institutionalized form defines itself primarily through exceptional states of misfortune, of which the mid-nineteenth-century founding of the Red Cross in response to war constitutes an oft-cited landmark. Whether motivated by religious faith or secular adherence to human empathy, the language of aid world humanitarianism is both moral and broadly medical, identifying well-being through species-level needs and health. Religiously inflected forms of humanitarianism, such as Mother Teresa's charitable order, Mahayana Buddhist humanitarian movements, Islamic *zakat*, and Hindu *dān* (all of which we will address in greater detail below), focus on the care of the soul or spiritual duties through the material world. Hence they differ in orientation from the life-saving norm of international aid, which at its core seeks to confront immediate suffering, usually understood as bodily or psychological anguish. In temporal terms this secular, contemporary strand of humanitarianism remains inherently presentist; the lives and welfare of those now living fundamentally matter and cannot be conscionably sacrificed in the pursuit of other goals.

In an even more crude heuristic, we might divide the aid world by professional expertise, noting that economists long played a lead role in development, that lawyers established a subspecialty in human rights, and that doctors and nurses have deep ties to humanitarianism. That said we would need to qualify such a suggestion immediately. Not only does humanitarian aid comprise a significant economic activity in many settings (whether or not calculated in terms of profit), but the Geneva Conventions hold a significant place in international legal tradition. Moreover, beyond the artificial preserve of aid professionals, humanitarianism's resemblance to religious charity and military action suggests alternative professions, from mission priest to quartermaster. Thus we ultimately find it most useful to think of these distinctions as historical orientations, trajectories, and tendencies rather than categorical certainties, focusing on when and how they appear in practice. At the same time, we emphasize again the tendency of contemporary humanitarian actors to focus on the immediate needs of living humans in distress. Amid the aid world's landscape of good works, such tasks as advocating reparations for dead victims or planning the happiness of future generations usually fall to others.

RELIGIOUS AND SECULAR CONCEPTIONS OF SUFFERING

Much writing on humanitarianism assumes the current framework of nation-states and international organizations, and thus presumes a secular division between politics and religion (see Barnett and Weiss 2008 for an excellent recent compilation). As anthropologists we seek to orient this project around a wider geography and a deeper history. Although the chapters that follow focus largely on contemporary experience, our discussions reference contours and limits to contemporary humanitarian concern for suffering and the ethical force of "care" (Wilson and Brown 2008; Tronto 1993). To better situate these structures of moral feeling, we briefly shift attention in the direction of comparative religious history.

States of suffering have long played a significant role in many strands of religious tradition. Most generally and superficially, we might note that religious practice has offered solace in response to moments of misfortune, whether in the form of small rituals of mourning or the construction of elaborate theological accounts of misery. Interpreting suffering as spiritual disequilibrium, a sign of divine displeasure, or the result of a greater Manichean struggle allows those who are afflicted the possibility of cosmological explanation, if not immediate relief. More directly and provocatively, we might also note that suffering at times offers the possibility of purification and the transcendence of bodily states. Thus coming-of-age ceremonies worldwide often feature forms of deprivation such as fasting, monastic orders from Buddhism to Christianity and Hinduism withdraw from the world to seek a more spiritual life, and the tribulations and sacrifices of Catholic martyrs and saints render their lives exemplary. As Talal Asad observes in reference to torture, physical pain has a proud pedigree in religious festivals (Asad 2003; see also Faubion 2003). However abhorrent pain might now appear in official forums of international law—which ensure the bodily comfort of even the most egregious offenders in trials and imprisonment—the longer profile of suffering in religious history has been as much that of a productive force as of a negative condition, inspiring both contemplation and action.

For our purposes we will focus on religious responses to suffering that have taken a this-worldly focus in the form of charity, ministration, and care, as well as different understandings of the gift. Acts of mercy may indeed represent something of a panhuman heritage, as the Red Cross museum in Geneva makes a valiant effort to suggest (ICRC 2000; see also Isaac 1993). Institutional interest in the needs of strangers appears more novel, however, and historically variable (Ignatieff 1984). World religious traditions have certainly featured provisions for charitable action, ranging from Buddhist doctrines of compassion, Jewish *tzedakah* and *tikkun olam*, Christian alms, and Islamic zakat, to Hindu *seva* and dān. However, these examples differ not only from the dominant assumptions of the contemporary aid world, but also from each other. Before outlining the background of dominant secular assumptions, therefore, we will first examine comparative religious understandings of the act of giving in greater detail. Although many religious groups claim ancient scriptural heritage for the contemporary humanitarian imperatives of their members, as anthropologists we emphasize the significance of historical context and caution against treating any tradition as timeless.

In his classic essay, *The Gift* (1990), Marcel Mauss highlighted the role of giving in maintaining social and moral order. He argued that as a collective action performed by groups, giving involves social contracts and reciprocity. Noting that the Arabic and Hebrew terms for "alms" derive from the word for "justice," Mauss (1990:15–16) drew an explicit linguistic tie between gifts and a larger moral field. Giving, he argued, has less to do with utility and the circulation of goods than with a type of social solidarity. It is through the exchange of gifts that individuals are connected to a larger society and hierarchy is established. Since this classic work, an extensive literature on the gift has emerged, including significant elaborations, inversions, and critiques of Mauss's analysis (for example, Bataille 1989; Derrida 1992; Godelier 1999; Gregory 1982; Laidlaw 2000; Parry 1986, 1989, 1994; Raheja 1988; Schrift 1997; Strathern 1988; Weiner 1992). Nonetheless, the original insight that the act of giving mobilizes a distinctively moral category of person remains highly relevant to the topic of suffering.

Salvational religions define giving as a sacred act with other-worldly incentives (Weber 1946a, 1993). In Islam, zakat is a religious duty in which the practice of almsgiving purifies the giver (Baeck 1991; Benthall 1999). The Islamic injunction for charitable giving has found institutionalized form in Islamic charities (Benthall and Bellion-Jourdan 2009) just as the Christian injunction for "good works" has produced Christian missions (Bornstein 2005; Bowie, Kirkwood, and Ardener 1993; McCarthy 1990; Tucker 1988). Religious giving explicitly demarcates boundaries between sacred practice and its profane alternative—the dangerous failure to recognize moral obligation. The injunction to engage in religious giving speaks to what will happen, whether in this world or the next, if one does *not* give, and challenges one's status as a properly virtuous person.

Within this shared understanding of the potential moral value of gifts, however, lie significant differences. In some traditions of religious giving, the worthiness of a particular recipient or group is an important consideration. For example, in the messianic religion of Judaism, it is the suffering of a *community* rather than the suffering of individuals that offers the hope for religious salvation (see Weber 1946b for a comparative account of approaches to suffering and injustice).[2] As Benthall (1999, this volume) notes for Islam in the case of zakat granted to "the poor," the Qur'an specifies the appropriate qualities of those who should receive it. Beyond the destitute, this scriptural injunction includes the administrators of alms, as well as potential converts and those who might further the cause of Islam. In the case of Hinduism, sacred writings such as the Manu Smriti (the Laws of Manu) and the Bhagavad Gita dictate worthy recipients of dān as well as appropriate contexts for giving (Heim 2004). Given that the relative purity (or impurity, as the case may be) of the recipient reflects back upon the merit of the giver, scriptural Hindu dān directs giving to specific types of people, such as Brahmin priests and world renouncers. Contemporary forms of zakat and dān may model themselves more along the lines of secular humanitarianism, as Benthall and Bornstein suggest in this volume. Nonetheless, the moral logic of both Islamic and Hindu traditions identifies appropriate recipients of aid by other criteria than simple suffering. Not just any human will do.

The study of traditions of Islamic zakat and Hindu dān de-center other basic assumptions surrounding aid world versions of humanitarianism, including the liberal emphasis on individual choice and the modernist focus on the present. Benthall and Bellion-Jourdan's work on zakat (2009; also see Benthall 1999) demonstrates how this form of giving itself constitutes a form of worship. Zakat is a social and religious duty—not an individual moral choice. As religiously structured action in some cases, it can take the form of literal taxation, collected by a religious state. In other cases, specific zakat committees structured as nongovernmental organizations provide for the welfare and emergency relief of specific local communities. Although Hindu dān, similarly, may now manifest itself in the form of NGOs receiving donations, it remains articulated as a duty of charitable assistance, offered without any expectation of benefit or return (Bornstein 2009). The examples of zakat and dān offer radical contrasts to forms of religious humanitarianism that focus on a universal moral "self" and its transformation. Hindu charitable dān, moreover, challenges the presentist, this-life focus of secular humanitarianism by emphasizing karma and the desire to be released from a repeating cycle of rebirth. In contrast to the problem-solving emphasis of most aid-world fund-raising, many who give dān speak explicitly of attaining merit toward their next life.

In addition—as highlighted by the case of Islamic zakat—religious giving does not necessarily aim to be neutral or even worldly at all. The post–September 11 denunciation of Islamic charities as inappropriately "interested" in political and spiritual terms (Benthall and Bellion-Jourdan 2009; Benthall, this volume) only reinforces the point that classic humanitarian concepts like neutrality and impartiality derive from a particularly secular political history (Redfield, this volume). There is, of course, a potential rhetorical double standard in play when some strategic giving to promote alliances—such as the military "interests" of Islamic charities—counts as terrorism, while other strategic giving—such as the charitable activities of Western military forces—counts as humanitarianism. But the point we want to emphasize here is that a case of social and relational assistance, such as the care of fellow Muslims, differs both from a generalized care of strangers (Sontag 2003 and Boltanski 1999) and from the neutral, impartial ideals of secular humanitarianism as advocated by the UN.[3]

Christianity, by contrast, makes fewer distinctions between worthy recipients at a scriptural level. The concept of "brotherly love" and the parable of the Good Samaritan are models for Christian giving in which all in need equally deserve care. Since all human beings can potentially be saved spiritually, they can also potentially be rescued through worldly action. Actual Christian behavior in response to this precept has obviously varied vastly through time. Nonetheless, the framing of the gift as an expansive expression of love resonates with the egalitarian sensibility of the aid world, even as it differs from its sense of self and care. The figure of Mother Teresa, a Catholic missionary who started her charitable order in India, offers an example of this religious tradition in contemporary practice.

Mother Teresa is both an icon of saintly Christian charity and a Nobel Prize–winning humanitarian. She has also been the subject of substantial critique from secular intellectuals for valorizing poverty while not attempting to change the structural conditions that produce it (Hitchens 1995; Prashad 1997) and for being part of bourgeois philanthropic ideology that, as Prashad argues, acts as the "mirror of bourgeois guilt." At the same time her aim of saving souls rather than lives has engendered criticism from secular humanitarians. Although the cosmological intent of humanitarianism inspired by the work of Mother Teresa addresses suffering in the moment, it is not oriented toward a presentist conception of life as is, say, the work of a medical organization like Médecins Sans Frontières (MSF) (Redfield 2005). To her critics, the sources of Mother Teresa's funding for the Missionaries of Charity (including dictators and wealthy criminals) as well as the use of the funds (medical care without medical training) suggest further grounds for hypocrisy. While these objections reveal aspects of the global context in which humanitarianism takes place, they also miss an essential element of this form of humanitarian practice. Religion designates more than ideological commitment here; it is also a specific habitus of the gift (see Bourdieu 1977).

As we outline below, Christianity played a particular role in the emergence of both the aid world and the secular order of institutions that surround it. While seeking to broaden the frame of reference for discussions of "faith-based humanitarian action" and to signal the significant distinctions between traditions, as well their differences from the secular universe of state-centered aid, we must also emphasize that these religious alternatives are hardly simple survivals of local tradition. Rather, the forms of belief involved in humanitarianism (Christianity, Islam, Hinduism, Judaism, and Mahayana Buddhism) are "world" religions with long histories and ever-evolving networks. Although the activities of religious-based humanitarian organizations may exist below the radar of state-level accounting, they frequently operate at their own expansive scale.

The Mata Amritanandamayi Mission, for example, is a transnational Hindu spiritual organization supporting the work of a guru named Amma whose "self-professed mission on earth is to alleviate the sorrows of humankind" (Warrier 2006:181, 2003). She is known for her particular style of interacting with her devotees, hugging each devotee individually and offering miracles and advice for personal needs. Like Mother Teresa, Amma attempts to alleviate and attend to humanity's everyday suffering, but in contrast to Mother Teresa her work embraces improvement and progress. To that end she has established schools, hospitals, and orphanages, as well as sponsored disaster relief, free food and clothing programs, and pensions for abandoned women and widows. The resulting institutional imprint is significant (an Indian newspaper claimed Amma's income to be around eighty million dollars in 2006), and she has mobilized tens of thousands of volunteers.[4] However, the best known calculation of Amma's impact comes in the form of personal interaction: over twenty-six million hugs, counted on a clicker as a testimonial to the number of people seeking her assistance.[5]

Devotee-driven forms of transnational humanitarianism can also adopt the more conventional techniques and institutional contours of an NGO. For example, the Buddhist Compassion Relief Tzu-Chi Foundation, a Mahayana Buddhist lay movement comprised of devotees running global outreach programs, emphasizes building a "pure land" in this world through the secular action of concrete contributions to humanity (see Huang 2005). Founded in 1966 by a nun and a group of housewife devotees, the group's initial goal was to defray medical costs for the poor through daily donations. In the first year, monthly charity funds came to less than US$30, but three decades later, Compassion Relief had five million members worldwide, with branches in twenty-eight countries, and gave away over US$157 million annually. The group runs a TV channel, a secular four-year university with a standard medical school, and two "state-of-the-Western-art 900 bed hospitals" (Huang 2005:187).[6]

Even when religious organizations surrounding the activities of charismatic leaders like the Mata Amritanandamayi Mission or Mother Teresa's Sisters of Charity inhabit recognizable institutional forms of the aid world, however, they do so uneasily. Much of the voluntarism in these types of devotee-institutions remains undocumented and uncalculated, since devotees and volunteers of these organizations are itinerant, informal humanitarians beyond the framework of government regulation. This can lead to tensions with state authorities, all the more when religious organizations respond to humanitarian emergencies in highly charged political environments or fill gaps of responsibility for the social welfare of citizens (cf. Bornstein 2005, 2009). Lay religious movements can either legitimize or become an opposition to oppressive state regimes when they blur the artificial line between humanitarianism and human rights (see Jordt 2007, for case of Buddhist monks in Burma).[7]

Accounts of humanitarianism, as we suggest below, usually assume a more secular focus in the frame of global politics (Minear 2002; Nichols and Loescher 1989; Nichols 1988; Weiss and Collins 1996). A faith in fundamental human equality plays a central role in this secular discourse, often appearing in tandem with efforts to spread democracy. Although actual practice often demands distinctions regarding who is most "in need" of humanitarian assistance, such decisions are inherently controversial (see Fassin 2007a and this volume on hierarchies of humanity; and Redfield 2008a on triage and sacrifice). Measures of lives saved or lives lost presume an ethical ideal of equality, echoing Christian ideas of brotherly love. They also recall the legacy of the Christian pastorate, which defined leadership through the care of a good shepherd who preserved the flock (Foucault 2000, 2007).

Secular humanitarianism likewise resonates with salvational narratives of rescue. However, in contrast to the legacy of Mother Teresa, the aid world redefines its worthy recipient in terms of a this-worldly, present conception of need. The growth of secularism and its temporal relation with internationalism (see Calhoun 2008) is evident in contexts where NGOs present themselves as helping all people rather than a particular group. Secular humanitarianism thus defines a new population: needy victims. Yet, as with forms of religious charity that specify the conditions of a worthy recipient, "need" likewise requires evaluation and confirmation, being weighed in a moral balance that abhors any suggestion of fraud or corruption. Secular neoliberal subjects are responsible selves, capable of their own development (Pandolfi 2008b; Englund 2006; Bornstein 2007a). Those who do not demonstrate the proper will to improve are morally suspect. Similarly, situations that fail to respond to repeated interventions provoke talk of "compassion fatigue." To follow such shifts in moral feeling from charity to philanthropy and humanitarianism we must first examine not only how pity entered politics (see Boltanski 1999; Arendt 1963), but also how humanistic feeling inspired moral fervor and forms of direct aid.

THE BIRTH OF HUMANITARIAN AID

Alongside centuries of colonial violence, European expansion also inspired counter-arguments about the moral significance of common human feeling. Following the conquest of what Europe considered a "New World," the Spanish priest Bartolomé de las Casas wrote *A Brief Account of the Destruction of the Indies* (1552), decrying atrocities committed against native peoples and emphasizing their humanity as potential Christians.[8] A few decades later the French author Michel de Montaigne penned his famous essay "On Cannibals" (1580), suggesting the need for comparative perspective when denouncing acts of savagery. When viewed from the present, such works appear ancestral to a broad complex of cosmopolitan humanisms, as well as the related assumption that even unfamiliar peoples and their lives might hold equal worth to one's own kin.

Contemporary humanitarianism, as described and understood in the aid world, has its most obvious roots in European experience from the eighteenth century onward. Here we will briefly cite four critical junctures that appear in the literature. Two are events—the formation of the Red Cross in 1863 and the response to the Lisbon earthquake in 1755—and two are longer historical shifts—the movement to abolish slavery and the efforts of administrators and missionaries to care for colonial populations. Navigating between them suggests ties both to specific historical events and to the larger trajectories of Enlightenment rationality, secularism, capitalism, and colonialism.

13

As mentioned above, one canonical landmark for humanitarian norms within international affairs is the emergence of the Red Cross movement and the subsequent adoption of the initial Geneva Conventions. Although Henry Dunant was but one of a wave of reformers horrified by the effects of modern warfare and lack of provision for the wounded, the publication in 1862 of his account of the battle of Solferino (Dunant 1986) prompted a distinctively international, as well as national, response. A deeply religious man, Dunant appealed openly to Christian sentiment and inspired a pragmatic attempt to "civilize" warfare. Once embraced by the sovereign powers of Europe, the movement spawned a complex of national Red Cross societies to provide aid, as well as an "international committee" (the ICRC, International Committee of the Red Cross) that strove to establish appropriate rules and monitor compliance (Hutchinson 1996; Moorehead 1998). Initially limited to the care of wounded soldiers, the scope of the organization's purview expanded to include sailors, prisoners, and civilians and responses to natural disaster. Although not, strictly speaking, a "nongovernmental organization,"[9] the ICRC figures prominently in the world system that NGOs would later help create (Boli and Thomas 1999).

The emergence of the Red Cross does serve as a convenient watershed and underscores the extent to which contemporary humanitarianism has been entangled with warfare and addressed legal states of exception. Certainly the combination of mechanized weaponry and conscript citizen armies with war correspondence and photography suggests a dramatic new template for regarding "the pain of others" (for example, Sontag 2003). Moreover, war is the classic edge of law, the moment in which norms can be altered or suspended (Agamben 2005). The effort of the Geneva Conventions to constrain its brutal effects clearly represents an effort to curtail the exercise of sovereign power by proposing "humane" limits and responsibilities. At the same time, however, the very convenience of this marker and the frequency of its citation risks exaggerating its historical significance. Neither the Red Cross nor the Geneva Conventions were the only expressions of humanitarian sentiment during the nineteenth century, and neither played a significant role in the colonized world until well into the twentieth. Moreover, the very symbol of a red cross used by the organization, and its presumed religious connotations, became a source of lasting controversy (Benthall 1997). And finally, the initial actions that inspired the Red Cross focused on easing death alongside saving life. "I spoke to him," Dunant wrote of a particular stricken soldier, "and he listened. He allowed himself to be soothed, comforted and consoled, to die at last with the straightforward simplicity of a child" (Dunant 1986:66).

Washing wounds and bringing solace to the dying, the Genevan business-man was as much a part of Christian lay charity as any secular, professional humanitarian tradition.

Another commonly cited formative moment in intellectual history is the dramatic Lisbon earthquake of 1755, news of which circulated across the continent and incited commentary from figures like Kant, Voltaire, and Rousseau. The event thus foreshadows the contemporary form of dis-aster, in which sudden rupture acquires enlarged significance through media representation and affects people well beyond its immediate reach. Reactions to the catastrophe varied widely, but left an imprint on the European history of ideas; Lisbon both inspired Kant to study seismology and likely shaped subsequent aesthetic and philosophical debates about the sublime (Ray 2004). The earthquake further featured in Voltaire's rejec-tion of theological optimism, one landmark in moral claims to Enlighten-ment reason. Rather than reconciling himself to the existence of evil and tragedy as part of a larger divine plan, the French satirist began to ridicule any suggestion that "all is well" or that this might be "the best of all possi-ble worlds." Finally, Voltaire's poem about the disaster also prompted a response from Rousseau, in which he noted the artificiality of "natural" dis-aster, created as much by urban crowding and hazardous construction as by geological instability. Such analysis, as Russell Dynes (2000) suggests, pre-figured that of later social science, in which events—even those of the most exceptional nature—are understood in relation to worldly experience rather than religious tradition or scriptural authority. Choosing this histor-ical moment as a foundation risks simply reproducing the linear self-nar-rative of Enlightenment history, as well as suggesting that elite ideas represent (or shape) popular sentiment. Nonetheless, it does suggest the possibility of catastrophe as both a moral sublime and a humanist justifica-tion for action, in social fact if not transcendent value.

Avoiding the seductions of a single event, we could focus on a more complex pattern of emergence around the international movement to abol-ish chattel slavery. As Craig Calhoun (2008) notes, the term "humanitarian" itself dates from the early nineteenth century, used first to describe a theo-logical position stressing the humanity of Christ, and subsequently efforts to alleviate suffering or advance the human race in general.[10] In this under-standing, instances of disaster or war were not necessary for action, and a feeling of kinship could extend across national and even colonial differ-ences. The most dramatic historical example of such humanitarian senti-ment is undoubtedly the long struggle of abolition (Hochschild 2005; Haskell 1995). Although the significance of the antislavery movement remains the subject of heated historical debate (for example, Bender 1992), for our purposes we might simply recognize both a connection to transformations in the wider political economy, and to shifting sensibilities about pain and suffering. The eventual abandonment of plantation slavery occurs amid the rise of industrial capital, new forms of labor, a wider wave of gradual reforms altering the practice of punishment and the treatment of animals, as well as the decline of blood sports as a form of entertainment (Foucault 2000; Elias 1978). The abolition movement is as much an ancestor to contemporary human rights discourse and political advocacy movements as to humanitarianism. Choosing this historical movement as a foundation therefore might blur as much as it distinguishes. Nonetheless, it does suggest the emergence and spread of a normative moral sentiment about the human amid the violence of market exchange, emphasizing bodily integrity as well as liberty.

We could also consider another broad historical pattern: the adoption of welfare provisions amid colonial rule, particularly the spread of missionary forms of medicine and the development of systematized famine response. Beyond attempting to extract resources from colonies, European empires also fitfully fostered civilizing projects to remake and reform their colonial subjects and landscapes. By the middle of the nineteenth century, medicine became a popular component of missionary work in Africa, and what medical infrastructure emerged on that continent grew largely out of religious activity (Comaroff and Comaroff 1997; Vaughn 1991). The figure of the saintly health worker, exemplified by Albert Schweitzer, would continue to play a significant role in the later colonial period. Conversely, state action and planning became a central focus in curbing famine in Asia and a matter of political dispute in British India (Davis 2001; Sharma 2001). Benevolent governance, meanwhile, emerged as a core principle of British colonial administrative policy in Africa (Lugard 1965; Gott 2002). By the twentieth century relieving hunger had become an administrative responsibility and starving masses elsewhere a moral concern (De Waal 1997; Vernon 2007). Whether condoning or condemning the motives and actors involved, this antecedent activity offers an obvious potential parallel for contemporary forms of international humanitarianism, one recalled by references to development and aid workers as the "new missionaries" (for example, Bornstein 2005; Manjhi and O'Coill 2002) and by media portrayals of hunger.

Whichever of these lineages we might favor and foreground, they all converge in the sensibility that perceives suffering as a preventable tragedy,

TABLE 1.1
Governmental Humanitarian Aid 2006 (Officially Designated)[1]

Donor	US$ million	Percentage
European Community & EU States (combined)	4327	50
US	3022	35
Norway	380	5
Canada	278	3
Japan	199	2
Australia	198	2
Switzerland	196	2
New Zealand	26	0.3

Recipient	US$ million	Percentage
Sudan	1201	18
Palestine	701	10
Indonesia	367	5
Lebanon	346	5
Ethiopia	314	5
Afghanistan	296	4
Somalia	275	4
Uganda	214	3
Kenya	202	3
Iraq	151	2
Burundi	136	2
179 Others	1956	29

1. Although this project does not focus on the political economy of aid, and some of the phenomena we mention here escape formal accounting, these tables offer a fiscal snapshot from one given year. Not all organizations report their budgets in identical terms or currencies, necessitating translation and conversion. The figures in Table 1.1 derive from the Development Initiatives report *Global Humanitarian Assistance*, 2007–08, p. 11. http://www.globalhumanitarianassistance.org/analyses-and-reports/gha-reports/gha-2007. This report estimates officially designated humanitarian aid from donors to have been in the order of US$9.2 billion in 2006 (about 9 percent of all aid), with an unofficial total of humanitarian assistance from all sources at 14.2 billion. To put this in perspective, the Stockholm International Peace Research Institute estimated military spending in 2006 at 1204 billion dollars. http://www.sipri.org/yearbook/2007/2008.

demanding a direct response. Humanitarianism in this sense is several things at once: a structure of feeling, a cluster of moral principles, a basis for ethical claims and political strategies, and a call for action. Although the contemporary form is certainly worldly, and often posed as a secular good, it evokes religious categories and legacies of the sacred. Moreover, in both nominal and operational terms it defines itself around the collective

TABLE 1.2

Selected Intergovernmental Agencies[1]

Agency	Year Established	Affiliation	2006 Budget Expenditure (US$ millions)
United Nations Children's Fund (UNICEF)	1946	UN	2343
World Health Organization (WHO)	1948	UN	3313
United Nations High Commission for Refugees (UNCHR)	1950	UN	1145
World Food Program (WFP)	1961	UN	2900
United Nations Office for the Coordination of Humanitarian Affairs (UNOCHA)	1991	UN	128.5
European Commission's Humanitarian Aid Office (ECHO)	1992	EU	1156

1. The figures in Table 1.2 derive from agency annual reports, as well as the Global Humanitarian Assistance report cited above; also see MSF (2007) and Aall, Miltenberger, and Weiss (2000). Our list is far from comprehensive; we provide it only to give a rough comparative sense of size and capacity between different organizations, state and nonstate, religious and secular. When more than one figure is available we have opted for the expenditure in the fiscal year noted. The number for the WHO is that of their 2006–07 budget cycle.

figure of the human, measured through basic needs and dignity. However stabilized in conceptual and rhetorical terms, this figure proves less stable in practice.

The institutional apparatus that composes the contemporary aid industry largely emerged over the second half of the twentieth century (see Tables 1.1, 1.2, and 1.3). Although forerunners like the ICRC and Save the Children have longer histories, the founding of the United Nations in the aftermath of the Second World War (as well as other entities of international governance like the World Bank) marks a clear watershed for humanitarianism as well as development and human rights discourse. Not only did the UN itself gradually burgeon into an ensemble of agencies, but internationally focused relief agencies also expanded as colonization receded, part of an exponential wave of NGOs that gave the acronym currency. Often founded in response to a particular crisis or concern, they expanded their ambitions over time. Despite this remarkable growth, and

TABLE 1.3

Selected Proto-NGOs and NGOs' Annual Expenditures[1]

Organization	Year Established	Country of Origin	2006 Budget Expenditure (US$ millions)
International Committee of the Red Cross (ICRC)	1863	Switzerland	771
The Salvation Army (US branch)	1865	Britain	2996
American Red Cross	1881	United States	5628
Jewish Joint Distribution Committee (JDC)	1914	United States	224
American Friends Service Committee (AFSC)	1917	United States	43
Save the Children International	1919	Britain	863
OXFAM International (originally Oxford Famine Relief Committee)	1942	Britain	638
International Rescue Committee (IRC)	1942	United States	211
Catholic Relief Services	1943	United States	561
Lutheran World Relief	1945	United States	34
CARE (originally Cooperative for American Remittances to Europe)	1945	United States	645
World Vision	1950	United States	2104
World Council of Churches	1948	International/ Switzerland	38
African Medical and Research Foundation (AMREF)	1957	International/US	44
Concern Worldwide	1968	Ireland	160
Médecins Sans Frontières/Doctors Without Borders (MSF)	1971	France	703
Action Contre La Faim /Action Against Hunger (ACF)	1979	France	125
Médecins du Monde/Doctors of the World (MDM)	1980	France	180
International Medical Corps (IMC)	1984	United States	116
Islamic Relief Worldwide	1984	Britain	77
American Jewish World Service	1985	United States	25
Partners in Health	1987	United States	30

1. The figures in Table 1.3 derive from the annual reports of organizations; also see MSF (2007) and Aall, Miltenberger, and Weiss (2000) and note for Table 1.1 above for qualifications. The organizations in this list also sponsor a range of diverse activities, and some, for example, the Salvation Army and the Jewish Joint Distribution Committee (JDC), maintain a strong religious focus (the JDC lists only 2.5 percent of their expenditure as nonsectarian). In addition we must reiterate that while these figures fluctuate annually, they generally trend upward, sometimes dramatically in response to major events like the South Asian tsunami. For a more quantitative perspective see Focus Report 2009—Public Support for Humanitarian Crises through NGOs (also posted at http://www.globalhumanitarianassistance.org/reports), which estimates that in 2006 NGOs collectively contributed some 40 percent of humanitarian aid, and that more than half of their share derived from public donations.

the economic gravity of Europe and North America within it, describing the new aid formation literally as a colonial substitute overstates its capacity. Although varying significantly in size and capacity (a few approach or even surpass UN agencies in financial terms), no international NGO can match the reach of a powerful state. Even as the humanitarian collective remains dwarfed by conventional military expenditure, its loose assemblage of affiliations and associations also lacks the centralized coordination of a modern fighting force, let alone a state or empire.

The postwar humanitarian turn was not just a question of institutional apparatus and material capacity. The period also saw the emergence of key conceptual elements of the aid world. As Paul Rabinow (1999:103) notes, by the founding of the UN, "dignity" had come to designate an essential component of human existence, rather than an attribute of reason or character. Dignity would continue to play a central role in documents and claims related to human rights and ethics and would serve as the primary supplement to physical well-being in humanitarian discourse.[11] Similarly, the new legal category of "genocide" and the historical referent of the Holocaust suggested that human populations and their potential suffering had intrinsic moral standing (see, for example, Hinton 2002). The full adoption of genocide as a lodestone for the international moral compass may have only occurred a generation later (Rabinow 2003:22; Ignatieff 1999:315). Nonetheless, the UN Convention on the Prevention and Punishment of the Crime of Genocide (1948) effectively assigned ordinary human lives equal value and inscribed them as a secular good within the emerging norms of international governance.

ANTHROPOLOGY AND HUMANITARIANISM

As Didier Fassin notes (this volume) humanitarianism is an uncomfortably intimate topic for anthropology. Not only does the discipline's intellectual coherence demand a fundamental recognition of humanity in some general form, but its institutional lineage also includes ties to the abolition movement and nineteenth-century philanthropy (Hiatt 1996). Compassion and empathy remain key values claimed by anthropologists in their representation of other humans across cultural difference. Moreover, anthropologists frequently make ethical and political claims in relation to human suffering and (knowingly or not) draw on humanitarian tropes when doing so. Within the world of secular value assumed by much anthropological writing, moral urgency often stems from threats to life and health. The prominence of the physician and anthropologist Paul Farmer as an exemplary figure attests to the allure of medical care beyond specific religious influences (Farmer 2003; Kidder 2003). Even moments of extreme professional dispute and vitriol can yield a remarkable convergence on the need to protect the well-being of specified others, for example the Yanomami controversy (Borofsky 2005). At the same time, most anthropologists remain intellectually and methodologically committed to the particularity of human experience and uncomfortable with universal claims of humanity. In addition, anthropologists are often of two minds when it comes to "doing good" (Fisher 1997) and more comfortable with the stance of critique than that of endorsement. The pronouncements and actions of international agencies and organizations seeking to pursue humanitarian goals on a global scale, therefore, provoke anxiety and mixed reactions that parallel the discipline's vexed relations with development and human rights (Ferguson 1997; Riles 2006).

In 1985 the Royal Anthropological Institute published an inaugural issue of a revamped newsletter entitled *Anthropology Today*. Attuned to the Live Aid era of Ethiopian famine response, it included a brief report surveying work on disasters since the founding of a small concern called the International Disaster Institute in 1979 (D'Souza 1985). Anthropologists not only had a natural interest in famine, the author, Frances D'Souza, suggested, but actually had generated some relevant research on social responses to it. Sadly, however, relief agencies and planners ignored longer term analysis, responding only to the immediacy of media reports of crisis and resulting political pressure. The report's assumptions about the potential benefits of social and cultural knowledge typify earlier work relating anthropology and humanitarianism: in a better world anthropologists might function as local experts and advisers. Over the ensuing decades, anthropologists would remain interested in disasters such as famine, social rupture, and displacement, and an increasing number worked as aid professionals. Their analytic lens, however, would widen beyond normative studies of affected populations to encompass both media representation and forms of aid response such as refugee camps (for example, Benthall 2010; De Waal 1997; Malkki 1995, 1996). Perceiving a reconfiguration of geopolitics after the Cold War, social science in general focused on more "global" phenomena, and new entities appeared such as the Center for Civil Society Studies at Johns Hopkins University and the International Society for Third Sector Research. Anthropologists were no exception to these trends. As ethnographic research sought to track more mobile and dispersed phenomena associated with globalization, it grew multisited (Marcus 1995; see also Inda and Rosaldo 2001; Rabinow 2003). It also began to include studies of nongovernmental organizations (for example,

Bornstein 2005; see Markowitz 2001 for review). Combined with accounts by reflective practitioners and other social scientists (for example, Barnett 2002; Keck and Sikkink 1998; Hyndman 2000), such studies helped introduce elements of the world aid system into anthropology's field of vision.

Two other interrelated factors also merit attention. First, anthropology not only developed a large applied sector over the second half of the twentieth century, but concerns for political relevance and ethical responsibility have motivated some academic anthropologists to seek a more "activist" role (for example, Hale 2006). Following the generational wave of attention to colonialism and forms of inequality, signs of political and moral commitment arguably became located in professional topics as well as personal sentiment. Anthropologists are thus now predisposed to engage in human rights struggles and truth and reconciliation commissions at more than one level and in more than one way. Moreover, the effects of both social rupture and humanitarian action have become increasingly unavoidable in many of the contexts within which anthropologists work. Topics such as violence and genocide, as well as recent crises like the Indian Ocean tsunami, appear as reference points in academic literature, alongside heightened unease over professional ethics, including recent debates over the involvement of anthropologists in military engagements and militarized forms of aid (for example, Gusterson 2007).

Several strands of anthropological literature frame discussions of humanitarianism. One returns to the classic interest in the gift outlined above, along with the social analysis of generosity and suffering. Unlike evolutionary accounts of altruism, which puzzle over instances of an individual or a species taking advantage of apparent acts of kindness, such work concerns itself more with the erasure of historical difference in claims of human universality. Given that discourses surrounding international conflicts and disasters regularly appeal to categories of the human, this pluralist legacy remains vital to any contribution anthropology might make on the topic.

A second line of literature focuses on exceptional states, and the growing ethnographic attention to disaster, conflict, and displacement. Drawing less on the comparative study of catastrophe or risk per se (as with Hoffman and Oliver-Smith 2002 or even Lakoff 2010) than on the philosophical legacy of figures like Walter Benjamin and Hannah Arendt, such work argues that moments of rupture are central to the contemporary legal-political order and its claims to "humanity." Given US foreign policy in the wake of September 11 and the ensuing emphasis on security and preparedness (see Lakoff 2007), the topic of legal exception has grown newly current, and the trend toward militarized forms of aid (Duffield 2001) all the more apparent. Moreover, following a distinction within the category of "life" made by Arendt (1998), and subsequently enlarged by Giorgio Agamben (1998), states of minimal existence increasingly characterize the fate of exceptional categories of people. Without necessarily accepting such theoretical claims in their entirety, anthropologists have found them generative for thinking about humanitarian practice. Thus a response to natural disaster could function as a moment of national political theology in Venezuela (Fassin and Vasquez 2005), even as the aid apparatus could appear to exert a form of "mobile sovereignty" in settings like Kosovo (Pandolfi 2000, 2003, also see this volume). Thus an international NGO with French roots could strive to preserve "life in crisis" worldwide (Redfield 2005, 2006), even as immigrants in France begin to make their claims to amnesty by appealing to humanitarian medical need rather than refugee status (Ticktin 2006b).

Current anthropological interest in the political status of life derives from the broad influence of Michel Foucault's (2003) concept of "biopower," from the emergence of new technologies and interventions in the biosciences (Franklin and Lock 2003), and from the discipline's greater engagement with medical topics. If "life itself" has emerged as a central component of liberal politics (Rose 2007), then we might talk about citizenship in biological terms, particularly in the wake of a catastrophe like Chernobyl when social welfare follows medical diagnosis (Petryna 2002). By extension, in a context where access to AIDS drugs means life, we might speak of "therapeutic citizenship" (Nguyen 2005) at the intersection of aid agencies and global pharmaceutical distribution (Petryna, Lakoff, and Kleinman 2006). Medical anthropology's concern for conceiving of suffering in social terms (Kleinman, Das, and Lock 1997) has produced both indictments of "structural violence" produced by the global political economy and calls for social justice (Farmer 2003; Kim et al. 2000), and concern about the figure of the "suffering stranger" that such calls deploy (Butt 2002). Studies of the HIV/AIDS pandemic in key contexts such as Brazil, South Africa, and China (Biehl 2007; Fassin 2007b; Hyde 2007) have reconfigured thinking about health and complex new relations between bodies, states, and the wider field of "nongovernmental" politics (Abélès 2010; Feher, Krikorian, and McKee 2007; Ferguson 2002). At the same time studies of organ transplants have further revealed the degree of fragmentation and circulation now affecting human bodies, as well as the complicated ethical fields evoked around gifts, commodities, and lives (Cohen 1999, 2004b; Lock 2002; Scheper-Hughes 2005). In a parallel manner humanitarian aid has performed its own selective transplantation, putting standardized equipment and models for intervention into circulation and deploying them in mission sites worldwide (Hyde and Feldman in this volume; Redfield 2008c). And finally, studies addressing trauma in terms of mental as well as physical well-being have underscored the production, circulation, and consumption of complex forms of subjectivity worldwide (Das et al. 2000, 2001; Fassin and Rechtman 2009; James 2004; Good et al. 2008).

Even as some anthropologists have focused on topics directly related to humanitarianism, through studies of institutions, professionals, and explicit moments of encounter, others have found aspects of humanitarianism in states and expectations of governance surrounding them. In the marginal settings where many anthropologists conduct their research, "the state" is far less of a given than political theory might indicate, and the disciplinary diagnosis of disorders focuses less on the failure of liberal forms to materialize than on the broader, often postcolonial context in which this "failure" occurs (Das and Poole 2004; Hansen and Stepputat 2001, 2005). In such "white jeep states" (Sampson 2003), international agencies and NGOs play a significant role in providing what welfare services exist. Between the scars of colonial history and the assumptions of neoliberal policies—not to mention episodic violence and warfare—politics and economics rarely conform to neat divisions between state and civil society, particularly in Africa (Comaroff and Comaroff 1999, 2006; Ferguson 2006; Mbembe 2001; Roitman 2005). War and peace also blur (Nordstrom 2004) while mass violence becomes more thinkable (Mamdani 2001); moments of violence produce multiple reverberations (Hoffman 2005; Theidon 2007; Wagner 2008). In such settings, encounters between elements of international advocacy and local populations result in as much friction as certainty (Englund 2006; Tsing 2005). On such ground neither the politics nor the ethics of "common human feeling" remain simple.

THIS VOLUME AND FUTURE RESEARCH

Humanitarian action has certainly provoked ample commentary, both with regard to specific crises and as a general pattern. Most analysis, however, remains either within the framework of specific policy or abstracted into sweeping theoretical claims (for example, Hardt and Negri 2000).[12] A number of more precise critical summations have emerged to occupy a middle ground, produced either by former aid workers and thoughtful fellow travelers (for example, Terry 2002; Rieff 2002; Kennedy 2004) or scholars with a background in international relations and generalizing social science (for example, Bass 2008; Weiss and Minear 1993; Hoffman and Weiss 2006; the introductory essay in Barnett and Weiss 2008 provides an excellent review). As of yet, however, there are relatively few in-depth ethnographic and historical accounts of humanitarian organizations, cosmologies, and encounters. This volume assembles a group of scholars engaged in precisely such studies and joins similar efforts to address the humanitarian action in specific detail (Feldman and Ticktin 2010; Fassin and Pandolfi 2010; Barnett and Weiss 2008; Wilson and Brown 2008). Informed by critique of the larger humanitarian project and related norms of international governance, such work also grapples with the specific elements that constitute and complicate actual practice. Our collective goal is to develop a more situated understanding of humanitarian action, solidifying the ground for its comparative analysis and engagement.

From the perspective of anthropology we confront two related, sometimes opposing tasks. One is to outline and examine the contemporary aid world, including its dominant practices, tensions, and beliefs about humanity. Another, however, is to place that world in comparative and historical relief by providing alternative histories and portraying different practices and beliefs.[13] The challenge thus becomes to navigate between these tasks with sufficient nuance and clarity to reveal humanitarianism as a particularly charged terrain between politics and ethics and to return to the question of why caring for strangers has become an urgent contemporary preoccupation.

This volume emerged from an intensive workshop held in March 2008 at the School for Advanced Research in Santa Fe. For scholars working on specific topics for an extended period of time (and at times in seeming isolation), it was an ecstatic experience to engage in extended conversation with people who shared common interests in such a serene and caring setting, and we remain extremely grateful to have had the opportunity to have our work benefit from such dialogue.[14] In accordance with the tried and tested formula for the Advanced Seminar program, our deliberations included four days of discussions around precirculated papers, as well as a final session focused on the volume as a whole. We engaged in an intense discussion ranging across the topics addressed in the volume, exploring the politics of intervention alongside religious diversity. Although the chapters that follow cluster thematically, the boundaries between them remain open, and we hope readers will approach them in the same spirit. Many topics overlap and complement or disrupt each other. Some chapters offer meta-level analyses (Benthall, Englund, Fassin, Pandolfi, Redfield) while others contribute detailed case studies (Bornstein, Feldman, Hyde, Ticktin). Some emphasize an ethical critique (Bornstein, Englund, Fassin, Pandolfi), others a political one (Benthall, Feldman, Redfield, Ticktin). As much as the lines between development, human rights, and humanitarianism are often porous, so are the boundaries between ethics and politics in these essays. In organizing the seminar we grouped papers according to initial intersections that we saw or anticipated might arise in discussion, pairing each author with another participant who led an analysis of it as a work in progress. The array and content of final submissions altered somewhat over time, but much of the original seminar architecture translated into the organization of this volume. In other words, the themes for the four sub-stantive working-discussion days roughly correspond to the four thematic parts of this book: Moral and Empirical Engagements, Cosmologies of Humanitarianism, Humanitarian Bodies, and Political Limits and Stakes.

To help readers navigate the book—recognizing that not everyone may approach its chapters in consecutive order—we offer short part introduc-tions. Readers who do follow a more linear path will no doubt realize that the organization of this book could have proceeded along a number of alternate paths, since individual chapters overlap in ways that supersede the structure of our volume. In the part introductions we seek both to make the organizational logic of connections explicit and to gesture beyond, imagining the chapters as moments in a much larger and dynamic conversation, with readers as participants. Further, we intend our collective contribution to be more generative than conclusive. Anthropology's gift to the intersection of scholarship and practice lies in its ability to engage ambiguity, to recognize concrete events and forms of action that fall between conceptual divides. By embracing a wider world and a deeper his-tory, it can question and unsettle even as it suggests and describes. To this end the authors in this volume accept the awkwardness of working in a gray zone between analytic registers, one initiated by the ambiguous, ambitious, and varied roles that ethnographers have with human practice: as partici-pant observers, expert witnesses, moral spectators, consultants, activists, critics, historians, outsiders, engaged sympathizers, and active members.

In closing we will make a generational observation. At universities where we have taught we have encountered a growing cohort of under-graduate students who want to get involved with NGOs broadly but do not know where to start and graduate students who enter anthropology with NGO experience and expect to continue their engagement, albeit with critical sensibilities. This generation of students—largely in their twenties in the early 2000s—brings a youthful urgency to their fascination with international development, human rights, and humanitarianism. At the same time global consumption practices—whether through Bono's "Red" campaign to fight AIDS in Africa or the "One Campaign" that mixes poverty reduction, AIDS relief, and humanitarianism—create possibilities to give to the world at every click of the computer mouse. Every opportunity for consumption presents a miniscule "choice" that seems to encompass the stakes at hand: a fair-trade cup of coffee, environmentalism through The Body Shop, an iPod that fights AIDS. If "the world" appears in need of urgent care, the fact that a field of intervention stands already conceptualized and marketed as such distinguishes our particular moment in history.

That youth of wealthy countries want to "do something" also appears as a significant shift from the apathy that followed the 1960s, or at least a resurgence and elaboration of the Live Aid moment of the 1980s. Certainly some crises (particularly the perception of genocide in Darfur) have evoked considerable emotional investment and organizational response (see Flint and De Waal 2005; Fadlalla 2008). For "doing something" at present primarily often means joining an NGO or forming a new one. Even more radical activists struggle with the critical dilemmas of funding amid the "nonprofit industrial complex" (for example, INCITE! 2007). The focus is on action and ethical engagement, regardless of religious heritage. Secondary students now fill their future résumés with community service, and student travel abroad increasingly includes aid endeavors along with traditional forms of study. And for every individual who realizes such a trajectory there are more who contemplate it and for whom it remains a nebulous dream. We make this observation not to dismiss the sincerity of the contemporary moment, but to rather emphasize the particularities of its formation and the central place of humanitarian sentiment within it. Clearly a desire to appear—and to be—a moral person remains strong.

One goal for research on humanitarianism, then, is to engage such dreams with the actual places they unfold and the larger histories they draw upon. As such this is a critical endeavor. But we claim no position of certainty beyond the phenomenon itself. When inflated to political abstraction the desire to aid demands a critical response; as MSF-France's former president, Rony Brauman (1996:28, 76), once acidly observed, Auschwitz today might be treated as a "humanitarian crisis," against which the fervent hand-wringing of television would provide little protection (see also Rieff 2002:75, 86, 166).[15] Nonetheless, we recognize that humanitarianism, like "Enlightenment," is not easy to oppose in general terms. (Who, after all, would be against clean drinking water?) Rather than sweeping denunciation, therefore, we suggest something more of an aporia, a puzzle viewed from within rather than from a distant mountaintop (Fassin 2007a, this volume). Perhaps one place to begin would be to suggest that we remember the narrative tradition of tragedy alongside that of romance, particularly when surveying political landscapes resulting from colonial history (Scott 2004). On a more modest scale, we might emphasize anthropological particularity, fragmenting grander human narratives with the concrete diversity of action. And finally we might also recognize the limits of our collective effort to expand a field vision: the geographic patchwork of these particular studies and the absence of other perspectives, including more elusive voices of varied aid recipients beyond the common filter of their need. This last absence underscores just how deeply perspectives on the topic remain mediated by relations of inequality and location, however cast on a global stage.

Notes

1. For an account that emphasizes the historical relations between humanitarianism and human rights see Wilson and Brown 2008.

2. Judaism provides two core concepts that address suffering: *tikkun olam* (heal the world) and *tzedakah* (the religious obligation to give to charity based on ideas of justice). Theological studies of Jewish humanitarianism emphasize how charitable works build communal Jewish identity (see Neusner 1990 on tzedakah; Shatz, Waxman, and Diament 1997 on tikkun olam in Jewish orthodoxy). Jewish philanthropy, even in its secularized form, has been considered by some to be a form of "civil religion" (see Steinberg 2002; Frisch 1924 for historical overview; also Meyerhoff's [1978] classic ethnography). Social scientific studies of Jewish humanitarian institutions echo the themes of identity and community. Historical accounts demonstrate that Jews cared for their poor in medieval Europe because the church and the guild—venues of charity available to gentiles—were not available to Jews (Penslar 1998; Frisch 1924).

3. Humanitarian analyses and controversies largely overlook Jewish charitable and humanitarian groups, which likewise long sought to help fellow Jews rather than generic others in need. Steinberg's (2002) comparative analysis of appeals by two Jewish organizations, (1) the Joint Jewish Distribution Committee's United Jewish Appeal founded in 1938 in response to Kristallnacht and focused on crisis resolution, and (2) the New Israel Fund founded 1979 and focused on social justice and peace in the Middle East, argues that humanitarian representations construct a global Jewish identity. Kavanaugh's (2008) study of ORT, a Russian-Jewish vocational training and relief organization whose acronym translates as The Society for Trades and Agricultural Labour, documents how Jewish organizations were active in post-Holocaust Jewish refugee relief. It is worth noting that while some Jewish humanitarian

organizations predate the Holocaust (ORT was founded in 1880, the JDC in 1914), their missions altered over time. ORT operated trade schools for European Jewish refugees in ghettos and continued its rehabilitation work with Holocaust survivors in displaced persons camps. The JDC expanded its domain beyond its central focus on assisting co-religionists to include some nonsectarian relief and development worldwide.

4. http://edition.cnn.com/2007/WORLD/asiapcf/08/22/hugging.guru, accessed June 10, 2010.

5. http://news.bbc.co.uk/1/hi/magazine/7130151.stm, accessed June 10, 2010. While the work of Amma is a fairly recent intervention into the spiritual, guru-driven institutional model of devotee-structured humanitarianism in India (Amma was born in 1953), there are also much older examples, such as the Ramakrishna Mission.

6. It has delivered relief to disaster victims all over the world including China, Bangladesh, South Africa, Guinea-Bissau, Nepal, Rwanda, Chechnya, Azerbaijan, Outer Mongolia, Ethiopia, northern Thailand, and Cambodia. Like any self-respecting NGO, the foundation also maintains a website (http://www.tzuchi.org). It explains that the goal of international relief work is to "solidify and practice the spirit of Buddha—great love" and that volunteer devotees of Tzu Chi follow the five principles of "directness, priority, respect, timeliness, conservation" in their relief work and follow three "no's" that include "no politics, no propaganda, and no religion, especially in mainland China."

7. This is of concern to some governments such as the government of India, which is currently attempting to regulate and control the millions of dollars in undocumented funds that are donated to religious and charitable organizations (see Bornstein 2009; Sidel 2004; Sidel and Zaman 2004).

8. The arguments of Las Casas infamously served as one justification for the substitution of enslaved Africans for Amerindians, a development he came to regret (Blackburn 1997:135–136).

9. Activities of the ICRC not only predate the emergence of the term "nongovernmental organization," but the organization's mandated role in international law vis-à-vis the Geneva Conventions places it in a unique position as private guarantor with official status.

10. In the *Oxford English Dictionary*, the term is defined as an explicitly secular concept: "One who affirms the humanity (but denies the divinity) of Christ" or "One who professes the 'Religion of Humanity.'" Although much contemporary humanitarianism defines itself as secular, its philosophical background has long intertwined with specifically religious conceptions of giving as suggested above. Humanitarianism involves implicit conceptions of "humanity" and what it means to be "human." These

are not strictly secular concepts—as they often intersect with religious cosmologies of the sacred and of spiritual purification—but have taken on secular valence in international moral discourse (see, for example, Asad 2003). When applied to human welfare the term first carried the pejorative connotation of an idealistic do-gooder before stabilizing as a technical category of action. Laqueur (1987) connects the increasing compassion evoked by the fate of individual bodies with the rise of detailed accounts of them in narrative forms such as the novel. Such particularistic compassion—never certain nor proportional—extended to both the living and the dead (Laqueur 2009).

11. Determining more precise relations between secular and religious understandings of dignity, as well as their historical influence on the aid world, remains a point for further research. For historical analysis of the religious and secular background to the "French Doctor" movement, see Taithe 2004 and Lachenal and Taithe 2009.

12. For policy discussions of humanitarian issues see the Humanitarian Practice Network at http://www.odihpn.org/, accessed June 10, 2010. Friedrich Nietzsche's *On the Genealogy of Morals* offers another potential point of reference on the theoretical front.

13. Although we do not address them here, efforts by corporations to present an ethical profile through gestures of "citizenship" and "social responsibility" also abut the terrain of contemporary humanitarianism and lie tangled in its history (see, for example, Ecks 2008; Hopgood 2008).

14. Two participants in the seminar, Lawrence Cohen and Liisa Malkki, were unfortunately not able to contribute chapters to the volume. Lawrence attended the seminar in Santa Fe and contributed extensively to both the discussions and the shaping of this book. Liisa was not able to attend the seminar, although she did submit a working paper in advance, which we discussed via telephone in Santa Fe. The influence of the work of both is visible in this book, through the papers that cite them, but extends much deeper. In addition to providing generous commentary throughout, Lawrence suggested the title for the volume at the tail end of our intense seminar week.

15. Some of this is translated and printed in "From Philanthropy to Humanitarianism: Remarks and an Interview," *South Atlantic Quarterly* 103, no. 2/3 (Spring/Summer 2004): 397–417. There the comment is on page 411. At a later point in the longer French interview he notes that it is absurd to think that TV images will save us.

PART I

Moral and Empirical Engagements

The first part of this book begins with a question posed directly by Didier Fassin's chapter: how does one approach humanitarianism anthropologically? Fassin offers a meditation on the "inextricable impasse"—or aporia—that humanitarianism poses for anthropological critique. The space for critique, he suggests, emerges at the interstices of institutional process, most precisely where there is conflict and disagreement over proper moral action. Only by paying attention to fissures of dissent and controversy can an anthropologist reach beyond the sacred quality of humanitarian ideals, otherwise untouchable through familiar modes of critical engagement. By questioning humanitarianism as a research object, Fassin urges us to refrain from taking sides and to steer clear of simplistic binaries such as victims and institutions. Instead, he suggests taking the stance of what he calls a "liminal critique." Humanitarianism is a difficult research object because it exceeds what can be said about it. It is simultaneously sacred and already questioned from within. Because of this, Fassin suggests, "criticism becomes critical." As a non-member but active participant in two prominent medical aid organizations in France, Médecins Sans Frontières and Médecins du Monde, he suggests adopting a position of "distanced interiority" and a form of a truth-telling that exposes the teller. Fassin elaborates the potential of this position through twin case studies in

Iraq and Palestine where fissures within the organizations exposed the limits of their humanitarian projects. He urges anthropologists to adopt an uncomfortable form of critique that recognizes the fundamental questions at stake—what risks to take, whose lives to risk, and whose lives are to be saved—presented in such a way that humanitarian actors can hear it as well.

Peter Redfield dissects the concept of neutrality historically, suggesting that the apparent contradictions of refusing political alignment in principle should not blind us to its productive variability in historical practice or its potential as a strategic form of "negative politics" employed by humanitarian actors. Redfield explores how neutrality represents "an effort to define parameters for situated action." Beginning with the historic emergence of neutrality in the conduct of warfare, he then demonstrates how it is used in the work of the aid organization Médecins Sans Frontières. Neutrality, Redfield argues, is not disinterested, but rather an instrumental claim, a political strategy that under particular conditions can serve the interests of the weak as well as the dominion of the powerful. Situating the analysis of neutrality in the work of MSF underscores the importance of understanding the relationship between medicine and humanitarianism and the manner in which health care could become a moral and legal category defended by aid organizations. By delimiting its engagement in medical terms, MSF seeks to redefine the situation away from directly political objectives. At the same time the organization engages with political events, practicing varieties of witnessing (*témoignage*) that can include public denunciation as well as quieter advocacy. In departure from the more principled tradition of the Red Cross, MSF's neutrality does not mean silence or even consistency. Rather the group operates amid the tension between its rival objectives: protecting its "humanitarian space" by claiming an operational sense of neutrality as a professional right and claiming moral authority through the engaged stance of speaking out or witnessing. Neutrality in humanitarian practice, then, appears to be a necessary fiction and a mutable strategy, one that can take partial and contradictory forms.

Harri Englund's chapter helps us link economic development, human rights, and humanitarianism by urging us to consider them through a common lens. Development workers, like their humanitarian counterparts, engage daily with human suffering, albeit through its slower, deeper roots in structural inequality and economic deprivation. However, their approach is defined by their focus on technical problems as professional poverty-alleviators. Confronted with the death of a young Malawian worker involved in a literacy training program, Englund is forced to reconsider not only the limits of technical expertise, but also his relationship as an ethnographer to his informants, his own sensibilities, and by proxy, the relationship of development workers to the communities with whom they ostensibly collaborate. It is through this frame that Englund critically examines the language of collaboration, which now pervades both development practice and anthropological approaches to poverty and suffering. Englund argues that development professionalism enforces boundaries between those who offer technical expertise and those who are considered its beneficiaries. Rather than viewing such incompatibility of understanding as a dead end, however, Englund suggests that it can itself prove productive when recognized and analyzed. Just as the crisis of the death of a development worker in this chapter reveals different responses from the anthropologist and his informants, the realization that collaboration must negotiate difference at a fundamental level is productive. Like Fassin and Redfield, Englund argues for an acceptance of incommensurability, or misrecognition, between the perceptions and intents of anthropologists and their subjects. In Englund's case the disciplinary stakes grow even clearer, as anthropology offers humanitarianism the uneasy gift of critical distance, through which even categorically "good" strategies such as participation, grassroots empowerment, collaboration, and witnessing emerge as sites for contest, negotiation, and reflection. Considering the theme of community empowerment embedded in contemporary aid work, human rights activism, and collaborative ethnography, Englund concludes that being external to a group can actually generate productive difference. He underscores the significance of arguing from divergent interests because argument "invokes relationships between and beyond particular viewpoints." When bearing witness means translating the conditions of a Malawian township to those elsewhere, it remains essential not to erase conflicting perspectives in the name of solidarity.

Taken together, all three of these chapters recall that the issues of life and death raised by contemporary humanitarian action pose unsettling questions when placed alongside the disciplinary tradition of anthropology and its inherited concerns for specificity, variability, loyalty, and difference. Examining strategies employed (and sometimes shared) by life-saving humanitarians and their ethnographic observers, the authors find a complex and impure mix of ethical and political engagement. Rather than seeking to resolve the lines of tension such inquiry reveals, they advocate for a recognition of the productive potential of incompatibilities, inconsistencies, and aporia.

2

Noli Me Tangere

The Moral Untouchability of Humanitarianism

Didier Fassin

Parrhesia is when truth is told in conditions that may incur a high cost for those who tell or have told that truth. In other words, in *parrhesia*, the true discourse reaches the interlocutor not through its internal structure or its purpose, but through the teller, or rather through the risk that telling truth incurs for the teller himself.

—*Michel Foucault,* Le gouvernement de soi et des autres, *1983*

For the anthropologist the world of humanitarianism is in many ways a unique research object. First, its manifestations are so diverse and indeed contradictory that its purpose seems nearly impossible to apprehend. Ranging from programs for assisting Central Asians in refugee camps to Seattle street demonstrations against globalization policies, from the struggle against famine in Africa to the defense of the national social protection system in France, from nongovernmental organizations decrying armed intervention to military operations justified in terms of assistance, the humanitarian world always exceeds what we can say about it. Second, it appears saturated with discourses that often turn out to have been authored by its own actors. Regardless of whether those humanitarian workers speak in the first person or proceed by way of their authorized commentators, whether they denounce world disorders or their own errors, they themselves are the ones to circumscribe the relevant questions and define what may legitimately be said about them. Finally—and this point follows in part from the two preceding ones—the world of humanitarianism tends to elude critical analysis. Because it is a valued good that many are seeking to appropriate for themselves by qualifying their own activities as "humanitarian," even when they are warlike, and because it operates by internalizing debate on the meaning and effects of its actions, it resists the inquiry of social sciences. It is this resistance that I am particularly interested in here, but I will also try to draw conclusions likely to improve our understanding of the "humanitarian world" itself. In other words, though I will focus on the conditions of possibility for studying the humanitarian world anthropologically, I will try to identify some of the blind spots of this anthropological study.

"Can any- and everything be laughed off?" one sometimes wonders. The Danish scandal known as the "caricatures of Mohammed" and the violent reactions it gave rise to in many Muslim countries remind us that the question cannot be thought of as a mere scholarly philosophical exercise— it is charged with political and moral issues. Here I will use a similar turn of phrase: not exactly "Can any- and everything be criticized?" (which would imply a normative position) but rather "Can any- and everything be submitted to critical analysis?" (implying a scientific approach). This question comes up every time we handle subjects that simultaneously involve persons trying to deal with painful situations—poverty, immigration, asylum, serious illness, childhood with AIDS, violence against women, to name only those I myself have worked on—and institutions whose mission is to help those persons. Deconstructing the obviousness of those categories, demonstrating that individuals assumed to be vulnerable also know how to use tactics for obtaining what they want, showing that the organizations or agents that take charge of them may have cynical attitudes and behaviors of their own and may actually be indifferent or cruel, is an undertaking that implies upsetting a kind of compassion consensus wherein the ill fortune or distress of some and the solicitude of others are understood to harmoniously respond to each other, pressured only by the impersonal, inhuman forces of the market, bureaucracy, or globalization, these last entities being easier to condemn than humanitarian actors and their sentiments. As anthropologists we may even feel embarrassed by such empirical observations and may hesitate to let them be known. In that case we practice self-censorship so as not to endanger, even abstractly or collectively, the men and women whose discourses we have collected and whose practices we have observed, fearing to betray their trust in us. We may also occasionally perceive reluctance on the part of our listeners and readers to learn about such matters, and it is not always easy in this case to know if what bothers them is the content of what we report or the very fact that we are speaking of it. Some matters would thus seem more sensitive than others. But how can we characterize them?

One thing they have in common is that they bring affects and values into play around two figures: victims of poverty, illness, or oppression and benefactors who assist, protect, and struggle to defend them. A third figure—examples of which are the money-grubbing boss, the insensitive bureaucrat, the cruel soldier—is obviously easier to criticize. The first two figures are linked by moral sentiments in Adam Smith's sense, beginning with "sympathy," that "emotion which we feel for the misery of others, when we either see it, or are made to conceive it in a very lively manner" (Smith 1982:1). According to the Scottish philosopher, this affective dimension is what underlies the moral sense as it is inscribed in the actors' virtues, judgments, or the actions they take. Compassion and pity are not only emotions but good feelings in that they manifest attachment to others. Humanitarian government, which can indeed be defined as "the introduction of moral sentiments into the political and policy spheres" (Fassin 2010a:269), paradigmatically crystallizes the emotion-charged encounter between victims and benefactors within the many different scenes of planetary tragedy it operates on. It extends the gesture of traditional charity or rather shifts it from nearby victims (the poor person one can see) to distant ones (victims of disaster, war, epidemics). It thus goes beyond Hannah Arendt's (1963) conceptual distinction between compassion as direct attention to individual suffering and pity as abstract consideration for the suffering of the masses in that it makes possible a paradoxical form of long-distance compassion where those masses (of disaster victims, refugees, the sick) become real (in tents, camps, hospitals), if only through media-delivered images. In this connection, the exercise in critical analysis that focuses on humanitarian government exemplifies the difficulties that may be encountered in any anthropological study of morally prized social activities, precisely because those activities involve persons and institutions believed to be above suspicion because they are acting for the good of individuals and groups understood to be vulnerable.

Noli me tangere—"Do not touch me," said Christ to Mary Magdalene when she extended her fingers toward him after his resurrection. It is the "untouchability" of certain actors and the values they incarnate that is of interest to me here. The Christian reference (noli me tangere) and the dimension of sacredness (untouchability) are central to my remarks. The humanitarian world is heir to a religious tradition of caring for the other and giving of oneself; it has become the secular expression of that tradition. As Craig Calhoun (2009) recalls, Florence Nightingale and Henri

Dunant led their fight for the right to treat wounded soldiers on battle-fields in the name of religion, and the very choice of the name "Red Cross" and the accompanying symbol refer back to Christian imagery—the Islamic response being the Red Crescent. The "second age of humanitarian action," that of "bearing witness" (Fassin 2008a:536), presumably broke free of these religious references; many of the founders of Médecins Sans Frontières (Doctors Without Borders) and Médecins du Monde (Doctors of the World) were previously linked to either the worlds of communism or leftism rather than Catholicism or Protestantism. But in addition to the fact that the cross (a white one) has long been the emblem of the first of these humanitarian organizations and the dove, a biblical symbol, is still the emblem of the second, the concept of humanitarian work is still strongly marked by the history of Western thinking on charity. Specifically, humanitarian government links up with "pastoral power" as characterized by Michel Foucault: it is exercised on "a multiplicity," that is the "flock"; it is "fundamentally beneficent" in the sense that "its only *raison d'être* is doing good"; and it is "an individualizing power" in that "the shepherd directs the whole flock, but he can only really direct it insofar as not a single sheep escapes him, and the shepherd owes everything to his flock to the extent of agreeing to sacrifice himself for its salvation" (Foucault 2007:126, 127, 130, 132). This was precisely the language used by the president of Médecins Sans Frontières to establish an opposition between the "cannibal ideal" of states and their armies, which, by their murderous actions, organize "the premature deaths of a part of humanity," and "the humanitarian spirit," which has taken on "the radical, arbitrary challenge of trying to succor those the society itself sacrifices" and whose responsibility is "to save as many lives as possible" (Bradol 2003:17, 32). This mystical language of salvation and sacrifice, this moral language about absolute evil and supreme good, attains here a sort of paroxysm to which many humanitarian actors would probably not subscribe. Still, a euphemized version of it may be heard daily in the offices of nongovernmental organizations and on their fields of action.

Under these circumstances, how can any independent analysis be permitted—or even possible? What autonomy is left for using a moral anthropology approach to apprehend a social world that presents itself as imbued with a sort of moral supremacy—a world, therefore, that claims it need not submit to any external oversight? It is this situation, *where criticism becomes critical,* that interests me here. I will be making use of my experience in the world of humanitarian organizations and of a series of studies I have conducted. I first define an epistemological position that can be described as distanced interiority. I then present two case studies that will illustrate my approach and its uncertainties and complications. Lastly, I draw a set of conclusions, putting forward two concepts that I hope will be granted some validity over and above the two examples. I would like this text to be read as a contribution to broader thinking on the conditions of possibility for criticizing practices and institutions that involve heavy moral investment, and on how to develop methods and concepts that will make noncomplacent and openly critical studies doable and receivable. The *parrhesia* that Michel Foucault (2008:67) spoke of—"truth-telling" that exposes the teller—seems to me a particularly decisive political issue for humanitarian government that, as mentioned, tends to elude just such truth-telling.

ON THE THRESHOLD OF THE CAVE

At the outset of a study he conducted on twentieth-century social criticism, Michael Walzer restates his own moral-philosophical position: "Over a number of years, I have been arguing against the claim that moral principles are necessarily external to the world of everyday experience, waiting *out there* to be discovered by detached and dispassionate philosophers. In fact, it seems to me, the everyday world is a moral world, and we would do better to study its internal rules, maxims, conventions, and ideals, rather than to detach ourselves from it in search of a universal and transcendent standpoint" (Walzer 1988:ix). Explaining that he has been criticized for this position by some who think that working from inside the social world amounts to eluding any radical thought coming from outside, he evokes Plato's celebrated allegory, suggesting that as far as he is concerned it is possible and necessary to analyze what "life in the cave" is, though others may choose to come out of the cave and examine it from a distance, "in sight of the sun." Ultimately, the question as he sees it is, "What further company should critics keep?" With whom should they have a conversation? "Some critics seek only the acquaintance of other critics; they find their peers only outside the cave, in the blaze of Truth. Others find peers and sometimes even comrades inside, in the shadow of contingent and uncertain truths" (Walzer 1988:ix–x). The author of *Spheres of Justice*, of course, belongs to the second group, though he recognizes the importance of the first. He advocates "connected" criticism rather than the classic representation of the solitary critic denouncing the power of the dominant, lamenting the ignorance of the dominated, doomed to tragic isolation.

The critical position I advocate is situated on the threshold of the cave, where a step in one or the other direction puts one either inside or outside. The humanitarian world I am concerned with here is a world I chose to mix with, collaborate with, and even belong to for a time, though I preserved a certain critical distance from it even while operating inside it. For fifteen years or so, starting in the mid-1980s, I had regular exchanges with nongovernmental organizations, particularly Médecins du Monde. Without being a member myself, I organized training for the organization's volunteer workers before they set out for their mission sites, and I myself did several missions, one for developing a program in Ecuador following the earthquake there, another with a fellow anthropologist in two West African countries to study policies for combating AIDS. In the late 1990s, the French section of Médecins Sans Frontières invited me to join its administrative board, and I accepted; I was later elected to the position of vice president of this organization, actively partaking in collective thinking on actions to be taken in the areas of assistance and bearing witness. Throughout those years I made a point of maintaining my critical independence, including within the organizations I was working with—a stance facilitated, of course, by the fact that I never received any remuneration and that I long remained a nonmember. Thus, when the organization would ask me to intervene "as an anthropologist" to help them understand what had caused the difficulties they encountered during a particular mission, expecting me to give them "cultural keys" for interpreting "resistance from the population," I would explain that, as I saw it, the analysis should encompass the entire intervention scene—that is, not just aid receivers but the association and its members. And when I became administrator of what was the largest French nongovernmental organization, I sought to pursue my critical discussion of the presuppositions of its leaders and volunteer workers, such as their relative indifference to the sovereignty of the states whose populations they were assisting. My position occasionally caused tension, but it was generally respected by the humanitarian actors. My critique, then, sought to reconcile my intellectual autonomy with my solidarity with the organization.

In the late 1980s, with the growing success of the French humanitarian epic, the discursive field came to be saturated first by humanitarian actors themselves, then by their authorized commentators.[1] These writings were not devoid of critical spirit, but what criticism they did make was circumscribed either by humanitarian actors themselves—several of whom have made their lives into novels (Jean-Christophe Rufin won the Prix Interallié for *Les Causes Perdues* [Lost Causes])—or their biographers, several having produced works that quite literally amount to hagiographies (Michel-Antoine Burnier relates *Les Sept Vies du Dr. Kouchner* [The Seven Lives of Dr. Kouchner]). These works criticized not the humanitarian world as such but rather other actors, accused or suspected of profiting from it. Some authors took out after the "charity business" and the "humanitarian trap"; others lambasted "predators of humanitarian action," the argument being that media or states manipulate nongovernmental organizations. In contrast, "the French doctors" were seen as "peace warriors" going about the world "succoring life." They did, of course, run into difficulties in the field, but according to these sympathizers, the moral force of their mission made its justice evident and irrefutable to all. Some have actually been quite clear-minded when it comes to internalizing criticism; namely, Rony Brauman (1993), who showed how, by keeping silent, humanitarian actors had facilitated the displacement of Ethiopian populations by an authoritarian government in 1985, and how in Rwanda in 1994 they had been helpless to save Tutsi staff members. But even in these cases, the target was not so much the organizations themselves as the governments of the countries involved, or the Western powers, or international institutions, starting with the United Nations. Overall, then, for nearly two decades, directly or indirectly, humanitarian workers themselves have been the ones to reflect critically, from the inside, on their own actions. And they have done so often in heroic mode, sometimes in a more sober style, rarely beyond testimony. Few authors produced studies based on their experience but substantiated by research carried out in an academic framework. Notable exceptions are Alex de Waal's 1989 book, written after he worked at Oxfam, and Fiona Terry's 2002 study, based on her activity at Médecins Sans Frontières.

External views of the humanitarian world began appearing later, first in the form of essays taking one of two diametrically opposed stances. On the one hand, a minority of these authors presented their works as praise of humanitarian action; more exactly, they set out to paraphrase the discourse of the protagonists of that action. This applies to a 1995 lecture by Renée Fox, a pioneering text in the sociology of humanitarian action. The author adopts the discourse of her interlocutors without critical discussion or analysis; she thus unconsciously becomes a spokesperson for Médecins Sans Frontières and Médecins du Monde, either by justifying their actions or by disqualifying competing international aid organizations. In this her text hardly differs from Nicholas Stockton's 1998 plea "in defense of humanitarianism" or Fiona Fox's 2001 argument in favor of the "new humanitarianism," the former speaking out for Oxfam and the latter for the Catholic Agency for Overseas Development (CAFOD). On the other hand, a larger group of authors chose instead to denounce humanitarianism. Their targets are not humanitarian actors per se (it was considered good form to recognize those workers' devotion and courage) but a certain ideology, understood to have overtaken them. This is the substance of Bernard Hours's 2000 work, which sarcastically lambastes not only humanitarian actors' presuppositions but also their social function of making the distress of the world acceptable. For him, the humanitarian ideology works hand in glove with market logic and military policy, concealing inequalities and serving domination. This grim view is also present in the writings of Robert Redeker (1996), for whom humanitarianism corresponds to an age void of significant ideological or intellectual innovation and Jean Bricmont (2005), who rejects the empire of humanitarianism and its right to intervene. Though these two sets of texts make opposite arguments—panegyrics on the one hand, scathing indictments on the other—they do have one significant point in common: they give priority to the normative perspective rather than an ethnographic approach. We can say that the first are in the cave and settle for mimicking its shadows, while the second are outside but tell us nothing of what is getting played out inside. That the issues involved are complex, that argumentation is dialectic, that positions may be ambiguous, that actors may be uncertain—these realities are not reflected anywhere in these analyses, as they contain nothing that cannot be simplified or readily evaluated.

Given these circumstances, the question I would raise is, can a critical discourse be produced on the threshold of the cave? A discourse that critically analyzes what those in the cave are doing while remaining "audible" to them? Both points are important. It is crucial to give a critical account of humanitarian actors' action, but that critique has to be audible to whom it is directed. The difficulty of developing a critique that is both autonomous and engaged is thus twofold: the actors have to recognize themselves in what is said of the way they act, but at the same moment, they have to perceive the distance that is being established. To put it more forcefully, the critical stance I am advocating necessitates for my interlocutors a dual sentiment of recognition and betrayal. Criticism is both loyalty and displacement. This is why I am particularly concerned in my work to examine "where it hurts"; in other words, where an institution or group is divided, what tears it apart. This is not intellectual sadism, but a theoretical choice: in periods of conflict, in the interstices of disagreement, a certain truth gets told that would not be told otherwise. An anthropologist who attempts to grasp that truth does not usually emerge from the experience entirely intact himself: the truth-telling ordeal puts him in a difficult position too. This is not mere rhetoric. It often seems to me that the accuracy of an analysis can be measured by the discomfort it causes in both the person who produces it and the person who receives it. With regard to humanitarian organizations, neither (of course) admiring support nor (paradoxically) virulent denunciation constitutes a moment of truth; the truth will only rise toward the surface if we stick as close as possible to the action. From this perspective, the distinction proposed by Iris Jean-Klein and Annelise Riles (2005) between two possible stances that anthropological studies of human rights can adopt is not entirely satisfactory, whether this distinction is meant to be prescriptive or descriptive. In their introduction to a series of articles on the issue, they first identify a "co-construction" mode, wherein the ethnologist is situated on the side of victims of violence and abuse, and a "denunciation" mode, wherein the ethnologist studies the bureaucracies whose tasks are to take charge of the victims, judge offenses, and repair damage. But they later seem to accept this duality, as if it were obvious that the anthropologist should take the side of the vulnerable and look harshly on institutions. The critical stance I am advocating is an attempt to escape this alternative.

SITUATIONS OF CRISIS

I propose to illustrate this stance by way of two case studies. My aim is to show that being attentive to the often tense debates that go on within the humanitarian world makes it possible to shed light on questions that are usually either hidden or simply invisible, both because they touch particularly sensitive nerves and because they do not get formulated adequately in the usual discourses on humanitarian action.[2] I do not want to assume a superior overview position, but rather to develop a critique that will resonate with the actors' own discussions—simply by taking those discussions a bit further than they allow themselves to do, something I can do both because the social sciences have familiarized me with a certain "unveiling" practice and because my somewhat marginal situation makes the cost of making such revelations much lower for me than for those who live for and from humanitarian work. There is thus no specific merit for using my critical sense; I simply felt it was the space I could usefully occupy. And in the explicit contract I had with my interlocutors in these organizations, I told them from the outset that this was perhaps the only thing I could bring with me.

The first scene, which I have recounted in detail elsewhere (Fassin 2007a), takes place at Médecins Sans Frontières, an organization founded in 1971 by a small group of doctors and medical journalists. Some of them (the most renowned being Bernard Kouchner) were "veterans" of the war in Biafra. They had worked there two years earlier for the International

Committee of the Red Cross, and had experienced that organization's neutrality principle as a genuine "law of silence." On the basis of what they had learned there, they decided to base future humanitarian action on two areas of activity: assisting populations and bearing witness. Three decades later, this group of friends had developed into an influential international nongovernmental organization; its original French section was the largest in the French humanitarian world, with more than four hundred positions in approximately one hundred "field" missions, one thousand volunteers per year being sent to work in those missions, and a budget of approximately $200 million, raised almost exclusively from private donors, a guarantee of financial independence. Being awarded the Nobel Peace Prize in 1999 gave Médecins Sans Frontières international legitimacy and made it an actor to be reckoned with in every conflict it was present in. It was in this context—that is, after the association had become a sort of humanitarian force or power—that the following scene took place.

In March 2003, just before the United States' air attack against Iraq, a Médecins Sans Frontières mission made up of six persons, including the president of the international bureau in charge of coordinating the nineteen national sections, chose to remain in Baghdad. The decision was a source of painful tension. Two of the six were not in favor of staying but did so to show their solidarity. Some in the headquarters were against this option but they constituted a minority on the executive committee. The question posed during the administrative council meeting a few days later was quite simple: Why take such a heavy risk (getting caught between American bombs and Iraqi resistants) for such modest anticipated results (six volunteers alongside several hundred qualified Iraqi medical personnel spread out among the capital city's thirty-five hospitals)? Both the president and the director-general argued in favor of keeping the team on the scene, the understanding being that even that minimal presence would save lives. However several members of the executive committee and administrative board had their doubts, and events proved them right. Twelve days after the first attacks by the United States and its allies, two members of the Médecins Sans Frontières team were taken hostage—the organization had not even set to work yet and there it was, paralyzed both locally and internationally. The wounded, meanwhile, began pouring into the hospitals. After eight days, the hostages were released—and revealed they had been kidnapped by Iraqi policemen. The Marines were already entering Baghdad. Traumatized by the hostage-taking, the association's head officials in Paris decided—against the recommendation of their colleagues on the scene, who were now in a position to help the local population—to shut down their mission and repatriate the volunteers to France, at just the time the other two Médecins Sans Frontières sections and most of the other humanitarian organizations were getting down to work. To justify their sudden departure, it was claimed that there was no real humanitarian emergency.

The violence of the disagreement on the executive committee and later on the administrative board about whether or not to stay in Iraq suggests that what was at issue was more than the technical matter of assessing the danger involved and the potential benefits. This is what I tried to explain during the debate. In fact, up against an army that was massively bombing the territory, causing high numbers of deaths in the Iraqi civilian population mostly to avoid losses of its own, the decision to remain was a courageous symbolic gesture aimed at establishing a kind of balance: by exposing themselves in this way, the humanitarian workers seemed to be showing that their lives were just as vulnerable as those of Iraqi civilians. However, this gesture revealed a twofold tension—theoretical and empirical. First, the notion of symmetrical exposure of lives did not hold up to analysis: in reality, Iraqi civilians were being sacrificed whereas humanitarian actors were sacrificing themselves—one group passive victims; the other committed heroes. Second, the notion of symmetrical exposure of lives did not hold up against the facts either: the humanitarian actors were free to pull out of the ordeal, whereas the civilian population had no other option but to remain—the former could protect themselves; the latter simply had to endure. This tension is not circumstantial but structural. To reveal it is to unveil a hidden truth of humanitarian work, a sort of family secret not even mentioned by the actors when they are among themselves. The humanitarian "gift" of assistance to the suffering is founded on two unrevealed facts. First, that the gift is unequal in that there can be no counter-gift: recipients of humanitarian assistance cannot offer anything in return, except in the highly asymmetric form of gratitude or in narratives of their distress. Second, that the gift cannot be complete in that those proffering assistance always protect themselves as much as they actually help, and everybody finds this normal because, after all, they are not there to lose their lives. The Iraqi scene, the spectacular exposure of organization members and the subsequent withdrawal of the team in response to the danger, thus functioned as a moment of truth-telling—or more precisely of *véridiction*, in Michel Foucault's (2007) words in his last lectures at the Collège de France.

The second scene, which I have also mentioned in another text (2004), involves Médecins du Monde, a humanitarian organization founded in 1979 out of a schism in Médecins Sans Frontières between certain founders (led by Bernard Kouchner) and a segment of the newcomers (including the president Claude Malhuret); the conflict came to a head around the question of chartering a ship to help Vietnamese boat people in the China Sea. The first group considered the object to be to save the lives of civilians fleeing communist persecution, but to the second group, the action appeared dangerous and primarily conceived to attract media attention. One can only be struck by the parallel with the scene just analyzed, which took place twenty-four years later. Finding itself outvoted by the young guard, the veterans' group favoring intervention seceded and left to found a new organization: Médecins du Monde. That organization considers this episode emblematic. Its motto is "There are no good or bad victims," a reference to the presumed indifference of leftist humanitarian workers to the Vietnamese boat people because they were victims of communism. A quarter of a century later, this dissident organization has consolidated itself and operates on a budget of approximately $65 million—one-third that of the French section of Médecins Sans Frontières. Like the older organization, Médecins du Monde gives special emphasis to one of its missions: the one it has set up in the Palestinian territories. The second scene thus concerns Médecins du Monde's presence there and unfolds in the context of the second Intifada.

When the Palestinian revolt against Israeli oppression broke out anew in September 2000 after Ariel Sharon's visit to the Esplanade of the Mosques known to Muslims as the Noble Sanctuary, Médecins du Monde had already been present for several years in Jerusalem and the territories, namely through its surgical assistance, psychological aid, and drug addiction prevention programs. The new violence led the organization to undertake new actions, particularly testifying actions, as was the case for Médecins Sans Frontières during the same period. In early 2002, it carried out a joint mission with the Fédération Internationale des ligues des Droits de l'Homme (FIDH; International Federation for Human Rights) in the city of Nablus, where a Tzahal military operation had killed 85 and wounded 289, a third of them civilians according to Palestinian hospital sources. The acts of violence committed by the Israeli army were recorded and violations of international law identified on the basis of eyewitness accounts by health professionals and services, municipal authority estimates, press articles, and direct observation by members of the Médecins du Monde mission—of building destruction, for example. The fully substantiated report concluded that the state of Israel had failed to abide by the "body of international law that governs armed conflict" and called upon it to carry out the necessary investigations, punish the guilty parties, and repair the damage done. Publication of the report elicited contradictory reactions within the organization, specifically on its administrative board. Some said they were satisfied with the report, which objectified war crimes and allowed for envisioning judiciary responses; others deemed it entirely one-sided and were indignant at what they considered its biased perspective. In this particularly stormy context, the decision was made to conduct another investigation, this time in Israel, to show the damage caused by Palestinian attacks. The FIDH refused to participate in this second study. The information collected came from Israeli police statistics and accounts by individuals who may not all have been directly involved in the violent acts. The attacks were termed "crimes against humanity," and the neologism "democide" was coined to signify murder of civilians. In the section assessing consequences, emphasis was placed on psychic trauma, which, it was explained, affected not only direct victims but also persons exposed by way of television coverage. This report was published together with the first report, and the cover bore the association's watchword, a direct reference to its founding moment: "There are no good or bad victims."

Published in the summer of 2003, the text provoked intense internal debate and wounding accusations. Initiators of the second investigation, including the organization's acting and honorary presidents, were openly suspected of having conducted it for reasons of religious group affinity: clearly they were accused of defending Israel because they were Jews. This was a hard blow for Médicins du Monde, which of course claimed to be above all partisan allegiance and to be working to promote universal ideals. But the point here is to understand the real implications of the organization's watchword about victims. We might think of the expression as amounting to a kind of founding credo not only for this nongovernmental organization but for the humanitarian world as a whole. Humanitarian workers who succor civilians in conflicts are not there to choose sides—this is what differentiates them from the military, as humanitarians themselves like to recall, especially since, in the field, some organizations actually confuse sides. This presumably obvious point is nonetheless misleading. On the one hand, sides are often chosen: humanitarian workers recently intervened in favor of the Kosovars rather than the Serbs, just as some time ago they intervened in favor of the Biafrans rather than the Nigerians and the Afghanis rather than the Soviets. On the other hand, not to choose may involve complex issues. Thus in the Israeli-Palestinian conflict, the organization's apparent neutrality has two consequences. First, it reduces actors in the conflict to the status of victims, a status to which they then have to conform so as to enable humanitarian testimony to follow its expected course: in the case of the Palestinians, we agree to consider them trauma victims, not combatants or martyrs. Second, in order for the organization to more effectively claim victim equivalence, its apparent neutrality abolishes collective and individual history: insisting on the shared experience of psychic trauma cancels out the meaning of the violence and, in this case, the historicity of Israeli occupation and oppression. This twofold impasse is revealed by publication of the second report, meant simply to "supplement" the first one.

FROM CONTRADICTIONS TO APORIA

I first outlined the preceding discussion—of Médecins Sans Frontières' politics of life in Iraq and Médecins du Monde's politics of victims in Palestine—with those two organizations at or near the time they were making their decisions. In other words, this critique is not being made from any retrospective heights; it was made earlier—and is made again here—in the interests of reopening dialogue with humanitarian actors. As explained, I mean to position myself on the threshold of the cave—as I did when I was on the administrative board of Médecins Sans Frontières and as I did again, in connection with the scene involving Médecins du Monde, by participating in a special issue of a journal on humanitarianism. Each of these organizations was in a crisis situation, which I tried to understand while sharing my analyses with my interlocutors. Their reactions—actually the presidents'—were sharp, probably because the distancing I was trying to manage touched on particularly sensitive points: the sacredness of life for Médecins Sans Frontières (the president's reaction was most virulent when I suggested that staying in Baghdad seemed comparable to a type of sacrifice); the issue of choosing victims for Médecins du Monde (it was when I showed how the maps of Palestine presented in the two reports differed, since the first was historical and political whereas those dimensions had entirely disappeared in the second, that the president asked the review to publish a response). Before further clarifying these two points, I would like to put forward the two levels of discussion I perceived during these crises. At the first level, humanitarian actors were debating together—inside the cave, as it were—and the issues raised did not ultimately affect the foundation on which their practices are based. At the second level, an internal foreigner came to dispute the normal proceedings. He was situated on the threshold of the cave, neither truly outside nor entirely within, and the questions he asked were troubling precisely because of this liminal position. Paradoxically, a possible third level—namely, contesting from "outside" the cave by asserting that humanitarian work can actually facilitate military action and that humanitarian actors partake of a neocolonial order—would not have shaken my interlocutors so much. They would either have rejected those accusations or even appropriated them for their own purposes, probably to call into question the work of other organizations. The idea I am defending here is that this liminal position is a specific one. Let us push the distinction further, bringing to light two orders of argument and confrontation.

At the first level, that of internal dispute, protagonists themselves point out the contradictions in their action; in other words, they themselves observe that the facts are running counter to their values and norms. Contradiction, then, can be thought of as "the relation that exists between affirmation and negation of one and the same piece of knowledge" (Lalande 1993:183). In the case of Médecins Sans Frontières, members' criticism of the decision to remain in Baghdad bore on the contradiction between the high level of risk incurred and the slim benefits to be expected. The organization's charter made clear to those taking action that they were there to "bring help to the population" and that they had to "measure the risks and perils of the missions they set out to accomplish." The president and director-general's reply, of course, was that lives would be saved and that the risks incurred were no greater than usual. In the case of Médecins du Monde, the suspicion that the organization leaders provoked when they decided to conduct an investigation in Israel and later to publish the report on it concerned their presumed "denominational" or "ethnic" allegiance, as any such allegiance would contradict the "neutrality principle" that is the cornerstone of humanitarian intervention and the very condition for ensuring that such intervention remains legitimate. Obviously the accused rejected that interpretation, arguing that their moves actually reflected a return to the organization's origins; in other words, concern for all victims, regardless of side. The advantage of contradictions of the sort brought to light by the actors at the first level is that they can be uttered, demonstrated, and even overcome. In Baghdad, later developments proved the accusers right: Médecins Sans Frontières picked up stakes after its kidnapped workers were returned and left without having succored a single Iraqi. The risk was shown to be real, and the organization's ineffectiveness was clearly demonstrated. In Palestine, conclusions were harder to reach: media support of the second report and the approval it received from Jewish organizations in France were not sufficient evidence to establish that the leaders had particular affinities. However that may be, contradiction could be overcome in both these cases.

At the second level of what I am calling liminal critique, an internal foreigner raises questions that reveal an aporia—an inextricable impasse. I am using the modern, strong sense of the word: aporia are "logical difficulties that cannot be gotten out of" (Lalande 1993:69). I would be tempted to rephrase that definition for anthropological aporia; in this case I would call them questions that touch on the very foundations of humanitarian action and admit of no solution given the state of the contemporary world. Contrary to contradictions, aporia are not a matter of organizational dysfunction but rather of the dysfunction intrinsic to their very functioning. For Médecins Sans Frontières (I am, of course, only citing this example for its general import), the aporia lie in the impossibility of actually maintaining the "equality of lives" promoted by humanitarianism. As I suggested—and above and beyond any rational risks/benefits calculation—the point of staying in Baghdad was not to sacrifice oneself but rather to recall that the lives of Westerners could be as vulnerable as the lives of Iraqis and that Westerners were morally capable of endangering themselves in order to protect Iraqis—in sum, that all lives were equally sacred. The fact is that in addition to the asymmetry of the exchange, due, as mentioned, to the fact that the victims can never offer a "counter-gift" in return for the "gift" of their benefactors, the hostage-taking revealed a vulnerability specific to such organizations, as well as a hidden truth: the lives of humanitarian workers are actually deemed to be much more precious than those of local civilians—even (as was discovered then) within the organization itself. The lives of "expatriates" are valued more than those of "nationals" in matters of wages, social protection, freedom to associate, recognition—to the point where the belligerents themselves, when attacking humanitarian mission sites, always differentiate between the two, demanding ransoms for Western hostages and simply killing local workers. The fact that there is a hierarchy of equally "sacred" lives represents a sort of anthropological nonsense—a fairly unbearable one. In the case of Médecins du Monde (but once again, the illustration only matters for its paradigmatic relevance), the aporia lie in the impossibility of maintaining victim equivalence as the humanitarian world claims to do. The suffering of Israelis threatened by Palestinian attacks can only be considered equivalent to the suffering of Palestinians crushed by the Israeli army if we reduce the social experiences involved to wounds and trauma—in other words, to the physical and psychic body—and eschew any grim accounting, which would quickly show a casualty ratio between the two sides of one to ten—one to one hundred in some instances. Above all, deciding to focus on suffering means deciding not to attend to either the historical dimension or the political issues of the conflict, though these, too, correspond to what victims are going through. More than bodies fall under bullets or bombs— though many more bodies fall on one side than the other. What fall are human beings who have not been and are not treated with equal dignity. The Palestinians experience daily oppression, humiliation, negation; this is not true of the Israelis. When Médicins du Monde forgot this, it was called to order by its own members, who spoke of injustice at the very moment their leaders explained that they were only defending all victims equally.

CONCLUSION

What I am calling anthropological aporia here concern humanitarianism precisely because they are inscribed in contemporary moral economies. The fact that lives and victims are not equal is not specific to the humanitarian world. The truths thus revealed go beyond the framework of nongovernmental organizations and their volunteer workers (though these organizations and volunteers do represent a kind of moral core in our societies and deserve particular attention). We therefore cannot hold these groups entirely responsible for the complex tensions and insurmountable problems with which they are confronted. But we can expect them to be more clear-sighted than they often appear. Discovering that they actually partake of certain realities that they condemn and that the principles of equal lives and equivalent victims that they identify as their own cannot be realized, due to the very foundations of their action— in other words, asymmetrical, ahistorical solidarity—means that they would have to surrender a certain representation of the moral hero in our time. That is, of course, hard to do.

As is uttering these truths publicly. The liminal critical position I have advocated exposes its defenders to virulent reactions from actors who feel they possess a legitimate truth and whose authority—together with the authority of what they represent—may be shaken by such revelations. As Michel Foucault suggests, we can perhaps judge such "truth-telling" precisely in terms of the risk it involves for the teller. But to suggest that my interlocutors have not heard my scientific criticism would be to yield, in my turn, to the power of another representation: that of the misunderstood, even accursed researcher—which is far from true. My critique *has* been heard, but, of course, more by those seeking to probe and question the humanitarian order than by those seeking to maintain it in its present state. In democracy, however, that amounts to a quite ordinary sociological fact.

Translated by Amy Jacobs

Notes

1. The many books written by French humanitarian actors themselves include Rony Brauman, *Humanitaire: Le Dilemme* (Paris: Textuel, 1996), *Penser dans l'Urgence: Parcours Critique d'un Humanitaire* (Paris: Seuil, 2006), *Aider, Sauver: Pourquoi? Comment?* (Paris: Bayard, 2006); Xavier Emmanuelli, *Les Prédateurs de l'Action Humanitaire* (Paris: Albin Michel, 1991), *Au Vent du Monde* (Paris: Flammarion, 1992), *Au Secours de la Vie: La Médecine d'Urgence* (Paris: Gallimard, 1996); Bernard Kouchner, *Charité Business* (Paris: Le Pré aux Clercs, 1986), *Le Malheur des Autres* (Paris: Odile Jacob, 1991), *Les Guerriers de la Paix* (Paris: Grasset, 2004); Jean-Christophe Rufin, *Le Piège; Quand l'Aide Humanitaire Remplace la Guerre* (Paris: Jean-Claude Lattès, 1986), *L'Aventure Humanitaire* (Paris: Gallimard, 1996), *Les Causes Perdues* (Paris: Gallimard, 1999). Works glorifying French humanitarian organizations or their heroes include Olivier Weber, *French Doctors: L'Epopée des Hommes et des Femmes qui Ont Inventé l'Humanitaire* (Paris: Robert Laffont, 1999); David Rieff, *A Bed for the Night: Humanitarianism in Crisis* (New York: Simon and Schuster, 2002); Anne Valleys, *Médecins Sans Frontières: La Biographie* (Paris: Fayard, 2004); Alain Guillemoles, *Bernard Kouchner: La Biographie* (Paris: Bayard, 2002); Michel-Antoine Burnier, *Les Sept Vies du Dr. Kouchner* (Paris: Editions XO, 2008).

2. For the case study of Médecins Sans Frontières I used the organization's *Rapport d'Activities 2002–2003* (May 2003), 123 p.; *Compte-rendu de la Réunion du Conseil d'Administration*, March 23, 2003; and *DazibaG* (May 2003), 125. For the case study of Médecins du Monde I used the organization's *Rapport Moral 1999* (October 2000), 175 p.; *Opération Mur de Protection Naplouse: Mission d'enquête conjointe Médecins du Monde-Fédération Internationale des Droits de l'Homme, West Bank* (May 2002), 64 p. and *Les Civils Israeliens Victimes des Attaques des Groupes Armés Palestiniens: Mission d'enquête Médecins du Monde, Jerusalem* (August 2003), 70 p.

3

The Impossible Problem of Neutrality

Peter Redfield

"Neutrality was never an issue outside the minds of humanitarians."

—*Rony Brauman (MSF-Holland 2000:16)*

The concept of neutrality now carries a hopeless burden of critique. On the far side of veiled interests, positioned subjects, and situated knowledge, it has become second nature in some quarters of contemporary scholarship to dismiss claims to neutrality, along with related concepts such as objectivity and impartiality, as naive surface representations or techniques to leach away political consciousness. There are many good reasons for this impulse and little doubt—in the comfortable preserve of academic disputes, at least—that the concept of neutrality constitutes a depoliticized and ahistorical fiction. But the dismissal of neutrality has a weakness: when reduced to a truism it grows ethnographically thin. Actual human practice is intricate and the practice of neutrality no less complex and thorny than other useful fictions people deploy.

In this essay I consider neutrality not as an absence of political positioning, but rather as an "impossible" or negative form of politics: a strategic refusal with moral inflections, actively problematic and generative.[1] Rather than engaging in critique at a global level, I seek to follow the more specific trajectory of neutrality as a problem amid shifting political and ethical norms related to life and death. My primary object of study will be the humanitarian organization Doctors Without Borders/Médecins Sans

Frontières (MSF). As both the inheritor of humanitarianism's neutral legacy and a sometime heretic within it, the group embodies critical tensions of the concept relative to shifting modes of practice. Examining MSF's statements and actions, then, may illuminate aspects of the larger problem of neutrality in a particular and grounded way—long the promise of anthropological case studies. As with humanitarianism itself, the classic ethnographic move of worrying less about the veracity or consistency of people's claims, and more about the manner in which they do or don't make and pursue them, serves to highlight the variability of historical experience. A neutral stance, I will emphasize, has served more than one end, and its strategic significance varies under different regimes of power. Recognizing variability and complexity in turn shifts the terms of question and critique. Rather than evaluating neutrality as an abstract principle, the goal becomes to evaluate the claim and relative practice of neutrality under given conditions.

The ethical standing of neutrality grows particularly vexed and contradictory when defined in relation to human suffering. On the one hand, war is the classic venue in which neutrality takes shape. To the degree that humanitarians evaluate organized violence in terms other than victory and defeat, they stand apart from military alliances and their political objectives. On the other hand, the humanitarian conscience responds to spectacles of human tragedy and remains haunted by the specter of genocide. To the degree that humanitarians involve themselves in delivering aid they are obviously engaged in any field of action, and to the extent they oppose any regime that fosters death they are clearly committed to its alteration or demise.

The current moment is a particularly fraught and telling one for this discussion. Recent trends in international politics toward humanitarian justification of military action and moves to legislate a moral "right to intervene," as well as the US led "war on terror," have presented humanitarian organizations with renewed quandaries about defining and proclaiming their allegiances (see, for example, Allen and Styan 2000; HPN 2003; Harroff-Tavel 2003; Shetty 2007; Lischer 2007). Thus neutrality has again emerged as a relevant topic in aid circles, reconfigured anew after an earlier round of concern about post–Cold War conflict and genocide in the 1990s (Duffield 2001). In an era when military conflict primarily produces civilian death and frequently involves strategic displacements, when political powers deploy the language of human rights and humanitarianism, when actors display keen awareness of the presence or absence of cameras and regularly communicate across context and distance, the process of defining terms of involvement is unlikely to be clear or simple. Rather, the heightened struggles over definition may themselves reveal older contours in the larger problem of not taking sides.

THE POLITICAL ART OF ABSTAINING

What might this term, "neutrality," signify? Before examining humanitarian understandings and MSF's particular travails with the term, I will take a historical detour. My purpose in doing so is to expand the concept, and thereby suggest the extent to which current assumptions may be anachronistic in more than one direction. Just as with "war" itself, "neutrality" may be an impossible word (Nordstrom 2004:5), one that appears sharp and sure on the surface, but rapidly dissolves under close examination into a wide range of forms and events. Current discussions cast the neutral state as fixed and inviolable when it is not a facade, a moral condition of purity akin to virginity, deeply associated with inaction. Neutrals are disinterested observers, bystanders to oppression or even genocide, invested above all else in maintaining a status quo. But it has not always been so, or at least not to the same degree.

Etymologically the Latin root (*ne-uter*) suggests a state of being neither one thing nor another, a condition of refraining or abstaining (Haug 1996). The possibility of standing apart during a conflict is a common enough human experience, as mediated by obligations of kinship and other alliances. However, relationships formally *defined* through degrees of abstinence present a more unusual and anthropologically interesting phenomenon. For the purposes of this essay I will concentrate on the modern tradition as understood in international relations and law, which dates from at least the seventeenth century. This legal trajectory has the advantage of both representing more than a specific case, as it constitutes an ostensive lineage extending to the present. Whether or not the edifice of treaties, principles, and precedents currently invoked or ignored represents a monument of human progress, it carries traces of a longer history of practice.[2]

In European military and legal history a formal category of neutrality emerged in relation to questions of arbitrage and trade between warring parties. Thus a sovereign power might claim the right to stand apart from the conflict of others and by making that claim seek protections for its political and economic affairs. Likewise, it might seek to serve as a diplomatic intermediary during conflict or a geographic buffer between potential adversaries in times of peace. Neutrals, then, were as much active as passive figures on the political landscape. Moreover, theirs was hardly an absolute condition: the state of neutrality extended only to particular conflicts and to certain relationships within them. In this sense it represented an effort to define parameters for situated action.

Several additional points become quickly apparent when looking at the historical emergence of neutrality as a political and legal concept in early modern Europe. First, the tradition derives from human practice far more than from abstract principle or Enlightenment reason. As Stephen Neff notes in his historical survey of the topic, "The law of neutrality, in short, was made not, as it were, from the top-down by scholars and commentators, but rather from the bottom-up by statesmen, generals, admirals and traders" (2000:7). Although standing apart might not conform to medieval theories of "just war," the record suggests a considerable body of custom that recognized precisely this possibility. Second, neutrality rarely appears disinterested or selfless. A concern for commerce and exchange is particularly evident: given that war might interfere with such other interests, it could be restricted for their sake. Third, the practice of war itself—its technologies, goals, and legitimate parameters—varies significantly over time. The importance of neutrality has waxed and waned in different periods, depending on moral framings of war and justice, the relative professionalism of armies, and the strategic scale of conflict. The eighteenth-century revolutionary version of "total war," for example, targeted economic exchange and thereby altered the manner and extent to which noncombatants could stand apart. Finally, neutrality was rarely certain or guaranteed; rather it was a claim, one that might or might not prove successful. Neutrals had duties as much as rights, primarily to abstain from open conflict and show impartiality in relations with combatants (Neff 2000:13). Whether or not they fulfilled such duties, or claimed legal rights as they developed, however, neutrals could be—and often were—invaded or otherwise compromised.

From the perspective of the present the historical record underscores a significant, often overlooked point: the refusal of political positioning not only has political effects, it is also a political strategy. Like any strategy, neutrality might or might not succeed in furthering specific aims under given circumstances. But its very claim suggests a potential limit to the sovereignty of another. Instead of denying self-interest, then, neutrality expresses it through an attempt to restrict or alter the terms of engagement. By expressing a desire to stand apart, the would-be neutral asserts independence, and by implication the capacity to maintain or form an alternative connection. Whatever neutrality has been about in the longer run of European historical experience, it has rarely expressed attachment to abstract virtue and certainly not altruistic justice (Neff 2000; Walzer 1977).

Rather, a broader principle of limitation emerges from a cobble of limited, and distinctly self-centered, aims.

Two additional historical observations help further undermine contemporary certainties about neutrality. First, minor states feature conspicuously in the collective record related to the topic. Declarations of neutrality offered "small powers" a means to survive amid larger neighbors; by avoiding conflict they could assert independence and sometimes enjoy the prospect of profit. At the same time, the existence of small neutrals could also periodically serve the commercial and diplomatic interests of larger states, including expansionistic ones. Even as Europe produced a series of major empires, odd corners managed not only to stand apart, but also eventually to present themselves as exceptional zones. Prominent among these was Switzerland, which would later play a central role in international affairs—and humanitarianism—as a distinctly neutral ground. Thus neutrality might appear as much a strategic weapon of the weak as a hegemonic assumption of the powerful.

Second, only in the nineteenth century did neutrality come to be defined as an absolute state. Prior to that time degrees of "imperfect" or "partial" neutrality enjoyed some recognition; for example, states might continue to honor arrangements that predated the onset of hostilities (Neff 2000:103). Amid royal disputes waged by mercenary armies, allegiances were fluid, and a measure of accommodation had reigned in war as well as peace. The wider scope of total war, however, recast both conflict and neutrality in more absolute terms. As civilians and their livelihood began to play a larger role in military strategy, neutrality entered law as a more permanent and restrictive condition. To dampen potential conflict in the aftermath of the Napoleonic era, states such as Belgium were designated as being "perpetually" neutral. As custom gelled into elaborated law, temporary or partial abstinence faded before permanent renunciation. Thus the image of neutrality as an inviolable principle appears a relatively recent inheritance, one that may be as inappropriate to many contemporary circumstances as the equivalent image of warfare that presumes neatly arrayed, uniformed lines of troops. In this respect at least, our present may have more in common with earlier European experience than with the more immediate past.[3]

MSF, THE RED CROSS, AND NEUTRALITY

Thus equipped with a measure of historical uncertainty, let us now return to the problems of the present. MSF has a famously complex relationship to neutrality, embracing and denying aspects of the concept at one and the same time. In genealogical terms, the group descends from the International Committee of the Red Cross (ICRC), an entity constituted around a moral response to the suffering of wounded soldiers and a commitment to circumspect operational neutrality (Hutchinson 1996). The Red Cross helped establish a skeleton for international humanitarian law with the first Geneva Convention held in 1864 and built itself around the emerging order of nation-states. MSF, by contrast, originally conceived of itself as an alternative to both. Even if moral testimony may not have been as central to the group's formation as later myth would suggest, its very name embodied independence and global ambition (Vallaeys 2004). In 1971 claims to neutrality and an international order of sovereign nation-states were political norms. The decolonization of European empire both reinforced the centrality of the nation-state form and embedded it into a new field of historical instability. At the same time the Cold War struggle produced numerous proxy conflicts, and technical developments in communications and transport reworked the speed and scale of international connections. Thus television could broadcast tragedy from afar, and middle-class European youth could travel to engage the world without having to rely on state conveyance (Boltanski 1999; Brauman 1996; Tanguy 1999). Moreover, in richer countries emergency medicine was moving off battlefields and into hospitals as part of a routine response to crisis. When the oppositional spirit identified with the period called for direct action, the biomedical context increasingly had means to realize a form of direct and rapid intervention.

The generation that most shaped MSF's early history saw the Red Cross's silence during the Holocaust as a failure and was quick to embrace the media, even as it sought to avoid bureaucratic entanglements and diplomatic niceties. Over the following decades, the group would deviate dramatically from Red Cross orthodoxy in several different directions. To cite just a few prominent and formative examples, in Afghanistan at the beginning of the 1980s, MSF operated a clandestine mission essentially in support of the mujahideen. In 1985, the era of Live Aid, the original French section of the organization found itself evicted from Ethiopia after speaking out against government resettlement policy. In Rwanda in 1994, MSF denounced the genocide and even issued a frustrated call for armed intervention. Nonetheless, much of the time the group's work on the ground has resembled that of the ICRC, albeit with a more informal and flamboyant twist. Furthermore, despite episodic internal debate, it has never removed the term "neutrality" from its charter. This last point, I suggest, merits particular attention, for it suggests that humanitarian claims to neutral status may run deeper than at first it might appear.

In order to grasp the historical force of the ICRC, one must first denaturalize humanitarian norms. At the point when the Red Cross emerged, the status of battlefield medicine was uncertain in principle as well as practice. Wounded soldiers and medical personnel had no uniform standing, and their protection depended on the calculations or consciences of individual commanders. Even if the greater Red Cross movement ultimately reinforced state interests by effectively creating an auxiliary civilian medical corps (Hutchinson 1996), it also repositioned ordinary suffering within moral sensibility. Through its sustained effort a red cross on a white background grew into an accepted symbol on the battlefields of Europe as well as in civilian settings. And even if the same armies ignored Genevan niceties in colonial contexts (Lindqvist 2000), key elements were in place for projection into more universal claims.

The point is not that humanitarianism lacks historical precedents; the ICRC itself now proudly catalogs potential antecedents to humanitarian thought worldwide, and many warrior traditions have included precepts of honorable behavior, mercy, and sanctuary (Barnett and Weiss 2008; Ignatieff 1997; ICRC 2000; Cox 1911). Instead, the project of nineteenth-century humanitarianism refashioned a matter of virtue into a moral and legal category focused on health care. The fiction of standing outside battle (*hors de combat*) could now be predetermined by professional status as a medical worker and bodily states related to suffering.

The Red Cross variant of neutrality, then, developed in a historical context where it represented the very possibility of delimited engagement, as defined through medicine. The ICRC's strategy depended on the extension of international legal conventions, into which it was subsequently written. It also anticipated the existence of clear sovereignty to work through and against. As the tendrils of the Red Cross movement expanded beyond care for wounded soldiers into a more general response to suffering, they provided a civil, state-sanctioned mode of welfare protection amid disaster. In addition they suggested a limit to state discretion in the form of international humanitarian law. Sovereign power might still declare a state of war, and claim legal exceptions through it, but would now confront a field of specific expectations to meet or ignore. At stake would be an appearance of humanity, as displayed through relative restraint.

Once transported beyond nineteenth-century European warfare, the Red Cross strategy faced serious structural "challenges" (to use the all-purpose euphemism of the aid world). Its legal claim anticipated a defined order of nation-states and clear sovereigns, not contexts of civil war and ethnic conflict. Even so, the ICRC maintained a creed of seven principles, including impartiality and neutrality. Neutrality constituted a disciplined refusal of involvement beyond the core mission: "In order to continue to enjoy the confidence of all, the Movement may not take sides in hostilities or engage at any time in controversies of a political, racial, religious or ideological nature" (Plattner 1996). Although the work might embody a greater ethic of compassion for human suffering, it should not give way to passions of any lesser sort. My portrayal here simplifies for the sake of emphasis. The ICRC now acknowledges its limits more openly and recognizes possible exceptions to its principle of confidentiality (Harroff-Tavel 2003). Nonetheless, its neutrality continues to define humanitarian orthodoxy, and the organization's legacy remains one of deep and abiding consistency. In schematic mappings of humanitarian types created by analysts, the Red Cross inevitably occupies the "classic" or prophetically "Dunantist" pole (for example, Hoffman and Weiss 2006:99; Slim 1998; Weiss 1999).

MSF's rebellion against this orthodoxy gained both clarity and nuance over time. Born in association with a medical journal, the initial group included a few journalists amid its doctors. Moreover, its name connoted a rejection of state authority alongside a more general refusal of limitations. Still, the organization's actual charter mirrored Red Cross principles, with neutrality, impartiality, and even confidentiality firmly in place. Media involvement grew more central during its tumultuous first decade, along with hints of assertive moral vision that suggested humanitarian needs took precedence over political order. This sense of moral primacy both reflected a longer tradition of French universalist impulses and anticipated the "right to interfere" later championed by Bernard Kouchner (Fox 1995; Taithe 2004; Vallaeys 2004). After losing a power struggle within MSF, Kouchner founded a rival group, Médecins du Monde (Doctors of the World or MDM). Initially distinguished from MSF by personality and style, MDM would push even further beyond the Red Cross model by embracing elements of human rights discourse in opposition to suffering. MSF, meanwhile, continued to grow and rupture with the emergence of new, largely autonomous sections elsewhere in Europe.[4] Following a bitter early controversy over the politics of "third-worldism" and a series of disputes in the wake of major crises in the mid-1990s, the greater assemblage quarreled its way into a loose consensus about its humanitarian perspective.

Like the Red Cross, MSF would generally concentrate on limited and short-term goals, avoiding appeals for development on the one hand and a full embrace of human rights on the other. MSF's version of neutrality, however, was more openly instrumental than that of its ancestor. The greater ethic of impartiality would find its sharpest definition through medical care. Operational neutrality, by contrast, must always allow for moral duty and its potential politics. To describe this delicate balance in the precise terms of its engagement, MSF gradually adopted the term *témoignage* to imply an active sense of witnessing, as motivated by humanitarian concern for suffering. In extreme circumstances, témoignage would take the form of "speaking out" and public denunciation. However much it might resemble political advocacy in practice, MSF would present its public speech as an exceptional act, deriving from a sense of moral obligation rather than the pursuit of political objectives (Terry 2001; MSF-Holland 2000; MSF 2006).[5]

MSF's variant of neutrality, then, developed in a historical context where engagement was no longer fully predicated on states. Independence, rather than reliance on international law, would serve to guarantee virtue. MSF constituted itself as a nongovernmental organization and jealously guarded its autonomy, even largely weaning itself away from state funding during the 1990s. Engagement remained rigorously medical but practiced with heretical zeal. Compassion now acknowledged passion and public speech, if still resisting formal politics. Thus MSF challenged sovereignty more directly than the ICRC, while avoiding any final determination of its own placement or responsibility. At the same time it only reinforced a medical vision of the humanitarian mission, its vision of advocacy nominally that of a collective doctor (Redfield 2006). Human life, health, and dignity constituted the core values, through which all political formations would be measured.

During the 1980s and 1990s, the claim of a "right to interfere" (*le droit d'ingérence*) on humanitarian grounds migrated from nongovernmental to governmental terrain, even as Bernard Kouchner became a significant political figure in France (Allen and Styan 2000). The phrase lurked in the background of the international intervention in Somalia and even more prominently in the NATO operation in Kosovo. By the time the "war on terror" was proclaimed by the United States in 2001, humanitarian justifications for military action and occupation had become a topic of dispute in their own right.

Although fundamentally committed to a sense of moral duty for intervention on their own part, MSF expressed deepening reservations about any general "right to interfere" on the part of political powers, particularly military action justified in the name of alleviating suffering. During its Rwandan agony the group had called for military intervention, noting bitterly "you can't stop genocide with doctors."[6] But Kouchner's successors never joined in his larger campaign, and in the aftermath of September 11

MSF only redoubled its denunciation of "military humanitarianism" (for example, Weissman 2004; MSF CRASH 2002; Dachy 2001). Instead, the group's rhetoric has focused on what it calls "humanitarian space" (Brauman 1996). This abstract formulation refers to the ability of humanitarians to work freely in a given set of circumstances. In effect, it seeks to define the situation so that humanitarianism—materialized in medical practice—will stand apart as a recognized exception. In this sense it follows the historical strategy of the larger concept of neutrality, defining a limited relationship outside conflict that permits the pursuit of another interest. At the same time the spatial metaphor suggests a mobile variant of religious sanctuary, in which certain ground would grant immunity from profane conflict (Cox 1911; Lippert 2004). As with the Red Cross, this assertion ultimately relies on moral appeal and persuasion. Although sometimes referenced against legal precept, its real calibration stems from practice and the reiterative normalization of humanitarian action.

Like most aid agencies, MSF seeks to actively signal its neutrality through both the form and content of its missions. From the uniform T-shirts and ubiquitous white vehicles, every object associated with the organization normally carries its logo, signaling a status that is at once distinctive and recognizably generic. Vehicles and key buildings also commonly carry a no-weapons logo to indicate their refusal of arms. Moreover, the group takes every opportunity to remind all actors on the ground of its medical focus and underscores the noncommercial and professional nature of its involvement by offering its treatments free of charge, under criteria it defines as medical need. In this sense it asserts humanitarian space by occupying it. Although claiming international humanitarian law as an authorizing precedent, as an independent, nongovernmental organization MSF depends less on treaties than on personalities and a fragile web of local agreements. Whenever possible, mission field coordinators take care to pay regular respects to all local potentates, with ritual visits a recognized part of operational routine.

Humanitarian space is a fragile fiction, easily disrupted by state strategy or violence. When military forces undertake missions pursuing humanitarian goals, the humanitarian space demarcated by MSF blurs back into a larger continuum of conflict. The case of Afghanistan is instructive in this regard. Following the romantic adventure in the early 1980s, MSF spent another two decades in the country, staying on through dark days of civil war and Taliban rule. The organization protested against food drops by US forces during their 2001 campaign and sought to maintain distance from state-sponsored reconstruction efforts. Nonetheless, MSF found itself—like all foreign agencies—increasingly identified with the American effort.[7] After the murder of five team members in 2004 the group withdrew. The deaths of project personnel, together with the absence of a meaningful state response, effectively collapsed MSF's definition of the situation.

Even as it maintained a version of operational neutrality in pursuit of projects on the ground, MSF also elaborated various forms of advocacy under the tradition of témoignage described above. In practice the term now can indicate a wide variety of activities undertaken with conscience in mind, from diplomatic encouragement to the production of statistics, in addition to "speaking out" through public appeals and protest (Redfield 2006). As its reputation readily attests, MSF's threshold for publicity and protest has proven far lower than that of the ICRC. Nonetheless, the group stops short of promoting human rights per se or directly pursuing legal redress for war crimes; indeed, with the emergence of an international juridical system it has sought to narrowly define its role as a medical actor rather than as a potential participant in juridical proceedings (Bouchet-Saulnier and Dubuet 2007:49–50).[8] Thus speaking out constitutes MSF's most overt ethical gesture toward justice. The form and limits of this engagement have varied through time along with its target and at times include a measure of self-interrogation, in addition to ready critique of the larger aid apparatus of which it is a part (Soussan 2008).

The precise balance between MSF's conception of humanitarian space and its practice of speaking out remains unclear. Speaking out certainly breaks with medical and humanitarian traditions of discrete silence and stands in implied contradiction with strict neutrality. Most prominent instances of the group's public speech involve moments of major humanitarian disaster and operational frustration or collapse.[9] Moreover, as Didier Fassin (2004, 2007a) suggests, in certain limit cases like Palestine, MSF's presence itself is primarily an act of advocacy, having minimal medical justification. At the same time instances of kidnapping or murder affecting members of the organization's staff trigger particularly passionate and loud response, even as they reveal uncomfortable inequities between the relative worth of particular lives.[10] Under extreme conditions, the group has few strategic options available to it other than withdrawal and denunciation. As it agonized over its public response during the Rwandan genocide and issued frantic declarations, MSF was only able to stay in the country by removing its own compromised insignia and working under the flag of the ICRC (Orbinski 2008:193). The rebel had returned home.

Even in comparatively placid—and more typical—settings, tensions surrounding the degree of desirable outspokenness periodically emerge. In Uganda, for example, different branches of MSF have sponsored a variety of projects in the country for over two decades. While most have worked in relative cooperation with the government, the upsurge of violence and displacement in the north in 2003–04 prompted some soul-searching on the part of field staff about why they had so long accepted government accounts. A head of mission for MSF-Holland at the time mused to me that Uganda had been "cursed by its good image" and aid agencies thereby lulled into collaboration. She advocated taking more risks on behalf of northern populations, expanding operations and publicly denouncing conditions in displacement camps. Although that section later did release a report proclaiming alarm about the health status of displaced people with some fanfare, matters never escalated into an open breach. Operations continued, while MSF's report joined a larger wave of advocacy produced at the time. Yet people I talked to on later trips to the northern region remained only marginally less suspicious of government intensions than those of the rebel forces. They did not wish MSF's activity in this context to be taken as endorsement of official policies. At the same time they wished to provide care, and with peace negotiations again on the horizon the political situation remained tantalizingly uncertain.

Given the political complexity of many field situations, it is no surprise that neutrality has remained a topic of continuing concern for MSF and figured in its internal debates. One of the most astute analyses came in 2001 from Fiona Terry, then a researcher at MSF-France's internal foundation. Raising the question of whether the principle of neutrality remained relevant to the organization, she surveyed its origin, perversions, and contradictions, while noting the significance of perceptions and tensions with the practice of speaking out. On the basis of this last point she proposed that MSF acknowledge its history of engagement and adopt a pending motion to finally drop the principle from its charter. After all, "it is not possible to be a little bit neutral, or subscribe to a 'spirit of neutrality'" (Terry 2001:5). Following a year of extended discussion across the movement, however, the general assembly of MSF endorsed a statement favoring retention of the charter's reference to neutrality. The statement noted that neutrality continued to be associated with humanitarian action, that the reference had not impeded the organization's ability to speak out, and indeed, that dropping it might actually weaken MSF's position at moments when it is already suspected of taking sides (Bradol 2001). MSF would remain, as it were, a little bit neutral.

THE PRINCIPLES OF THE WEAK

MSF's trajectory with regard to neutrality is only one variant in the broader field of humanitarian actors. Others have gone much further in aligning themselves with political crusades or human rights ideals and negotiated collaboration with military reconstruction with far fewer qualms (for example, CARE). However, MSF presents a particularly telling case, I suggest, precisely because it deviates from the inherited understanding of ICRC tradition without ever fully rejecting it. Although this elasticity may upset classificatory schemas, in which MSF is only uncertainly "classical" or "solidarist" (Weiss 1999; Tanguy and Terry 1999), it helpfully returns topics like neutrality from the realm of abstraction to the more fluid ground of historical practice. It also serves as a reminder that radical commitment to an overarching value, such as the minimization of suffering, may consequently render other principles less absolute.

As the tradition of guerrilla warfare suggests, open struggle can be particularly fraught from a position of strategic weakness. The risk of defeat can prove worthwhile, but only if a logic of sacrifice and the moral force of suffering can transform present loss into later political gain. Thus the slaughter of civilians, even supportive ones, can serve strategic ends from a military perspective. For humanitarians, however, such forms of sacrifice are morally unacceptable. By openly committing to the protection and well-being of the living, NGOs like MSF reduce their room for political maneuver. When faced with unacceptable circumstances, they can only negotiate, resort to denunciation, or withdraw.[11] Thus the humanitarian position is politically weak in the strategic sense and must rely on moral persuasion and the actions of others.

In humanitarian discussions of neutrality, protagonists often appeal to additional principles, particularly that of impartiality. For the most part MSF adheres strongly to impartiality, in the sense of providing aid "in proportion to need and without discrimination" and stressing financial independence to forestall undue political and economic influence on its decision-making (Tanguy and Terry 1999). Unsurprisingly, this approach conforms to the tenants of modernist medicine, emphasizing physical need over social position, only reinforced by the organization's engagement with the statistical logic of epidemiology. Where neutrality may carry deep scars of critique, impartiality appears somewhat less scathed, perhaps due to its intimate role in liberal conceptions of justice that forbid discrimination.

Once put into practice, however, impartiality can carry its own risks and political complications. As Terry notes in her essay on neutrality, from a medical perspective the needs of opposing sides are rarely equal. By acting impartially one can thereby appear aligned, directly contributing goods and services unequally between combatants. In Bosnia even accepting the terms for safe passage led to accusations of concession and threatened the collapse of "humanitarian space." The risks of impartiality extend to a wider field of representation, however, as made clear by another case Terry cites:

> In the current conflict in the Molucca Islands of Indonesia, for example, it is the Christian population who are most in need of assistance. But as an essentially European NGO, MSF is perceived as being pro-Christian. Thus MSF is searching for ways to assist Muslim communities to avoid accusations of partiality in the conflict. The need to be perceived as neutral in order to remain present outweighs the importance of basing assistance on the greatest need. [Terry 2001:4]

Impartiality, then, is as much dependent on perception as neutrality and offers no universal safeguard to either operational access or moral standing.

As a former executive director of MSF-USA pointed out in response to an earlier version of this paper, considering neutrality as an imperfect claim rather than an absolute principle does little to alter its ultimate dependence on the perceptions of actors involved. Anecdotal evidence and field experience indicate that people on the ground often have a hard time distinguishing between aid agencies or grasping the nuances of their ideological commitments.[12] Principles of neutrality, or impartiality for that matter, are likely less crucial than a reputation for positive engagement across locales. Given this, the question for humanitarian organizations then becomes how best to influence perception to further their ideals. The classic Red Cross adherence to neutrality traded public silence for operational access and cast its moral appeal at the level of formal agreements and long-term influence. Its aura of moral authenticity thus relied on consistent adherence to principle and recognition by political powers. MSF modified this classic equation by claiming independence, adding public speech, and minimizing its patience for violations. Its moral authenticity therefore shifted to a more oppositional framing of virtue and realistic adjustment of principle to the humanitarian needs of the moment. Neither approach guarantees universal success in achieving humanitarian ends. But MSF's looser style reveals the political edge of a humanitarian ethic, as well as its strategic weakness. The organization's internal debate over neutrality occurred on the eve of 9/11. After subsequent shifts in US foreign policy and a new scale of militarized action co-opting humanitarian rhetoric, the debate quietly subsided: claiming neutrality clearly still had some uses.

BY WAY OF CONCLUSION

When the ethics of life intersect with the blunter politics of death, humanitarianism reaches a limit. Medical assistance pales before genocide and a concerted campaign against aid personnel generally forces their withdrawal. Humanitarian neutrality ultimately relies on recognition. Thus it comprises a position of formal weakness alongside its partial counterclaim to sovereignty. At the same time it resists the full sovereignty of political definition, preferring a negative formation of refusal. In this sense neutrality constitutes an "impossible" problem. Nonetheless, it remains actively generative, rearticulating the significance of suffering in moral terms. Humanitarian sensibility now filters back through human rights discourse, through development, and through state policies of immigration (Ticktin 2006a). Humanitarianism even emerges in warfare, reworking the very form that gave it birth and playing again into strategic calculations. Throughout, the medical vision remains two edged: attention to biological life can both clarify the terms of humanity at stake and reduce it to a suffering body.

By prefacing this brief survey of MSF's relationship with neutrality with a brief history of the concept, I have sought to emphasize its variability. The point is not that neutrality in contemporary humanitarianism mirrors that of medieval warfare in any direct fashion, but rather that the concept itself might prove more unstable and thus more potentially generative than we often assume. If one looks beyond nineteenth-century norms as a starting point, then neutrality appears less of a perfect practice and rather as something partial, temporary, and always negotiated. The key, as Terry's article and the MSF board's statement quoted above both note, lies in perception. Given that MSF emerged and grew during an era in which conflict occurred increasingly at the edges of law (even as treaties and resolutions continued to proliferate), it should come as no surprise that the group would retain a formal claim to neutral status while modifying its practices in accordance with circumstance. In this sense contemporary humanitarians may have reinvented something like that European custom under which imperfect neutrality was not only conceivable, but also quite permissible, provided one could get away with it.

On one of my initial visits to MSF, in this case to an office in Amsterdam, I interviewed a veteran staff member, then readying to work for another organization. After a lengthy discussion of the politics of intervention, he paused, lit another cigarette, and noted with a wry smile: "The beauty of MSF is the anarchy as well. We're not always consistent." The comment stayed with me throughout subsequent research. Beyond reflecting the essential style of the group, it also summed up and celebrated its de facto embrace of contradiction. This remains a significant point of divergence from the ICRC, which plays a role in international law and takes its principles more literally.[13] In the end, I suggest, MSF's inconsistency provides a more revealing reference point for principles such as neutrality. Yes, neutrality is a fiction and often a thin one. But the very inconsistencies of its practice recall that neutrality is also a strategy, one whose effects vary in different contexts. This obvious point is too often forgotten amid either affirmation or denunciation and dismissal, and thus I return to it by way of conclusion. The politics of ethics are rarely singular or stable. The effort to redefine a situation by standing outside, by abstaining and refusing positions, is no exception.

Notes

1. To emphasize contingent practice over categorical assumption I avoid the term "antipolitics" (as in, for example, the erasure of politics amid development planning described by Ferguson 1990).

2. Most writing in this area considers the emergence of neutrality as part of the progressive history of law and pays little attention to antecedents or comparative possibilities. See, however, Bauslaugh 1991, Frank 1992, Nevakivi 1993, and Knight 1920. Neff 2000 provides the most comprehensive recent overview I have found.

3. For a parallel argument about war and states see Nordstrom 2004. The larger point is that assumptions about linear, progressive time may at times actually generate analytic conundrums and confusion.

4. For the purposes of this argument I foreshorten the group's history and simplify its structure. MSF currently has nineteen national sections as well as a number of other offices. Not all these sections are equal, however, nor are they always aligned in practice; indeed, the French section has often quarreled with its Belgian and Dutch counterparts, the two other heavyweights.

5. For all that it appears regularly across the group's publications, training materials, and internal discussions, "témoignage" is by no means a stable term, its content shifting across eras alongside MSF's scope of activities and the expansion of international law (see Bouchet-Saulnier and Dubuet 2007; Soussan 2008). MSF's different subgroups have interpreted it differently, with the French section emphasizing a history of practice and even walking back from the term itself (Redfield 2006). In this context I simply underscore MSF's need to authorize its action along the ethical edge of politics.

6. MSF Press conference, June 17, 1994. In the event the group was far from pleased with the actual French action undertaken at the end of the genocide and with the new Rwandan government's later forcible repatriation of refugees. See Orbinski 2008 for a vivid personal account of events.

7. The blurring of military and humanitarian activities extended into appearance and equipment. A field coordinator for MSF told me an anecdote about how the US Army once purchased three hundred white Toyota Land Cruisers of the sort that NGOs commonly use in such settings. Stunned by the sheer scale of potential misrecognition suddenly confronting it, MSF could only plead with the military command to at least paint them green (author's notes, December 2004).

8. As an MSF Foundation study of the group's legal testimony notes, while the organization might wish to avoid establishing precedents of legal obligation and of speaking beyond its actual knowledge, "it is always possible for the volunteer to testify on his/her own account, without mentioning the name of the organization or its members and without using its internal documents" (Bouchet-Saulnier and Dubuet 2007:14). The degree of nuance presented in such self-analyses (see also Soussan 2008) itself indicates the extent to which MSF seeks to define itself as standing apart and, in that sense, potentially neutral.

9. MSF-France has sponsored an internal study series, *MSF Speaking Out/Prises de parole publiques de MSF*, to document the group's response to landmark catastrophes. A full four volumes address the extended crisis in Rwanda and Zaire, an indication of the compound severity of that experience. See also De Torrenté 1995 and Delvaux 2005.

10. Even beyond actual acts of violence, a sense of threatened security has pervaded many aid organizations in recent years and altered their perception of risk. Many older members of MSF regularly express disgust at travel restrictions that would forbid taking public transport and restrict vehicle movement and other cautions to protect expatriate team members that they view as unnecessary and counterproductive.

11. Another possibility—embracing the martyrdom of their staff—remains off the table, part of the unequal political economy of life in which humanitarian action occurs (Fassin 2007a).

12. Most people I talked to in Uganda recognized MSF's medical focus but little else. Preliminary results from a multicountry study undertaken by the organization indicate that it is at times perceived as having a religious or political agenda. See discussion archived at http://www.msf-crash.org/rencontre-debats/2009/07/09/305/dans-loeil-des-autres/, accessed June 10, 2010. Also see Donini et al. 2010. The group's commitment to a shorter term humanitarian vision and its general avoidance of development projects likewise do not always translate cleanly, generating consternation when it withdraws.

13. MSF prides itself on maintaining a culture of internal critique. In 2005, the nineteen sections of MSF engaged in a reflective project known as La Mancha (a conscious reference to Cervantes), inviting internal and external commentary, and engaging in debate over its core principles. In contrast to an international gathering a decade earlier at Chantilly, the project featured more consensus than friction, to the extent that some participants expressed disappointment (MSF 2006).

4

The Anthropologist and His Poor

Harri Englund

Dead bodies are rarely encountered in development work, and the dull condition of endemic, structural poverty stands in a sharp contrast to the urgent decisions demanded by humanitarian catastrophes. A clear-cut distinction between international development and global humanitarianism is, however, difficult to sustain. As both the early expositions of dependency (Amin 1976; Frank 1969) and the current critiques of participation (Cooke and Kothari 2001; Hickey and Mohan 2004) have made clear, the professionalization of poverty alleviation risks making human suffering look like a technical problem, lacking the urgency of humanitarian emergencies. At the same time, alternative approaches are themselves hard-pressed to avoid the routinization of their own procedures, the hierarchies they depend on barely concealed by the populist idioms of grassroots empowerment and community-based collaborative action. A closer look at one such approach, I argue in this chapter, not only suggests intellectual and pragmatic resources to reconsider the professionalization of poverty alleviation, it also engages a disquieting parallel between this mode of routinizing human suffering and the populism of anthropological practice evident in a recent call for collaborative ethnography.

A dead body was almost laid on the doorstep of the governmental and nongovernmental participants in a training workshop I attended in the southern African country of Malawi in 2003. A junior participant, whom I call here Boniface Mbewe, developed respiratory difficulties during the third night of the two-week workshop, was sent on a bus to his home district some 400 miles away, and died virtually as soon as he had disembarked from the bus. The symptoms had erupted suddenly, and the workshop convenors took the decision to send him away early in the morning before I was aware of the incident. Ethical doubt tormented me for the rest of the workshop, dismayed as I was at what seemed to be a lack of reflection on how the tragedy could have been averted. Senior participants later explained to me in private conversations why they had taken this course of action. Had they sought diagnosis and care themselves when Mbewe's kin were absent, they could have exposed themselves to criticism afterward, especially in the event of death. It was far better, they assured me, to send Mbewe to his own people whose responsibility it was to seek medical care. The underlying fear, I gathered after several conversations, was the possibility that his kin would have accused the participants of witchcraft (*ufiti*) if he had suddenly died in their hands. Enmity or sheer malevolence could have explained his death among colleagues, a misfortune that could have subjected the participants to occult reprisals or more overt acts of revenge.

Under the circumstances, with Mbewe dead and buried, I presumed that my best chance of eliciting critical reflection lay in my own profession, the production of descriptions of social relationships. I was struck with the fundamental similarity between the lifeworlds of these development professionals and those they objectified as their illiterate beneficiaries in villages. As I show in this chapter, the workshop deployed the populist idioms of grassroots participation and collaboration even as it asserted development professionals as the possessors of exclusive technical knowledge. These idioms, however egalitarian, did not permit the workshop participants to draw on their own situated and embodied experiences as relatives and neighbors of the poor, because such identification could have obliterated the very boundary that made them professionals in the first place. Mbewe's tragedy, including the workshop convenors' response to his sudden illness, could have started to indicate the need to question this boundary, if only by acknowledging the obligations that tied together the persons it seemingly separated.

It is unremarkable that my description, an assault on the status of development work as a distinct profession, appeared irrelevant to the workshop participants to whom I presented it. More interesting are the complexities that the incident and my description of it throw into relief. The humanitarian urge to save a stranger's life applied here to the anthropologist rather than to development professionals, whatever humanitarian imperatives development work might otherwise have. Yet these development professionals were not playing a politics of life (see Fassin 2007a and this volume). The workshop convenors did not question whether Mbewe's life was possible or legitimate to save; nor did they strip his personhood to the bare life of individuality. For them and for myself, human relationships were intrinsic to our assessment of the kind of action Mbewe's illness required. Whereas I assumed that our participation in the same residential workshop involved some solicitude for those who fell ill, the workshop convenors asserted Mbewe's belonging to relationships elsewhere. The case is complex also because the topic of the workshop did present an alternative to much rhetoric and practice in poverty alleviation. The topic was REFLECT (Regenerated Freirean Literacy Through Empowering Community Techniques), an approach to adult literacy that emphasizes not only the acquisition of literacy and numeracy skills but also the creation of opportunities for poor people to pursue tangible changes in their material circumstances. The outlook of REFLECT, as will be seen below, shares a good deal with anthropology, its methodology designed to blur the very boundary that development professionalism seems to entail.

As such, my initial interest in the workshop was not deconstructive, as though the tragic incident only confirmed my convictions of unpalatable professionalism. My interest in REFLECT had arisen in the context of my earlier work on human rights activism in Malawi (see Englund 2006). Preoccupied with dismantling autocratic rule, many Malawian human rights activists and their foreign sponsors put a premium on political and civil freedoms in their definition of human rights. Once a new constitution and competitive multiparty politics had been secured in the early 1990s, the activists embarked on educating the rural and urban poor on their new freedoms, with foreign funding poured into various governmental and nongovernmental programs of civic education. When human rights activism among the impoverished majority took the form of education rather than advocacy, it quickly assumed the long-established patterns of one-way communication between the elites and the poor, with a professional class of NGO activists emerging to provide their "civic education services." Although human rights NGOs, together with faith-based organizations, kept politicians on their toes through mass-mediated interventions, the expression of social and economic rights received little attention throughout the first decade of democracy. In this regard, REFLECT could offer a set of alternative concepts and imaginaries to foster critical analysis of Malawi's inequities. Indeed, precisely by asserting themselves as development professionals untouched by politics, REFLECT advocates could detach themselves from the association of human rights with narrowly defined politics and make explicit the injustices underlying impoverishment. The extent to which this happened in practice may be limited, but the space opened up for reflection should not be discounted.

What the tragic incident, and the workshop convenors' response to my description, compelled me to contemplate were the limits of collaboration—both between the convenors and the Malawian poor, and between the convenors and the anthropologist in their midst. A recent call for collaborative ethnography, particularly its evocation of grassroots empowerment (see Lassiter 2005a), offers an opportunity to explore those limits also in a disciplinary idiom. It is the desire to bridge the perceived gulf between grassroots knowledge and activist-anthropological knowledge that makes collaborative ethnography and the Malawian REFLECT workshop instances of the same contemporary moment. The idea of collaboration accompanying this order of knowledge production can be rather insidious, exhorting as it does the anthropologist-activist to reach out to his or her localized partner with the distinct advantage of having access to wider frames of knowing. This chapter issues an invitation to accept incompatibility between the positions and descriptions different people adopt in relation to poverty and human suffering. Collaboration, as Anna Lowenhaupt Tsing has pointed out, "is not a simple sharing of information" (2005:13). Collaborators need not share common goals. Incompatibility can, as such, be either productive or unproductive. If my encounter with the workshop convenors provides an example of unproductive incompatibility, an argument from a different fieldwork in an impoverished township may begin to indicate what productive incompatibility might involve. Crucial here is a move from populist to postpopulist egalitarianism.

FROM THE GROUND UP

In *The Philosopher and His Poor*, Jacques Rancière attributes to Plato the formula that has underpinned philosophers' meditations on the subject of the poor: "Let all do their business and develop the virtue specific to their condition" (Rancière 2004:220). Generations of philosophers, Rancière claims, have elucidated the virtues of the poor with this formula in mind, a pattern of philosophy that has given a priority to theorizing the "bottom" rather than the "top." And yet, Rancière points out, every shoemaker knows that there is no shoemaker virtue. A virtue, no less than a voice, has been a function of the philosophical discourse within which the poor have been summoned into being, with the consequential assumption that "the shoe-maker is someone who may not do anything else than shoemaking" (Rancière 2004:58). Lest this assumption is seen to separate philosophy from social science, Rancière proceeds to examine Pierre Bourdieu's soci-ology. Bourdieu's demystification of high culture and his disclosure of mis-recognition all amount, in Rancière's analysis, to the same order of knowing as in philosophy. The only difference is that the sociologist, taking the side of the wretched of the world, explains "backward *the same thing* as the philosopher" (Rancière 2004:179; emphasis original).[1]

Anthropologists, proudly immersed in ethnographic fieldwork among the poor, are likely to see such problems as intrinsic to armchair theorizing in philosophy and sociology. Yet anthropology is also driven by populist passions, not least when anthropologists, in Jean-Pierre Olivier de Sardan's words, "discover the people, pity their lot in life and/or marvel at their capacities, and decide to put themselves at the disposal of the people and to strive for their welfare" (2005:35).[2] Although decoupled from dema-gogic politics, anthropology's populism has an ambiguous relation to mis-erabilism (see Grignon and Passeron 1989). Interlocutors in the field can appear to be the miserabilist subjects of domination and privation no less than the resourceful subjects invoked by populism. Even when the injunc-tion is to study elites, the interest is often to uncover the ways in which mar-ginalization gets reproduced (see Nader 1972).

A recent call for collaborative ethnography, understood as the copro-duction of ethnographic texts, asserts a radical equality between the part-ners in anthropological knowledge production (see Lassiter 2005a). Still firmly embedded in anthropological populism, collaborative ethnography promises to contribute to "the larger anthropological project of social jus-tice and equity" (Lassiter 2005a:94). It emerges after decades of anthro-pologists criticizing their own knowledge practices. While the idiom of collaboration may have replaced the idiom of dialogue, which in turn had replaced the idiom of the text as a metaphor for anthropological knowl-edge production (Lassiter 2005a:93), enough has been said in the disci-pline to make the very process of coauthorship a subject of inquiry (see, for example, Abu-Lughod 1993; Caplan 1997; Clifford and Marcus 1986; Rabinow 1999). Yet some metaphors prove resilient and entice anthropol-ogists to embrace collaborative ethnography with their usual populism that can, once again, preserve the order of things, leaving, so to speak, the shoe-maker to his shoemaking.

Luke Eric Lassiter sees in collaborative ethnography an opportunity to build "a public anthropology from the ground up and the center out"

(2005a:97). "Grassroots collaborative action," whose concerns are "community-based," ensures the success of "larger public anthropology" (Lassiter 2005a:97). Radical equality, I argue in this chapter, is the first casualty of these metaphors through which collaborative ethnography is to be envisioned. Confined to the grass roots, the anthropologist's coauthors, or "consultants" (Lassiter 2005a:95), depend on the anthropologist for their insertion into "larger" frames of knowledge. Whatever high value is placed on grassroots knowledge, the scalar hierarchy informing this value brings anthropologists perilously close to state bureaucrats whose geographical and conceptual range always appears to be broader than those of their "local" subjects (see Ferguson 2002:987–988). Moreover, however attuned it is to activist agendas, this juxtaposition between collaborative ethnography and public anthropology also mimics an all too familiar distinction between ethnography and theory. Just as theory conventionally encompasses ethnography as an intellectual domain that permits cross-cultural elucidation (see, for example, Sperber 1985:9–34), so too does public anthropology encompass collaborative ethnography as a "larger" project.

The purpose of this chapter is to explore the collaborative impulse in the production of anthropological knowledge about poverty and human suffering and to ask what a postpopulist egalitarianism might look like.[3] The question arises not only as a response to Lassiter's (2005a:102–103) cogent call for a critique of collaborative ethnography, but also in recognition of unsettling similarities between the rhetoric of collaborative ethnography and that of many human rights activists and development professionals. The participatory rhetoric of "community-based" and "grassroots" interventions poses a dilemma to the anthropologist, whose engagement with the poor takes place within the context of a myriad of projects to improve their lot, some of which bear uncanny resemblance to the egalitarian sensibilities of anthropology itself. REFLECT provides a particularly gripping illustration of this dilemma.

FROM REFLECT TO REFLECTION

A fusion between the politicized pedagogy of the Brazilian educationalist Paolo Freire (1970) and the techniques of Participatory Rural Appraisal (PRA) (see, for example, Chambers 1994, 1997), REFLECT has since the early 1990s become an influential approach to combating poverty and inequality in Latin America, Asia, and Africa. In Malawi, as in many other countries, the pedagogical impetus has associated REFLECT with campaigns for adult literacy. Spearheaded by the British NGO ActionAid (see Archer and Cottingham 1996), REFLECT had been adopted by eleven agencies in Malawi by 2004, most of them development and faith-based NGOs working in consultation with the government's National Adult Literacy Programme. They combine the learning of writing, reading, and numeracy skills with various attempts to promote socioeconomic change among the poor, the collective and participatory projects known as "Action Points." In the words of a Malawian advocate of REFLECT, it "encourages and enables participants to critically assess their lives, take control of their future, enhances their literacy skills, generates a written vocabulary, which is relevant to their own community or situation, recognizes and builds upon their knowledge and mobilizes for individual and collective action" (Tizora 2004:1).

Although this emphasis on critical awareness does make REFLECT stand out among current approaches to poverty and inequality in Malawi, it is pursued in the context of a particular economic and political history that has to be understood before I proceed with my analysis. Paternalism, evident in but not reducible to strong presidentialism, has long informed campaigns for change in Malawi, its roots deep in the colonial period (Vail and White 1989:181). It has assumed different forms under Malawi's three postindependence administrations, with the authoritarianism of Kamuzu Banda's one-party state (1964 to 1994) modified by the wasteful neopatrimonialism of Bakili Muluzi's "democratic" regime (1994 to 2004) and the more technocratic approach of Bingu wa Mutharika's government (2004 to the present). Each style of governance has been attuned to the dominant development paradigms of its period, but the paternalism of those who consider development as their profession has never faded. Campaigns for adult literacy, the immediate context of REFLECT in Malawi, are a case in point. When the National Adult Literacy Policy was formulated in 1986, it not only promised "to support and save the precepts and cornerstones of the Republic of Malawi in a spirit of unswerving loyalty and dedication" (NALP 1986:20) but also adopted Functional Adult Literacy (FAL) as its approach to promoting literacy as "a part of development strategies in Malawi" (NALP 1986:22). FAL, not unlike REFLECT, combined the acquisition of literacy and numeracy skills with the teaching of agricultural techniques and what came to be known as civic education. These "economic, social and cultural messages" (NALP 1986:22) were often delivered by the Malawi Young Pioneers, a paramilitary wing of the ruling party, disbanded after the democratic transition in 1994.

The concern with development as the nation's redemptive and transcendental project did not wane with the change in governance. On the contrary, the government's proposal for a new "mass literacy campaign" suggested in 2005 that the name of the literacy schools should be changed from *Kwacha*, a Chichewa word for "dawn" or "sunrise" that came to depict the birth of the nation, to *Chitukuko*, the Chichewa word for "development" (see NALP 2005:13). The obvious reason for the new campaign was the persistently high levels of illiteracy in the country, the official illiteracy rate being 42 percent at the beginning of the new millennium (UNDP 2001:29). As a consequence, the technocratic thirst for development remained insatiable, as illustrated by the new campaign proposal's staggering estimate that the country of five million illiterates needed two hundred thousand literacy classes (NALP 2005:5). Malawi had four thousand literacy classes when this estimate was made.

The introduction of REFLECT has to be understood within this historical context that has professionalized the provision of development and made the poor a category of thought among Malawian policy makers and activists. The development professionals' descriptions of themselves have not, however, remained unchanged. Whereas the 1986 report noted that any initiative by the ruling party and its paramilitary wing "will be received with alacrity and acted upon with efficiency" (NALP 1986:31), the 2005 report urged "Civil Society and Private Sector to take a leading role" in the campaign for adult literacy (NALP 2005:10). It appealed to them as "service providers" who would design and implement "community-based activities" so that the private sector could "build a literate environment for its pool of labourers and consumers" (NALP 2005:10). The reference to community-based activities placed REFLECT at the level of local projects for poverty alleviation and, as I discuss below, made the approach virtually indistinguishable from the Participatory Rural Appraisal (PRA) that was supposedly a mere component in it. One evaluation of a REFLECT project echoed the predicament of many others by pointing out how little material and financial support communities had been able to solicit for their Action Points, the initiatives of practical action that were expected to make REFLECT a tool of empowerment (see Benediktsson and Kamtengeni 2004:26–28). In the absence of an effective link to the worlds beyond their own villages, people participating in REFLECT classes found themselves engaged in various small-scale building and income-generating endeavors far removed from the structural change demanded in Freirean pedagogy. Moreover, the above-mentioned view on citizens as laborers and consumers accorded with the way in which illiteracy had long been associated with backwardness and ignorance by Malawian elites (see Englund 2006:119–120). Not only were illiterate laborers and consumers an impediment to the growth of the private sector, they lacked the acuity and intelligence of a responsible citizenry. As far as I know, never did the REFLECT advocates in Malawi, let alone the country's other elites, consider literacies in the plural, with the elites' interpretative relation to texts quite distinct from the literacy of nonelites who were taught a submissive relation to texts (see Collins 1995:84).

THE ANTHROPOLOGIST AND HIS ACTIVISTS

It would be wrong to lose sight of REFLECT's distinct features by dismissing it as yet another depoliticized approach to socioeconomic change. Its persuasive rhetorics and methodology offer, rather, an opportunity to examine the blurring of boundaries between anthropology and activism in the ethos of collaborative ethnography.[4] The anthropology of human rights has produced particularly sophisticated perspectives on the discipline's uneasy relation to activists and development professionals who pursue justice and equality. According to Iris Jean-Klein and Annelise Riles (2005), co-construction and denunciation have been the two main modalities of anthropological engagement. The modalities can overlap and result in a double orientation in the same project, such as when the anthropologist chooses to advocate one set of actors rather than another or when he or she becomes a so-called expert witness or adviser. Yet as the ends of a continuum, co-construction and denunciation refer to the tendency among anthropologists either to express moral empathy with the subjects of their study, typically by giving them a "voice," or to denounce the proliferation and effects of technocratic regimes that claim to alleviate human suffering. Jean-Klein and Riles (2005:180) observe that denunciation speaks in "the external register of humanitarian outrage" and "the internal register of expertise and advice," in both cases proceeding as though the regimes it criticizes were interested in, and vulnerable to, anthropological critique. Moving beyond these strategies of anthropological engagement requires appreciation of the diversity of activist positions within contemporary discourses on human rights, humanitarianism, and development (see, for example, Cunningham 1999; Tate 2007). Technical capacity and moral voice may well be combined, rather than kept separate, in some emerging activist positions, and disinterest can give way to public interest as the preferred justification for witnessing and intervention (see Redfield 2006:5).

What co-construction and denunciation, if pursued as anthropological strategies, do not capture are the complex ways in which some activist and anthropological approaches at once dovetail and diverge. REFLECT in Malawi serves as an example of an approach that shares with anthropology not only its respect for other ways of knowing and being but also the concomitant invitation to reflect on one's own knowledge, as the following description of a training workshop shows. Yet the prospects for deploying collaborative ethnography as a tool to realize that shared vision are curtailed by an acute divergence between anthropological and activist interests in the orders of knowledge their reflections identify. To put it differently, collaborative ethnography in this context may conflate what is best kept separate, both for the sake of care for the discipline that Jean-Klein and Riles (2005) ingeniously call for and, *as a consequence*, for the renewal of anthropology's radical potential that makes engagement with issues such as human rights, humanitarianism, and development so productive in the first place. This divergence, in the form of various incompatibilities between ethnographic and other descriptions of human suffering, will become clearer as this chapter progresses, but it is necessary, before returning to the case of REFLECT in Malawi, to recognize the limited extent to which human rights anthropology has harnessed its insights into different orders of knowledge. While this field of interest has advanced rapidly from its early preoccupation with cultural relativism (see Engle 2001; Merry 2003; Riles 2006), its practitioners struggle to find an appropriate framework for elucidating competing perspectives on the meaning and practice of human rights. "Global" and "local" still appear as the conventions by which difference and its relation to power are described, at times in conjunction with a metaphor of translation that sees activists shifting between the two levels (see Merry 2005). Few anthropologists take the global-local divide as an empirical given, however, and Mark Goodale, for example, explains that it "evokes a self-consciously artificial verticality" (2007:23) that prevents him from describing the networks of human rights activism horizontally, as though those networks were devoid of hierarchy (Goodale 2007:20).

A fundamental concern in Goodale's conceptual scheme is to retain a sense of distinct sites where human rights are pursued and debated, a sense of, in fact, "places which can become law-like and coercive" (2007:13). Yet even if places matter, anthropologists' propensity to use spatial metaphors for describing different orders of knowing and being is itself an old disciplinary convention that comes with specific consequences (see Fardon 1990; Gupta and Ferguson 1997). One consequence relates to what I noted earlier, the tendency to portray "local knowledge," however acute and sophisticated in its own context, as more limited in scope than the conceptual abstractions that are at the anthropologist's disposal. As has been seen, this effect of spatial metaphors inadvertently accompanies the definition of collaborative ethnography as "grassroots public anthropology" that emanates "from the ground up and from the center out" (Lassiter 2005a:97). Whatever its merits in affording alternative perspectives on large-scale economic and political issues, collaborative ethnography that stakes its claim to the grass roots will always be hard-pressed to contest the actual ways in which the metaphor gets deployed by activists and development professionals (compare Riles 2000:5–6). In Malawi, for example, "the grass roots" became the term of choice in human rights activists' efforts to distinguish their knowledge from the misunderstandings and prejudices among the impoverished masses (Englund 2006:99–122).

More broadly, it is worth reflecting on the ultralocalism of a notion that "burrows into the earth itself" (Goodale 2007:23). When the challenge to apparently universalizing dispositions is posed in localist terms, a hierarchy of scale seems to underlie claims to knowledge. As mentioned, some anthropologists recognize this hierarchy in their juxtaposition of ethnography with theory. A post-localist epistemology, by contrast, begins with the realization that ethnography is "theoretical from the start" (Malkki 2007:170). Just as the categories by which anthropologists structure their research are never pretheoretical, so too is it instructive to consider their interlocutors during fieldwork as engaged in producing social theory rather than simply local knowledge (Moore 1996:3). Human rights anthropology can again offer a clue here, insofar as it advocates "open source theorizing" (Goodale 2007:26) as a way of involving a range of subjects, elites and nonelites, in debating the idea of human rights.

Does the world begin to appear flat in its constitution by multiple knowledge claims, best described by "the Flat-Earthers of social theory" (Latour 2005:172)? Anthropologists should not rush to declare everyone a social theorist before asking whether different techniques of theorizing share common ground (Strathern 1987:30). A democratization of knowledge claims is, however, what collaborative ethnography, as the latest illustration of anthropology's populism, seeks to achieve. Engagement, by contrast, necessarily involves remaking ideas and practices, not merely seeking or adding allies (Tsing 2005:212). Populist egalitarianism is too similar to the doctrine of tolerance by which "everyone talks and nothing is argued" (Strathern 2006:192). Indeed, *argument* rather than collaboration can be a more propitious idiom for an engaged anthropology that subscribes to the postpopulist view of equality as an "initial axiom" in human relationships (see Rancière 2004:223). The imperative of argument requires more than a capacity to disseminate viewpoints in a dialogue. It demands a simultaneous capacity to detach oneself from one's own viewpoint and, in effect, oneself from oneself.

"I LOVE THIS WORD 'DIALOGUE'"

The REFLECT workshop I observed in 2003 was known as a training of trainers course for practitioners working for both the government and NGOs. The theme of the workshop was "REFLECT as a Tool of Empowerment." It was convened by the newly established REFLECT Forum, with representatives from the government and NGOs taking turns to lead the proceedings. Among the twenty-six participants, the most senior ones included an experienced officer from a foreign-funded NGO and a teacher from the government's Magomero Community Development College. The others working for the government were either middle-ranking officers from the Ministry of Gender, Child Welfare, and Community Services in the capital Lilongwe, the ministry responsible for overseeing the campaign for adult literacy, or field officers from various districts, particularly community development assistants who were expected to implement REFLECT on the ground. All participants were Malawians, but the language of the workshop was English rather than Chichewa, the national lingua franca and the main language used in the implementation of REFLECT. However, as I discuss below, the comments and interjections expressed in Chichewa were important to the participants' critical awareness of the practical limitations of this approach. The workshop was held for two weeks in Dowa District, far from most participants' workplace and home, a significant detail for my subsequent discussion of the tragic incident.

The conduct of the workshop bore close resemblance to the many workshops that Malawian activists and practitioners attend (see Englund 2006:85–95). A paramount aspect, though largely unstated, was its monetary reward, with the daily allowances for a two-week workshop enabling the participants, particularly those employed by the government, to double their monthly salary. The workshop also deployed familiar methods of teaching and training, such as small-group discussions and lecturers' attempts to solicit views from the audience. It was clear, however, that REFLECT was an approach that had its own experts to elucidate it, a division between teachers and their audience asserted over and again in the workshop's agenda. Critical reflection, as I discuss below, did emerge, but its space was constantly curtailed by the leaders' inclination to codify their knowledge in jargon and techniques that made REFLECT lose much of its radical potential. For example, a senior NGO representative spent a whole session on the jargon that made the approach seem like an exclusive body of knowledge.

Well over twenty words or phrases were presented, all with their specific definitions and implications for techniques. They included *Matching Game, Buddy System, Fish Bowl, Spider Diagram, Buzz Session, Mixed Level Circle, Pair Work, Listening Pair, Simulation, Jigsaw, River of Life,* and *Fishbone*. Through a mastery of these concepts, the participants were invited to feel that they belonged to a group of experts, a collective of REFLECT professionals.

This sense of professionalism was also fostered by the close association of REFLECT with the Participatory Rural Appraisal (PRA). The participants were familiar with the PRA before this workshop through their previous training, and many of them had deployed its methods and concepts in their own work. On the first day, one of the workshop convenors stated that "in modern days, everybody is using PRA; that's why also in REFLECT we are going to that direction." He added, "Please make sure to use participatory methods as much as possible." A narrative derived from the work of Robert Chambers (for example, 1994, 1997) had become central to the participants' understanding of themselves as development professionals. Participation by the beneficiaries of development aid was seen to correct the mistakes of earlier "top-down" development paradigms through "changes and reversals" (Chambers 1997:103) in the relationship between outside experts and local communities. Yet as critics have observed in a number of settings, the professionalization of the PRA itself has involved increasing abstraction and codification of its methods and principles, with its emphasis on community development all too compatible with neoliberal economics and its notion of community rather lacking in historical and sociological nuance (see, for example, Bornstein 2005; Cooke and Kothari 2001; Green 2000; Hickey and Mohan 2004; Mosse 2005). The conflation of REFLECT and PRA diminished the chances of the former to reclaim the radical potential in the latter. However, the workshop participants' critical awareness had not been entirely dimmed by this professionalization; the limited material rewards of participation had not always been lost on them (see also Bornstein 2005: 124; Mosse 2005:173–175). As is described below, this frustration gave rise to sarcastic Chichewa remarks during the workshop.

The sessions on Paolo Freire's ideas touched, however superficially, on a set of issues that enhanced the participants' critical awareness. "Rights and dignity" appeared frequently in the speakers' talk about according the poor their due role in development. One clear criticism of Malawi's regime as it stood in 2003 was the speakers' insistence on rejecting handouts as a way of helping the poor, a method that President Muluzi had adopted as the main instrument in his paternalist bid for popularity and power. The workshop participants were asked to involve the poor in decision-making and to help them "take full control of their environment." "We have to give them complete power," one speaker enthused, adding, "We must empower them." Examples were given of development projects that, despite their high-profile presence, had failed because they did not involve "sustainability" and "ownership" by their beneficiaries. Freire's ideas about advocacy and political action were not presented in any detail, however, and the participants' opportunity to reflect critically on the practice of development did not go far beyond sloganeering about empowerment and the reiteration of how useful the PRA techniques were. "I love that word 'dialogue,'" one speaker confessed, telling the audience how the word evoked in his mind "something beautiful." Whether lobbying, protests, and other interventions would have stimulated equally pleasing sentiments was not discussed at the workshop.

A somewhat subversive discourse co-existed, however, with these rather standard statements about the poor and the role of participatory development. It came to the fore, if only briefly, when a speaker switched to Chichewa to reflect on what he or she had just said in English or when someone in the audience intervened with a comment. Laughter was the typical response to these moments of subversion, and their expression in Chichewa indicated the extent to which the participants' critical awareness was actually informed by their own experience of Malawian rural life. For example, when a speaker expounded on the importance of "multidisciplinary teams" for the PRA, he suggested that villagers had their own doctors, judges, and scientists. "There are healers who know lots of medicines" (*kuli asing'anga amene amadziwa mankhwala ambiri*), he added, immediately drawing laughter. The word for "healer," *sing'anga* (plural, *asing'anga*), is ambiguous in Chichewa, its scope encompassing morally neutral herbalists and immoral sorcerers, with some healers thought to combine both qualities in their practice. This ambiguity, compounded by some Christian churches' condemnation of all asing'anga, made the reference to local doctors rather more controversial than what the PRA's democratic sensibilities expected. Knowing "lots of medicines" was a morally ambiguous state, far removed from the scientific neutrality that multidisciplinary teams were supposed to exercise at the service of the local community. Another instance occurred when a speaker discussed the use of pictures and images in eliciting community participation. He pointed out how the pictures in the commonly used manual *Chuma Ndi Moyo* (Wealth Is Life/ Health) portrayed fine houses and cars as some of the wealth successful farmers could acquire. "That's what they get through agriculture" (*zimene amapeza muulimi*), the speaker commented wryly, amusing his audience, all too aware that food insecurity rather than car ownership was the prevalent condition among Malawian smallholders.

In the absence of pragmatic innovations through which to translate their critical awareness into transformative action, the participants were left with a diluted version of REFLECT. They were left, also, with a renewed sense of their professionalism. After all, they had come together to learn how REFLECT could assist them in their work to combat illiteracy. The illiterate were the "community" they were learning to empower through REFLECT, and various rhetorical devices during the workshop distinguished the participants from their local interlocutors. For instance, during an early session, one of the convenors observed that "experience has shown that adults, especially in rural areas, are illiterate." "Perhaps another experience I can share with you," he went on to say, "is that adults relapse into illiteracy if they are not supported." The participants were thereby invited to tap into the convenor's considerable experience and to recognize the predicament of their subjects in rural areas, never mind the fact that illiteracy was not nearly as universal as the convenor seemed to suggest. Moreover, although the drift of the workshop was to accord rights and dignity to rural people, the participants' access to other bodies of knowledge was also enunciated. With a suitable dose of jargon and techniques, the participants could themselves feel empowered to carry out their professional duties. "This course is a model for what you are going to do," one of the convenors announced on the first day.

THE DEATH OF BONIFACE MBEWE

A man in his twenties with a wife and a child, Boniface Mbewe had recently graduated from Magomero Community Development College. He had been posted to work as a community development assistant in Mangochi District and was still in the process of moving his young family there. This was the first workshop he had attended, and his inconspicuous presence accorded with the expectation that junior participants were there to learn from their more experienced coparticipants. After his death, a dispirited day ensued, the agenda interrupted by a prayer session and the collection of money for Mbewe's widow, but the workshop proceeded with minimal disruption. Mbewe's employer sent another community development assistant straight away to replace him, and no public discussions of the incident took place.

I was struck by the contrast between the workshop's hierarchical conduct and the fear its most junior participant was able inflict on others. However quiet and submissive Mbewe had been, his illness suddenly made him assume power over his superiors at the workshop. No one questioned whether the decision to send him home was in his best interest, and to that extent the threat he posed was defused by the convenors' prompt action. Yet the power he wielded was of the unstated kind, tacitly understood by all participants to bring more misfortune if appropriate precautions were not taken. Just as the Chichewa remarks mentioned above, the incident betrayed these development professionals' knowledge of how their world works beyond the vacuous evocations of empowerment. Mbewe did not need to be empowered by others more educated than himself, because he carried, as a person in relationships with both his colleagues and his kin, within himself the potential to cause further misfortune. Ironically, despite their familiarity with current human rights talk, none of the workshop participants seemed to contemplate the possibility that Mbewe's kin might sue them for negligence. Mbewe's individual right to care was overshadowed by his constitution in relationships with others.[5]

This relational view on persons and their effects on one another suggested, in my perspective, an alternative to the paternalistic, if well-meaning, approach disseminated in training workshops for activists and development professionals in Malawi. Hierarchies may be inevitable both in the conduct of workshops and in the actual campaigns for socioeconomic change, but a relational view qualifies them by identifying a more distributive sense of power. The fear of the occult is merely one instance of the interdependence that persons experience as an effect of their relationships. Transposed to a scale beyond interpersonal relationships, this perspective could prompt Malawian activists and development professionals to envision their work in relational terms, with categorical distinctions between the poor and their benefactors giving way to a sense of how all are related. The egalitarianism that I discerned was different from the kind proposed by both paternalism and populism. Rather than being handed down to the poor by their benefactors, equality is a presupposition, "an initial axiom" (Rancière 2004:223) without which no relationship could assume its specific qualities. Advocacy rather than education appeared as the logical mode of intervention under the circumstances of Malawi's structural inequalities. I felt obliged to leave its parameters open to discussion among Malawians themselves.

My egalitarian vision of collaboration between development professionals and their beneficiaries did not result in collaborative ethnography. The workshop participants to whom I presented my emerging description found it difficult to recognize its value. Mbewe's illness *was*, they insisted, a private affair that had nothing to do with the workshop's agenda, let alone how these professionals were to implement REFLECT in villages. I was left with a sense of impasse, an unproductive incompatibility between their description and mine. One description was not simply true and the other false, however, and nor were the workshop participants entangled in webs of self-mystification and misrecognition. Their reaction to my description had to become a part of it, an insight into how REFLECT, for all its promotion of critical awareness and egalitarianism, was instrumental to reproducing a structure of relationships that posed little challenge to Malawi's entrenched inequalities. Several years of ethnographic fieldwork in Malawi made my description possible, its conclusion by no means reducible to the views expressed by the workshop participants. Yet it is important to be clear that the difference between the descriptions was not a function of competing knowledge claims but of incompatible *interests*. I had no interest in maintaining the order of things I described because I had little personal investment in it. The incompatible descriptions could be contrasted, and one could even be used to criticize some aspects of the other, but separated by interests, they could never be put together as the outcome of a collaborative project.

PRODUCTIVE INCOMPATIBILITY

Rather than resulting in an unproductive impasse, incompatible descriptions can be productive of further engagement and knowledge if they emerge from argument between the anthropologist and his or her interlocutors. Another fieldwork, taking place in Chinsapo Township in the capital Lilongwe since 1996, illustrates productive incompatibility. The vast majority of the township's thirty thousand residents are first-generation migrants from rural areas, enticed by economic and political liberalization to seek employment or business opportunities in the city or forced to move to this underprivileged location by congestion in more established areas. In 2003, residents in this and other townships in Lilongwe became gripped by fear that unscrupulous politicians were involved in stealing human body parts (see Englund 2006:170–185).

The scare in Chinsapo concerned, in particular, the safety of children who were seen to come under the risk of abductions by traders in body parts. Rumors implicated local entrepreneurs, and some were said to store body parts in their refrigerators. On some occasions the police would arrive in the township to investigate the allegations, but because the information they offered was as implausible as it was minimal, further rumors quickly answered the popular demand for explanations. It was rumored that the reason why the police denied that anything criminal had taken place was the fact that the cases implicated the highest political authorities in the country. It was explained that when abductors and traders in body parts had been taken to a police station, they had pointed out that they were not working alone. After naming the cabinet ministers for whom they had acquired body parts, the police had allegedly called these ministers to ascertain the veracity of the claims. The cabinet ministers, in turn, had explained that they themselves had received orders from their *bwana* (boss), President Muluzi. The ministers had directed the police to release the detainees and to issue denials that anything criminal was involved.

As an ethnographer of these rumors, I did not hesitate, after several years of fieldwork in the township, to identify contexts for describing them. An immediate context was the economic hardship that liberalization had brought to impoverished urban and peri-urban dwellers, starkly contrasted with the perceived greed and corruption of the new regime. Beyond this immediate context was the way in which township dwellers' trust in the police had evaporated over a long period of time. One of the clenched fists of the one-party state, the police force had gained little popular credibility after the democratic transition. Township dwellers considered the police corrupt, all too often accomplices to criminals. Armed criminals were rumored to acquire their firearms from these apparent custodians of law and order, the deal stipulating that the owners of the weapons were entitled to a share in the loot. Thieves who had not struck a deal with the police could buy their way back to freedom by giving them the money they had stolen.

Township dwellers had no interest in my contextualizing efforts, if only because their own descriptions were never "rumors" (*mphekesera*) to them, however much this or that detail could be contested. They were ways of orienting oneself in the world, and my ethnography effectively *re*-described, rather than simply contextualized, their viewpoints.[6] What township dwellers sought to explain I re-described. Yet incompatible as our viewpoints were, I was expected to be a more sympathetic witness to township dwellers' predicament than the police and many human rights activists. Accordingly, my ethnography took issue with the condemnations of superstition and "mob justice" that littered human rights NGOs' and journalists' comments on these scares (see Englund 2006:180–185). By taking an explanation as a problem in need of a description of a different order, ethnography spoke to an audience of its own.

Here was an incompatibility that could be productive of connections and further engagement. My inclusion in the networks of "rumors" was an indication that I was considered able to appreciate them. It became somewhat dangerous to spread rumors, because the threat by the police to arrest rumor mongers was reinforced by a similar announcement on the national radio. My role as a witness to the public scare was itself predicated on long-term engagement with township dwellers. Yet it must be emphasized that I was a *witness* rather than another township dweller. It was precisely because of the entrenched inequalities in Malawian society that the white ethnographer in the township represented a resource, a point of access to the external world, and, as such, an embodiment of productive difference. Some anthropologists strive for a "radical reorientation of knowledge" (Miyazaki 2004:139) by seeking to replicate the knowledge practices of their interlocutors (see Strathern 1988). This is also my ambition, but the effect can take place the other way round too, with anthropological knowledge practices enabling the anthropologist's interlocutors to detach themselves from their own viewpoints. Ethnographic description, making their aspirations and ways of life accessible to far-flung audiences, struck township dwellers as a worthy pursuit, an opportunity to generate further connections.

They contrasted my approach with other white people's lives in gated communities elsewhere in the city. A major concern for township dwellers was the possibility that affluent whites, unable to speak Chichewa, were being deceived (*kunamizidwa*) by both top politicians and NGO executives. Many understood that bearing witness (*kuchita umboni*) required a capacity to relate what I experienced to the experiences of those who would never live in the township. My living in a house similar to their own, our eating similar food, and our speaking the same language were equally crucial preconditions, but a certain degree of incompatibility between my position and the positions of township dwellers was considered productive, not a hindrance to our engagement. Neither a binary opposition nor incommensurability arising from the lack of a common yardstick captures this sense of incompatibility (see Lambek 1998:109). Township dwellers recognized value in my description of the rumors about trade in body parts, not because it reproduced their version of events but because it made the seriousness of their predicament apparent to others, in contrast to Malawian human rights activists' condemnation of so-called mob justice. Unlike the development professionals described earlier, township dwellers were able to detach themselves from their viewpoints in order to acknowledge value in my description. The audiences of my ethnography were elsewhere, familiar to myself rather than to the residents of Chinsapo.

CONCLUSION

It would be an onerous task to separate human suffering as a topic of anthropological research from the study of practical measures to alleviate it. Few anthropologists would welcome such disconnection, the prospects of real-world engagement drawing them to this topic in the first place. I recognize similar aspirations in my own trajectory as an anthropologist (see Englund 2004), but this chapter has put forward some reasons for envisioning a rupture between activist engagement and ethnographic engagement. It should be clear that those reasons do not arise from a vain hope to assert the supremacy of academic knowledge production. Ethnographic engagement is distinct because its interests are distinct, opening up rather than closing down perspectives on human suffering, and so the ethnographer is rather diffident about solutions. The further refinement of ethnographic engagement with this topic will, however, discern more varieties of activist positions than what co-construction and denunciation (Jean-Klein and Riles 2005) and the well-worn theme of depoliticization, as in my own work (Englund 2006), have so far been able to identify. For anthropologists to have anything distinctive to say about poverty and human suffering, they have to attend to the diverse ideological commitments that drive political and technical involvements with them.

In Malawi after the democratic transition, as my discussion has indicated, human rights activists and development professionals shared a disposition that set them apart from "the grass roots" they claimed to empower. In accordance with trends that prevailed well beyond Malawi, empowerment was community-based, often exhorting local effort to address challenges that were fundamentally supralocal in nature. The freedom-focused human rights agenda in democratic Malawi co-existed, however, with alternative discourses on development. REFLECT was a key approach by which Malawian governmental and nongovernmental officers could imagine alternatives to both human rights activism and the machinations of the political class. Their commitment to development was deliberately nonpolitical in order to escape the narrow concept of politics that preoccupied both activists and politicians. As a consequence, REFLECT practitioners' view on empowering the poor was a direct assault on the practice of handouts that had become President Muluzi's trademark. It was in this context that the anthropologist had to ask why their critical awareness resulted neither in tangible improvements in villages nor in advocacy and popular mobilization. By contemplating such questions, the anthropologist at once betrayed the divergence between his perspective and that of the REFLECT practitioners. The sources of this divergence were thrown into sharp relief by the tragic incident at a training workshop.

Insofar as saving Boniface Mbewe's life is concerned, we will never know if my humanitarian urge to seek immediate medical assistance would have made a difference. Yet it is important to note that the alternative to my humanitarian urge was no less concerned with saving a human life. The alternative was to associate this life with a particular set of relationships that carried the responsibility for attending to it. The way in which Mbewe's illness exerted influence on the workshop, much more so than when he was in good health, accentuated my impression that the participants held convictions similar to their beneficiaries in villages, in spite of the professionalism that separated them and made advocacy an alien proposition. The critical awareness fostered by REFLECT was, under Malawi's historical conditions, too specialized to make this shared knowledge explicit or to allow enough detachment from the participants' own viewpoints to raise questions about the effects of their professionalism. Ethnographic engagement, by contrast, uncovered aspects of development professionalism that its practitioners preferred not to see.

Whether or not it is the newest idiom for anthropology's populism, collaboration risks ironing out the incompatibilities this chapter has identified in ethnographic engagement with poverty and human suffering. The coproduction of ethnographic texts is clearly desirable in some contexts, and its proponents are well aware of the complexities involved (see Lassiter 2005a:96). Yet when collaborative ethnography and public anthropology are summoned "to serve humankind more directly and more immediately" (Lassiter 2005a:85), it is necessary to pause and consider what services ethnographic engagement can render. Populist sentiments advise alignment with the poor, but their empirical identification is complicated in the Malawi case by the likelihood that many community development assistants, for example, are no less financially constrained than many entrepreneurs in Chinsapo Township. More illuminating are the positions different subjects assume in relation to poverty and human suffering, as revealed by ethnographic engagement. Neither development professionals nor residents in Chinsapo Township expressed any desire for collaborative ethnography, but they differed in the extent to which ethnographic engagement appeared productive to them. My re-description of township dwellers' accounts of their tribulations undermined the possibility of coauthorship, but it was precisely because my description was so different from theirs that it could yield value. The productive difference did not inhere in the proportions of our knowledge claims, as though my description increased the scale of their predicament beyond the township. The scale remained intact, only the audience changed as the description changed.

Collaboration, co-construction, and denunciation as modalities of ethnographic engagement with human suffering lack verve if they fail to convey a sense of argument. Subjects argue their positions on poverty and human suffering among themselves no less than in conversation with the anthropologist. Argument arises from divergent interests, and while some are more capable of pursuing their interests than others, a populist identification with the downtrodden is no guarantee of compatible interests between them and the anthropologist. In point of fact, as far as knowledge production goes, a compatibility of interests would be rather surprising, as though the anthropologist's interests were duplicated by his or her interlocutors' viewpoints. The accurate description of those viewpoints remains vital, of course, but argument invokes relationships between and beyond particular viewpoints. It is in postpopulist egalitarianism that ethnographic engagement with humanitarianism and development can find its own voice.

Notes

1. See Nordmann 2006 for a discussion of the differences and similarities in Bourdieu's and Rancière's views on political emancipation and intellectual equality.

2. Olivier de Sardan (2005:115–118) identifies several dimensions of populism among intellectuals who define "the poor" as their interlocutors, such as moral, cognitive, methodological, and ideological populism.

3. Collaborative ethnography, as outlined by Lassiter (2005a), is, of course, merely one of the many forms that collaborative research can take. It is hard to imagine how ethnographic fieldwork, for all its misunderstandings and impasse, could be anything else than collaborative. I applaud Lassiter's choice to confront some of the epistemological and ethical issues that are intrinsic to ethnographic fieldwork (see also Lassiter 2005b).

4. A superficially similar aspiration to close the analytical gap between anthropological and other knowledge practices appears in the burgeoning literature on expert knowledge (see, for example, Brenneis 1999; Holmes and Marcus 2005; Riles 2006; see also Maurer 2003). As this chapter suggests, however, development professionals' knowledge about poverty is, under Malawi's historical circumstances, of the kind that would make the closing of analytical distance rather futile.

5. Despite mass-mediated demands in Malawi for legislation to curb perceived

problems with witchcraft (see Englund 2006:175–176), the fears and conflicts involving suspicions of witchcraft usually fall outside the domain of law.

6. Richard Wilson (1997) identified decontextualization as a major problem in human rights reporting, usefully challenged by the ethnographer's familiarity with local contexts. Wilson's argument led Marilyn Strathern to question whether contextualization, which submits "supplementary circumstances for an action, reasons at a remove" (2004:230–231), is what ethnography does. Ethnography offers, Strathern pointed out, a qualitatively different description, not a method of adding context to a preexisting description.

PART II

Cosmologies of Humanitarianism

The second part of this book articulates humanitarian forms that de-center Western, secular, and Christian notions of humanitarian practice. Jonathan Benthall's chapter looks at controversies surrounding the Islamic practice of almsgiving known as *zakat* and explores the wider effects of the September 11, 2001, World Trade Center attacks on perceptions of Islamic charity. His study reveals the significance of theological directives that orient many contemporary practices of giving, in conflict with international directives toward aid that assume a secular divide between religion and political life. His chapter also highlights a double standard regarding not only who counts as a worthy beneficiary but also who can appear as an appropriate benefactor, under which Islamic forms of assistance meet exceptional political and legal scrutiny. Focusing on Islamic charities in Palestine and their sympathizers overseas—a particularly charged case in international relations—Benthall opens the larger cosmological framework that structures international moral discourse and the political interests invested in its articulation. After fielding requests to serve as an expert witness in trials defending Islamic charities from accusations of terrorism, he adopts the stance of an engaged anthropologist and provides a counter-narrative to that of counter-terrorist specialists. From this perspective we see Islamic charities as grassroots, faith-based organizations whose activities took on a different hue post–September 11. Benthall reminds us that Islam is no less universalistic than Christianity or secularism, a feature that renders it a particular threat on the global stage. Zakat, one of the five pillars of Islam, entails an obligation to donate a percentage of annual assets to worthy recipients as specified in the Qur'an. In this chapter we learn how zakat has grown into the central artery for contemporary Islamic aid, flowing in rhythm with a religious calendar and life cycle. When the aid system expanded post-1960s, coinciding with an "Islamic resurgence," local zakat committees in Palestine increasingly tapped into external funding from diaspora Muslim populations and international donor organizations. After outlining the types of programs that zakat now encompasses (including orphan care, schools and vocational training, and assistance to refugees and displaced people), Benthall examines the two legal cases in which he gave evidence or advice to demonstrate how the US government has blacklisted Islamic charities. He critically analyzes the "pyramid model" forwarded by terrorologists who link Palestinian zakat committees to Islamic militancy and proposes an alternative etic model that casts zakat committees as civil society institutions and "community based organizations." His examples suggest a parallel between Christian and Muslim international aid organizations. To the extent that both renounce proselytism and embrace international codes of conduct in their work, they seek an analogous "humanitarian space" to that of a secular organization such as Doctors Without Borders. Yet Islamic charities encounter far greater political suspicion than their Christian equivalents and legal challenges that reduce their action to its political allegiances. Such attempts to monopolize the charitable sector within a historically Western frame, according to Benthall, are both inaccurate and deeply misguided.

Erica Bornstein's chapter further expands the horizon of religious humanitarianism. The gift may embody a humanitarian act, but it only appears pure if free of self-interest. In New Delhi, India, the gift without a return (Hindu dān) presents a particular model of donation that encourages givers to release themselves of the gift while ensuring that they are giving to worthy recipients. From this vantage point Bornstein analyzes ethical engagements related to orphans and their particularly acute articulation of humanitarian value. Expanding on specific laws governing the adoption of orphans by Hindus, Muslims, and Christians, the chapter explores how in India orphans become children of the nation. When faced with the call to help an orphan, adoption presents one alternative, care by nongovernmental organizations (NGOs) or the state is another, and social sponsorship is yet a third. New Delhi boasts some of the most stringent adoption laws in the world, even as the category of the orphan remains an important target of humanitarian activity and value. Orphans, as children of the nation, are protected, saved, and managed by humanitarian institutions and the state. Other contexts of orphan care include institutions such as orphanages and social adoption, where the state remains the legal guardian and an individual (or family) economically supports an orphan's education and care. As subjects of secular legislation, orphans embody a generic national humanity, which must then be translated for adoption purposes into particular legal identities. Although a given orphan may know no religious identity, India's secular state maintains extensive legal procedures pertaining to adopting orphans that differ according to one's nationality and religious identity. As a result, in India, most orphans are not adopted. Instead, they are socially sponsored by the government of India in orphanages and supported by donors who pay monthly for their education, upkeep, and eventually for their marriage. Such an arrangement conforms to the broader logic of dān, as opposed to the potential commodification of orphans through human trafficking and the global adoption market. By examining the political economy of two adoption scandals in a transnational frame, Bornstein concludes that in terms of Indian humanitarianism state orphans are "good to give to" precisely because they are not kin: they involve no relation or self-interest and thus require no return.

Both contributions in this part pose alternate perspectives to aid world norms. Humanitarianism, however global, is not simply, or singularly, universal; indeed, rival formations of humanitarianism such as Islamic zakat and Hindu dān challenge fundamental assumptions of global regulatory bodies seeking to oversee charitable donations or the care of orphans. Tensions over which gifts are legitimate and which suffering strangers most deserve care (abstract humans or ones with whom one has cultural proximity) reflect a deep and active fault line between differing religious cosmologies and political interests. In both chapters, states reemerge as potentially mediating, and regulating actors in humanitarian practice. At the same time we glimpse the ongoing reconfiguration of religious traditions of social welfare—Islamic and Hindu as well as Christian—amid secular landscapes of international aid.

5

Islamic Humanitarianism in Adversarial Context

Jonathan Benthall

INTRODUCTION

As recently as 1991 a charity registered in the United States was accepting government funds to subsidize a magazine named *Afghan Jehad*. Typically of our century so far, a Pakistani charity, Jamaat-ud-Dawa, came to public attention when it provided effective relief aid after the devastating Kashmir earthquake in October 2005, but in 2008 it was accused of being a front for an Al-Qaida type terrorist organization and of being implicated in the November 26 attacks on Bombay. The silent majority of Islamic charities that follow a straight humanitarian calling can rarely escape the cloud of notoriety that now hangs over their sector.

Why is Islamic humanitarianism so controversial? I have begun the following chapter by summarizing the principles underlying Islamic humanitarianism and then thinking of them as being like a system of springs that feeds a river. This upstream system can be studied in itself, but the present-day realities when the river is observed downstream are of a different order. Others may condemn the river itself as an essentially disruptive force, but I see the consequences of September 11, 2001, and other international crises as being like weighty rockfalls altering the river's flow.

I have focused on Islamic charities in Palestine and their supporters overseas. The case is unique, but its interpretation depends on some knowledge of Islamic charities both in historical depth and in the context of present-day global flows of aid.

What started for me as an exercise in applied cultural anthropology—that is to say, in this context, as an attempt to apply anthropological methods of research with an explicit bias toward pro-poor initiatives (Benthall and Bellion-Jourdan 2009)—developed unforeseen dimensions. First, I became engaged with practical questions of charity regulation and capacity building, in support of a confidence-building program to help bona fide Islamic charities demonstrate, through voluntary adherence to internationally accepted codes, that they had nothing to do with terrorism. This was the Montreux Initiative, launched in 2005 by the Swiss Federal Department of Foreign Affairs (and recently recast as the Islamic Charities Project of the Graduate Institute of International and Development Studies, Geneva). Second, I was invited to serve as an expert witness and deponent, at the request of legal teams representing people involved in some of these charities—on which more below.

The focus of this chapter, with some short digressions to illustrate the breadth of Islamic charities as a social movement, is on the divergent ways in which Palestinian Islamic charities can be interpreted. I arrive at a more benign interpretation than that favored by the Israeli and US governments. These charities can be seen, I contend, as grassroots faith-based organizations that were beginning to tap effectively into the international aid system until their growth was suppressed as a result of the Middle East political predicament, sharpened by reaction to the September 11 attacks.

A familiar anthropological distinction between "outsider" and "insider" levels of analysis is used here with the aim of clarifying the argument about the Palestinian Islamic charities. I conclude by making an anthropological point—arguing that Islamic charities present a different intellectual challenge from the familiar conundrum of cultural relativism, since the ambitions of Islam are no less universalistic than those of Christianity or its successor, post-Judeo-Christian secularism. Indeed, the expansionist claims of Islam present new challenges to the discipline of cultural anthropology, much of whose distinctiveness in the past has lain in the respectful attention it gave to small-scale societies and subcultures.

ZAKAT IN ISLAMIC TRADITION

The principles of Islamic humanitarianism and how it works in practice will now be outlined. This should put the specifics of the Palestinian case in a wider, indeed global, context. I have documented elsewhere (for example,

Benthall 2006) how Islamic charities can operate smoothly and without political controversy when a society is not riven by religious conflict.

The key concept in Islamic humanitarianism is zakat. The closest English translation of the Arabic *zakat* is the now obsolescent word "alms." "Charity" includes connotations of spiritual love that are absent in zakat, which is associated more with purity and productivity. Zakat is mandatory on all Muslims, whereas *sadaqa*, which has connotations of justice, is what is given over and above one's obligation. Zakat is one of the five "pillars" of Islam—the others being faith, prayer, fasting, and the pilgrimage to Mecca. Prayer is considered to be effective only when accompanied by fulfillment of zakat. Zakat signifies the obligation to donate one-fortieth of one's assets each year—excluding the value of one's home and working necessities—to a list of eight categories of people specified in the Qur'an. These are, to borrow the most usual descriptions, poor people; the destitute; those employed to administer the zakat; those who might be converted to Islam or help in the cause; captives; debtors; those committed to the "way of God"; and, finally, travelers in need.

Islamic scholars have written extensively on the interpretation of these categories. "Captives," for instance, may be taken to include not only prisoners of war but the subjects of oppressive political regimes. The "way of God" is synonymous with *jihad*—an elusive concept whose nearest equivalent for Christians is the idea of the Church Militant warring against the powers of evil. Jihad can have military connotations in some contexts, but can also mean a spiritual commitment to master one's weaknesses and lead a better life. Effective compassion for the disadvantaged is a possible expression of this commitment.

The Qur'anic injunctions on zakat have much in common with the Hebraic tithe—the obligation to give a tenth of annual agricultural produce—which, though replaced in early Christianity by the idea of freewill offerings, was later revived in various forms by some churches. Some denominations, such as the Mormons, still practice strict tithing in the same way as devout Muslims. The Qur'an not only urges generosity, but also tells Muslims that they should encourage others to be generous. As in Judaism and Christianity, all wealth belongs to God. Zakat purifies both wealth itself and the individual. It is specially enjoined, and bestows special merit, during the holy month of Ramadan, which has become the major fund-raising season, similar to Christmas. Alms given discreetly rather than publicly are best. Those whose personal wealth is below a fixed threshold are exempt from almsgiving.

At various points in Islamic history, zakat became a mere vehicle for extracting taxes. In no present-day state is zakat organized exactly as Islamic teaching prescribes. However, great efforts have been made to explain how the original injunctions should be interpreted in response to economic realities. It is used as a fund-raising device by charities both in Muslim countries and among Muslims resident in Western countries. Such charities often supply their supporters with tables to enable them to calculate their zakat liability. Zakat is one of the two major Islamic institutions mobilized for modern fund-raising—the other being the *waqf*, which is, broadly speaking, the equivalent of the European charitable foundation.[1] It is clear in principle that zakat, if implemented with anything like the rigor enjoined in the Qur'an, could be a major vehicle for wealth redistribution, economic development, and reconstruction in conflict-torn areas. The ideal of a brotherhood of Muslims transcending national borders, the *umma*, remains just an ideal. However, zakat is the backbone of a number of effective Islamic charities, even if these remain small when compared with the huge resources that could in principle become available. Moreover, several of these charities are succeeding in building constructive relationships with non-Muslim relief and development agencies and donors and in complying with internationally accepted codes of practice relating to nondiscrimination and the like. Practical cooperation of this kind ought surely to be seen as a desirable counter-balance to the purported "clash of civilizations." This is recognized in Britain, where the Charity Commission has made a point of encouraging Muslims (and other minorities) to set up charities that can operate on a par with those of the mainstream. This has not been the case in the United States, where it seems that zakat is acquiring negative connotations comparable to those that accompany jihad (in its military aspects, its spiritual aspects being ignored). And what happens in the United States has wider repercussions, as we shall see from analysis of what the many legal cases involving the Palestinian zakat committees have in common.

COMMON FEATURES OF PRESENT-DAY ISLAMIC AID PROGRAMS

The Muslim world is no less varied than the Christian world. However, the shared religious tradition that underpins Islamic philanthropy has resulted in a family resemblance between Islamic agencies, and some common features may be distinguished.

Religious References

First, there are frequent references to zakat and sadaqa (explained above) and to waqf. In a country such as Britain where waqf is not a juridically recognized concept, donors are nonetheless encouraged to remit funds earmarked for specific projects that are labeled as waqf for fund-raising purposes. Campaigning literature frequently quotes from Qur'anic verses—such as "Whoever has saved a life, it is as if he has saved the whole of humanity"—and *hadiths*, the statements and actions attributed to the Prophet Muhammad. Favored visual motifs include the ear of corn (alluding to another Qur'anic verse that likens charitable giving to the grain of corn that "fructifies seven-hundredfold"), the minaret, the Dome of the Rock in Jerusalem, and the crescent. (The thirty or so Red Crescent National Societies—members of the International Red Cross and Red Crescent Movement that have opted to use the crescent rather than the cross as their emblem—are technically not Islamic charities, since the movement is strictly nondenominational, but in practice some of them have taken on an Islamic flavor.) Green is frequently used in Islamic charities' promotional literature, since it is a color associated with the Prophet Muhammad.

The Religious Calendar and Life Cycle

Islamic festivals are based on the lunar month and so move through the solar year. Islam requires all who can afford it to buy and slaughter an animal (such as a sheep, cow, or camel) and distribute the meat (though it is sometimes nowadays canned) to the poor on the occasion of the "great feast" at the end of the annual hajj to Mecca. This is in memory of the sacrifice that the Prophet Abraham made to God in substitution for his own son.

Some children are sent on the *umra* (lesser pilgrimage to Mecca) as a reward for good schoolwork. Islamic charities may also subsidize circumcision ceremonies for young boys, usually carried out at the age of about seven years, or sponsor programs to enable young men to marry—a high incidence of unmarried young people being widely seen in some countries such as Algeria as a social evil.

Orphans

There can be few Islamic charities without an orphan program. In the Palestinian context these programs have led to the suspicion that the zakat committees have been favoring the orphans of suicide bombers.

The Prophet Muhammad was an orphan himself, and many Islamic texts enjoin the care of orphans, defined as children who have lost their fathers, that is to say, the family breadwinner. The term "orphan" is also sometimes used as a euphemism for a child born out of wedlock who is rejected by a family. Residential orphanages are still built, but Islamic

Relief, for instance, has developed a program of orphan sponsorship, under which some thirty thousand orphans are currently sponsored world-wide. It has, in effect, translated the traditional Islamic concern for orphans into a mechanism that attempts to bring help to the poorest, which is notoriously the most difficult part of any development program.

Refugees and the Displaced

Aid to refugees is another widely recognized priority. In Islam, as in both Christianity and Judaism, the story of a forced journey has theological reso-nance. According to tradition, the Prophet Muhammad had to leave his hometown of Mecca and find refuge with his companions in Yathrib, later known as Medina, so that the year of his departure, the *hijra*, 622 CE, became the first year of the Muslim calendar. Refugees are eligible for zakat as "people of the road," and it is often pointed out that a large proportion of the world's refugees are Muslims. The UN Relief and Works Association (UNRWA), the (wholly secular) UN agency, is responsible for 4.77 million registered Palestinian refugees, of whom 1.40 million live in official "camps."

Interventions by Islamic charities on behalf of displaced people have sometimes proved controversial. For instance, Islamic charities based in northern Sudan were accused of exerting undue proselytizing pressure on displaced people from the non-Muslim south during the long-running civil war. During the Bosnian conflict in the 1990s, Islamic charities were con-cerned to keep refugees in place so that their Muslim identity could be maintained, contrary to the apparent policy of the UN High Commission for Refugees, which was to disperse them.

Schools and Vocational Training

Many Islamic charities are keen to encourage the transmission of prac-tical skills, such as computing, that have an economic value. However, the more traditional Islamic charities, such as those based in the Gulf States, also sponsor mosque-based madrasas with an emphasis on Qur'anic mem-orization. These can be controversial when there is competition between Islamic schools and secular or Christian schools, as in parts of Africa, and the educational value of rote learning is also disputed. However, the role of madrasas in promoting Islamist militancy is probably exaggerated.[2]

Gender

"Gender mainstreaming" has become almost a shibboleth of Western aid agencies, and local NGOs all over the world have become sophisticated in falling in with genderized policies imposed from abroad. In general, Islamic charities are conservative as regards gender relations. This may prove to be the most sensitive long-term ideological flashpoint between Muslim and non-Muslim development agencies.[3]

A SHADOW OVER THE SECTOR: THE DANISH AL-AQSA FOUNDATION CASE

Since the attacks on the United States on September 11, 2001, the whole sector of Islamic charities has been under a cloud. Many of these charities have been "designated," that is, blacklisted by the US government and by other authorities. A sector that was previously growing in scale has been pushed back on the defensive.

I will give a detailed account of a legal case focused on Palestinian Islamic charities and summarize in tabular form the surprisingly large number of other cases in different countries that hinge on the same issue.

Rachid Issa was born in a refugee camp in Lebanon, in a family that had lived in a village close to Nazareth. In his testimony he said that he went to school for about six years until 1982, when the school closed as a result of the war. He fled to Denmark in 1989 at the age of about twenty-one, as a result of Israel's bombing of Lebanon. He left behind his father, who in 2008 was aged eighty and had spent the last fifty-eight years in the camp. Mr. Issa had a wife and four children in Denmark. In 2008 he was stateless and unemployed. He received a pension and still was receiving medical treatment due to an accident that had occurred some years before. After a visit in 1999 from his father, who told him about conditions in Lebanon, he decided to do something for Palestinian orphans.

Ahmad Suleiman also came from Lebanon to Denmark, where he worked as a taxi driver. He and Mr. Issa were neighbors in Denmark and had been neighbors in Lebanon. Together with three others, who were hardly involved in decision-making, they founded the Al-Aqsa Foreningen (Al-Aqsa Foundation) as a charity for the benefit of Palestinians in Palestine and Lebanon, with a constitution drafted by a lawyer. The charity was named after the Al-Aqsa Mosque in Jerusalem, a landmark for all Palestinians. Mr. Issa was the chairman, making most of the decisions, and Mr. Suleiman the treasurer. They raised funds by means of bank transfer forms left in shops and through cash donations.

In March 2007, these two men were charged in the Copenhagen City Court with sending in 2002 the sums of €20,000 to the Islamic Charitable Society, Hebron (Al Khalil),[4] in the West Bank, and $51,000 to the World

Assembly of Muslim Youth (WAMY) in Gaza, to be remitted in turn to four zakat committees; also with accumulating the equivalent in Danish kroner of about $107,000 that they intended to remit to zakat committees. The grounds of the charge were that the various societies and committees were part of Hamas, designated in Denmark as a terrorist organization, and that some of the funds remitted were used or intended to be used for the families of suicide bombers. The prosecution asked for confiscation of the accumulated funds, custodial sentences for the two men, and the deportation of Mr. Issa. The court acquitted them. It questioned the cogency of the prosecutors' documents, which originated from Israeli sources.

Later in 2007, the Eastern High Court of Denmark heard an appeal, and in February 2008 it upheld the lower court's decision to acquit. I gave evidence for the defense in the appeal hearing, as an expert witness on Palestinian zakat committees. The prosecution imported two American experts on counter-terrorism. The bench of six judges split evenly on whether the zakat committees were connected to Hamas, and under Danish law the benefit of the doubt was given to the defendants. They were all agreed that there was no evidence that funds had been sent to families of suicide bombers.

Because Hamas has organized suicide bombings and is a proscribed organization under the Danish criminal code, the issue on which the Danish case hinged was whether the zakat committees to which the funds flowed were genuine charities or merely subsidiaries of Hamas. Though the Danish prosecution was launched against a pair of somewhat low-key charity organizers, this forensic issue has been at the heart of several other cases, summarized in Table 5.1.

It is clear then that the characterization of some 130 small- to medium-size charities in the Palestinian Territories—running orphan programs, food aid, medical services, income-generating schemes, dairies, schools, and the like—has become the deep structure of numerous juridical performances. The penalties at stake range from possible prison sentences of a few years (the Danish case) or life (the Holy Land Foundation [HLF] criminal case), to financial payments ranging from small (the Simon Wiesenthal case) to massive (the banking cases) damages, through exclusion from intellectual exchanges in the United States. Decisions are taken by single consuls, judges, or politicians (in the Tariq Ramadan visa case), or by panels of judges, or by juries supervised by judges, or by regulatory authorities (the inquiries by the UK Charity Commission into Interpal). The evidence of experts is evidently pivotal.

TABLE 5.1

Summary of Cases (All Outside Israel-Palestine) Bearing on the Question of the Independence of the Palestinian Zakat Committees

Country	Legal Case	Type of Case	Status as of July 2010
Denmark	Al-Aqsa Foundation	Criminal	Acquittal on appeal
UK	*Interpal v. British Board of Jewish Deputies*	Defamation	Public apology and damages secured in 2005
UK	Interpal	Regulation by the Charity Commission	Twice cleared; again cleared in 2009 with some directions to make changes
US	Tariq Ramadan visitor visa[1]	Exclusion from US	Ban upheld in New York courts in 2008, reversed by Secretary Hillary Clinton in 2010
France	Comité de Bienfaisance et de Secours aux Palestiniens	Defamation case against Centre Simon Wiesenthal	Damages awarded but reversed on appeal in 2008
US	David Boim case against Holy Land Foundation (HLF)[2] et al.	Civil	Damages awarded, reversed on appeal, but decision overridden by the Seventh Circuit Court of Appeals sitting en banc, referred back to lower court
US	Holy Land Foundation and its officers	Criminal	Mistrial in 2007 in Dallas. Retrial in 2008 resulted in convictions for supporting terrorism and jail sentences up to 65 years. Appeals pending
US	Arab Bank, Crédit Lyonnais, NatWest, UBS[3]	Civil	Cases pending, to be decided by juries in New York City
Sweden	Al-Aqsa Grain Foundation, Sweden	Criminal	Acquittal
Belgium, Germany, Italy, Netherlands	Various comparable cases		Pending

1. Ramadan, an influential Islamic academic based in Geneva and Oxford, widely considered to be a moderate, was denied a visa to enter the United States on the grounds that he had made donations totaling some $1,300 to a Swiss registered charity, Association de Bienfaisance aux Palestiniens.
2. HLF, founded in 1992, was during the 1990s the largest US Islamic charity. It and some other US entities were sued by the family of David Boim, a teenager killed presumably by Hamas gunmen in the West Bank in 1996.
3. These banks were alleged to have provided foreign exchange and remittance services involving zakat committees and similar charities supposedly connected to Hamas. The suits were being brought by survivors and families of suicide bombings.

THE "PYRAMID MODEL" OF THE PALESTINIAN ZAKAT COMMITTEES

I have done my best to inquire into the true status of the West Bank zakat committees and have reached the conclusion that the case against them is flawed. This case relies on what I will call the "pyramid model," as presented by Matthew Levitt (2006), according to which Hamas's political section is the apex of a structure resting on a military section that in turn rests on a social welfare section called the *da'wa*, which is the Arabic term for the call to Islam: for missionary activity and sometimes by extension the provision of religious education and social services with a view to reviving the faith of a community.

The first objection is that this is presented not as an analytical (outsider's or "etic") interpretation of the facts, but as if it were an insider's ("emic") description, that is to say an organization chart of Hamas.[5] In fact, da'wa is not in Arabic the name of a department or section, but refers to a principle or duty.

The second objection is that, even as an "etic" interpretation, it is mistaken. It neglects two foundation stones that have underpinned Hamas's popularity: first, religious conviction as a social determinant in itself, expressed with particular force in the idea of the umma, or brotherhood in Islam; and second, opposition to the Israeli military occupation that is by common consent responsible for much hardship. An alternative "etic" interpretation of Hamas's motivation contends that its military and political functions are subordinate to an overriding priority that has been to promote a moral and spiritual reawakening based on a particular reading of the Qur'an: the principle of da'wa as a primary objective, not as a means to a merely political end.

My criticisms of the pyramid model are available in more detail elsewhere (Benthall 2008a), and I will merely summarize here the various levels of allegation together with a rebuttal. It should be made clear that the evidence relied on here predates July 2007, when Hamas's takeover of the administration of Gaza resulted in a sharp division between Hamas and the rival party, Fatah, and in measures taken by the Fatah-led government in Ramallah since December 2007 to take centralized control of the zakat committees—measures that provoked a crisis. The Israeli government decided to raid and eradicate a number of Palestinian Islamic charities in the West Bank, eliciting protests from the Fatah government as well as other observers. The effect of the purported reforms has been further researched,[6] while the whole political and military context has changed since Israel's attacks on Gaza in the closing days of 2008.[7]

The evidence is incomplete, and it is difficult to arrive at certainty in such a contentious field of research where trust has broken down on almost every side. However, it is possible to reach a conclusion based on the balance of probabilities.

Allegation 1: That the Zakat Committees Were Subsidiaries of Hamas

Contrary to the allegation that the zakat committees were subsidiaries of Hamas, they were constituted independently and operated within Palestinian law. This is not to deny that there may have been affiliations of sympathy between some zakat committee members and Hamas. This is to be expected since Hamas has consistently since 1996 attracted support from between 25 and 50 percent or more of the Palestinian population. The zakat committees were controlled by the Ministry of Religious Affairs, under the Palestinian Authority, and all their members had to be approved by the ministry. Other ministries, such as the Ministry of Health and Agriculture, supervised the committees' specialized operations. Each committee consisted of between seven and fifteen members who were banned from taking any financial benefit themselves, and decisions were taken by majority vote. Several of the committees predated the foundation of Hamas in 1988. Both the Israeli and the Palestinian security services compiled reports alleging that various committees were controlled by Hamas, but these reports are heavily biased and neglect to mention that many zakat committee members supported Fatah or other political factions, while others were not politically involved.

Allegation 2: That the Zakat Committees Actively Supported Suicide Bombing by Guaranteeing to Prospective Bombers That Their Families Would Be Provided For

The committees claimed that they supported bereaved families on the basis of needs assessment, regardless of how the parent died. Some confusion has been caused by the Arabic word for martyr, *shahīd*, which is often assumed by the Israeli authorities to refer to suicide bombers, whereas it is used more generally in Palestine to refer to anyone who has died in a just cause.

Allegation 3: That the Zakat Committees Provided Services Selectively so as to Build Up a Sense of Individual Indebtedness to Hamas

No solid evidence has been produced to support this allegation, which is belied by the evidence of public trust (see below).

Allegation 4: That the Zakat Committees, by Collecting Funds for Charitable Activities, Relieved Pressure on Hamas's Budget so that It Could Spend More Money on Bombing Missions

This is the doctrine of "asset substitution," which—even if the premise that the committees are fronts for Hamas were true—surely presents real ethical difficulties. The provision of medical services, food aid, and so forth in militarily occupied territories is enjoined and protected under International Humanitarian Law.

Allegation 5: That, Even If None of the Above Can Be Demonstrated, the Zakat Committees Were Nonetheless Winning "Hearts and Minds" for Hamas

This should surely be too inchoate an accusation to be properly admissible in a court of law. It is impossible to disprove an allegation that seeks to probe into the motivations of hearts and minds, but it may be submitted on the other side that the zakat committees were specially valued by the public for their independence and honesty, by contrast with the corruption that has notoriously afflicted Fatah.

The Clinching Points That Confirm for Me That the Pyramid Model Is Almost Certainly Wrong Are as Follows:

1. Two successive public opinion polls were published by the Human Development Studies Program, Bir Zeit University, Ramallah, in 2000 and 2004 inquiring into the degree of confidence felt by the Palestinian public in various categories of civil society institutions. The zakat committees scored second highest (58 to 67 percent), after universities (62 to 81 percent), with Palestinian opposition groups second to last (32 to 36 percent) and political parties last (27 to 29 percent). (In the middle were, in order, NGOs other than zakat committees, the local press, the judicial system, and trade unions. An earlier poll with similar results had been conducted in 1998–99.)

2. Contrary to many misconceptions, the voluntary sector in the Palestinian territories is tightly regulated and monitored. All schools, for instance, follow the Palestinian national curriculum.

3. Extensive documentation shows that from 1992 to 2006 the zakat committees were receiving grants and contracts from a wide variety of donor agencies. Apart from the fact that, as far as I know, no non-Muslim donors have been pursued in the courts for supporting the zakat committees, major donors demand a high standard of

professionalism in grant applications and reports, and they conduct regular inspections, audits, and evaluations.

4. The Palestinian zakat committees operated openly and transparently but did not have an umbrella body to represent them collectively.

5. The findings of a number of other researchers and observers are consistent with the view put forward here (see Schaeublin 2009 for a summary).

The case against the zakat committees relies to a great extent on Israeli military intelligence reports and on the principle of "guilt by association," as do the prosecution cases that are advanced against their donors. I concede below that such investigations have their place. However, higher standards of evidence apply both in the social sciences and in courts of law. Both insist on cross-checking of evidence against different sources (including the viewpoints of all the relevant protagonists). The inevitable bias that creeps into any interpretation of contentious human relationships is balanced in the social sciences—especially in anthropology—by academic training and in the law courts by the adversarial process.

When giving expert evidence myself in support of those accused of supporting the Palestinian zakat committees, I have stressed the difficulty of arriving at certainty. I would certainly admit that I was mistaken if those accusing the zakat committees were able to produce solid or "smoking gun" evidence, such as an organization chart emanating from Hamas showing the committees as subsidiaries, or a reliable record of committee meetings at which decisions were made with an obvious intent to serve Hamas's interests, or statistics showing that families of deceased suicide bombers could have received preferential help from the committees compared to other families in need. But nothing like this has been produced. Of course, those who condemn the committees would argue that they were part of a gigantic conspiracy that ipso facto conceals its true motivations, but I am not convinced that the managers of hospitals, dairies, and food aid programs think this way—and the burden of proof should be on those attacking them. It is impossible to disprove any conspiratorial theory since its adherents can dismiss all evidence against them as mendacious.

The prosecution in the Holy Land Foundation criminal case (see Table 5.1) made much of extensive, secretly obtained recordings of conversations between the charity's founders during the early 1990s and some written documents that also came to light, which (it was claimed) demonstrate that they were more concerned with spreading the religio-political message of Islamism, and specifically with opposition to the Oslo peace process, than with purely charitable objectives. These recordings all predated the black-listing of Hamas by the US government in 1995. It does appear that the directors of the Holy Land Foundation were Islamists—that is to say, Muslims committed to social and political action in the name of Islamic principles—and may have strayed, in what they thought were private exchanges, into expressing personal approval of political violence. Unfortunately for Islamic charities in general, they were not charismatic personalities like Britain's Hany El-Banna, the founder of Islamic Relief Worldwide. The US and Israeli governments have lumped all Islamists together as "Hamas," though many Palestinians have Islamist sympathies without agreeing with all of Hamas's policies. It is fallacious to believe that the rival party, Fatah, is purely secular: many of its members have been reli-gious, and there is some evidence of competition between Hamas and Fatah to have influence in the zakat committees. If some members of Hamas ever did intend to dominate and control the zakat committees, it would appear that such a policy evolved toward the more nuanced goal of encouraging the Islamic voluntary sector.

One is entitled, as a field researcher, to make judgments as to the integrity of one's informants. In 1996 and 2009 I visited Nablus, the historic West Bank town. The treasurer of the committee had been Haj Adli Yaish until the old zakat committees were all dissolved in December 2007. He was elected mayor of Nablus in 2005 on the "Change and Reform" ticket, which was a coalition group of Hamas and other opposition groups, but also on the strength of his high personal reputation. It is true that "Change and Reform" was widely seen as equivalent to Hamas, but the fact that some Christians stood on the Change and Reform ticket suggests that opposition to Fatah, with its reputation for corruption and cronyism, was the domi-nant attraction. Adli Yaish was later arrested and detained in an Israeli prison, but in 2009 he was back in his mayoral office. He seems to me a typ-ical businessman with a social conscience—an importer of Mercedes cars and owner of a motor spare-parts store—such as you would find filling civic and charitable positions in medium-size towns all over the world.

It is easy to understand how Israeli and US analysts have reached their view of the zakat committees. We are, I suggest, confronted with an idée fixe emanating from the Israeli government and endorsed by powerful sec-tions of the US government and its advisers. I do not doubt the sincerity of those who construct ideological edifices such as the "pyramid model" and are hostile to Hamas because of its aim of dismantling the Jewish state, its record of suicide bombings against civilians, and its poisonously anti-Semitic charter.

There are, however, three disturbing factors. The first is the disinclination to listen to voices opposed to the Israeli political and military establishment as credible witnesses (though Levitt has conducted interviews with Palestinian prisoners in Israeli jails) and the unquestioning acceptance of the reliability of secret intelligence sources and information extracted under duress. The second is the willingness to conflate the issue of Palestinian nationalism with the fight against Al-Qaida, whereas it is more likely that the continued failure to resolve the Israeli–Palestinian conflict is opening the door to Al-Qaida by fostering despair and vengefulness among young Palestinians. The third is the increasing evidence that attempts to dry out the funding sources of "terrorism" by attacking charitable organizations are not only ineffective (since there are many other ways in which terrorism can be funded) but even counter-productive, since they drive money underground—outside the purview of banking regulators.

AN ALTERNATIVE "ETIC" MODEL

I propose an alternative model, "etic" in the sense that it is imposed as an interpretation, not necessarily as it seen by the protagonists. The Palestinian zakat committees are an instance of "civil society institutions" or "community-based organizations" (to use the jargon of development professionals) such as had been operating unobtrusively for centuries not only in Palestine but across the Muslim world, distributing funds to the poor and needy in the vicinity of individual mosques. At the global level, the international aid system had begun to expand since the 1960s, and by the 1980s—when the Palestinian territories were under direct Israeli occupation—the zakat committees were beginning to find ways of tapping into external sources of funding. These included the wealthy Persian Gulf states, the Muslim diaspora, and also major international donor agencies.

These developments coincided with the "Islamic resurgence," which drew its energies from the Muslim Brotherhood of Egypt, founded in Egypt in 1928, and other opposition movements. Hamas was founded in 1987–88 as a successor to the Muslim Brotherhood's Palestinian branch, which was founded in Jerusalem in 1946, two years before the establishment of the state of Israel. The Muslim Brotherhood is not a tightly organized "Islamist international" but has splintered into numerous national movements varying greatly in their degree of radicalism, degree of nationalism, and degree of commitment to violence. The rise of the Muslim Brotherhood must be seen historically as part of a wider Islamic resurgence with counterparts in the Indian subcontinent and elsewhere.

During the first years after Israel's victory in 1967, Palestinians were incorporated into the Israeli labor force, many vocational training courses were set up in the Occupied Territories, improved varieties of seeds for vegetables and food crops were provided for farmers, and hundreds of thousands of trees were planted. The effect of the Oslo Accords was to "outsource" the Occupation to the Palestinian Authority, and in particular responsibility for welfare. This has resulted in escalating insecurity, which, as an Israeli scholar has commented, "has no doubt benefited Hamas, not only because of its ability to fill in the institutional vacuum, but also because of its ideological conviction. Simply put, within a context of widespread destruction and absolute uncertainty a worldview that accentuates the importance of faith, fate, and divine ordinance gains ground" (Gordon 2008:221).

Hamas set out to "re-Islamize" the Palestinians, especially their youth, as a means to restoring their dignity and reclaiming Palestinian lands. This re-Islamization included attracting people back to the mosques and the encouragement of Islamic dress and morals. But the program also included almsgiving, and here it was possible for those who sympathized with re-Islamization to engage with the old committees—such as the Nablus committee, registered in 1977, or the Hebron charitable society, registered as long ago as 1963 under an Ottoman law of 1909—and with new committees founded since 1988. Re-Islamization has also harmonized with the practice and motivation of traditional observant Muslims uninterested in politics. It would thus appear that the zakat committees provided a "social coalition" between the new-style Islamism and the old-style Muslim piety. Hence it was not necessary for Hamas to establish control over the zakat committees. The re-Islamization policy led to the translation of Islamic principles and values into effective charitable relief and welfare. The Palestinian Authority, dominated by Fatah, and the Israeli state have both viewed these committees with suspicion, sometimes detaining committee members or closing offices, but on the whole the committees were—until recently—allowed to operate and to receive and disburse funds, even though Israel has had complete control over financial flows into the Palestinian territories through the banking system. Only relatively recently, in 2002, did the Israeli state declare some thirty zakat committees to be illegal.

One testimony to the efficacy of the zakat committees is that in 2003, the Food and Agriculture Organization of the UN reported that "the Islamic social welfare organizations (including zakat committees) were collectively the largest food donor in the occupied Palestinian territories after UNRWA [the UN Relief and Works Association, which is mandated only to help refugees]." But those who criticize the zakat committees' record during this period do not seem to challenge their efficacy or personal probity, only the motivations of their members.

The zakat committees also received donations from the international Islamic aid agencies that began to be founded from the 1980s onward. If we look at the wider regional context, the zakat committees fit into a pattern.

In Britain particularly, thanks to the sympathetic environment for Muslim charities fostered by the Charity Commission, some major NGOs such as Islamic Relief Worldwide and Muslim Aid emerged. These followed the lead of Christian agencies such as Christian Aid and the Catholic Agency for Overseas Development (CAFOD, the English branch of Caritas Internationalis) by renouncing all proselytism and embracing international codes of conduct such as the commitment to nondiscrimination.[8] They are beginning to conform to Raphaël Liogier's description of faith-based organizations as manifestations of individuo-globalism (Liogier 2007),[9] and in particular to project a public image of Islam that contradicts widely held negative stereotypes, even to offer implicitly in their new bureaucracies an alternative focus of authority for Muslims to traditional religious hierarchies based on the mosque. Islamic Relief Worldwide cooperates harmoniously with CAFOD and is a prominent member of the Disasters Emergency Committee, the consortium of elite British NGOs that coordinates emergency appeals. Muslim Aid cooperates with Oxfam and has negotiated a long-term agreement with the United Methodist Committee on Relief (UMCOR), the US Methodists' humanitarian agency. Secular agencies, too, such as Cooperative for Assistance and Relief Everywhere, Inc. and Médicins Sans Frontières, are interested in collaboration with Islamic charities, partly in the hope of being able to find ways to deliver aid more safely in militantly anti-Western Muslim countries.

Lack of transparency remains a problem with the large Gulf-based Islamic charities. In Saudi Arabia, for instance, it is still widely felt that they need be accountable only to their donors, not to the public at large. This has left them in a weak position to defend themselves when they have been accused of complicity in laundering funds for the benefit of terrorists.

CHARITIES AND TERROROLOGY

Having been engaged in research on Islamic charities since 1993, I was at first hesitant when invited since 2004 to serve as an expert witness to rebut various attacks on them. My hesitancy relaxed when I realized to what extent governments and law courts rely on experts who claim knowledge of terrorism, but no special knowledge either of aid and development or of religion.

Terrorology (as it has been called pejoratively) should not be condemned as such, for we all depend on police and intelligence work for our safety if we travel by air or train or visit crowded places. Most of us are willing to accept that innocent people are sometimes detained or arrested in the wider interests of security—provided that habeas corpus and other safeguards are observed. However, when apparently humanitarian organizations and their financial supporters overseas are accused of being, according to Israeli and US law, tantamount to terrorists, the solidity of the evidence against them becomes an important question, and if one has developed a skeptical view it is surely right to express it publicly when invited. Anthony Good (2008) has persuasively argued, in the different context of anthropologists giving expert evidence in asylum cases, that expert witnesses are often unduly pressured to give yes/no answers. No researcher today who has absorbed the precepts of a serious social science discipline lays claim to neutrality as an unproblematic academic position. However, it is possible to set oneself a standard for relative objectivity. Anthropology dictates that one should try to make allowance for one's own prejudices and to take account of different kinds of evidence and points of view in the widest analytical context. The Israel–Palestine conflict as seen in this perspective is a classic example of a Hegelian tragedy where two rights have collided.

The charity sector is always especially vulnerable to abuse because it is based on trust (Rosen 2008). For instance, Noraid, or Irish Northern Aid, the New York–based charity that since 1969 has raised funds in the United States for Irish Republican—that is to say, Catholic—charities in Northern Ireland, was regularly accused of spending some of the funds on weapons until the Irish Republican Army accepted the peace process in 1996. Some past connections between Islamic charities and terrorist or military activities are clear, but it does not follow that blanket condemnation of Islamic charities is justified.

During the 1980s, the US, Saudi, and Pakistani governments combined with the mujahideen to bring down the Soviet-backed regime in Afghanistan. As far as I know, no academic study has yet been undertaken of the use of the American charity sector to pursue this aim as a supplement to direct government funding: the many books published about the conflict barely touch on this aspect. A number of US nonprofit organizations with tax-exempt status (technically, (501)(c)(3) organizations), such as American Friends of Afghanistan, were formed to channel US government funds through USAID and the National Endowment for Democracy (NED), to engage in such activities as publishing a magazine, *Afghan Jehad*, arranging for injured mujahideen to be flown to the United States for medical treatment, training journalists to comment favorably on the mujahideen, and publishing leaflets for religious scholars.[10] It was reported by an independent commentator in 1990 that the activities of some seventy advocacy NGOs worldwide had created an atmosphere of unconditional sympathy for the "freedom fighters," as they were then called by the US government, in which "anyone criticizing the rebels for their human rights violations or the alliance's lack of legitimacy is automatically seen as an apologist for the Soviet and Afghan armies" (Baitenmann 1990:78). Meanwhile the Soviets objected that the US administration was supporting international terrorism (Donini 2004:121).

American aid for Afghanistan soon came to an end in the 1990s as the freedom fighters began to be redefined as terrorists. It is now a commonplace that, as an anonymous US law enforcement official remarked to a *New York Times* journalist in 1993, "the mujahedeen went to fight the Soviets when the Soviets were our enemies. Now...our former allies have turned their skills against the US in favor of terrorism. The obvious conclusion is this is coming back to haunt us."[11]

Clearly some jihadists in the bin Laden mold would have taken advantage of the privileges of charities to further their aims without scruple, regardless of any actions by the US government. But it is worth examining the possibility that some Muslims whose charitable activities in the United States during the 1990s have been criminalized may simply have been slow in noticing the change in American foreign policy, were following what they took to be legitimate religious leadership, and had become accustomed to a relaxed regime of charity regulation.[12] In any case, the majority opinion reached in 2008 by the Seventh Circuit Court of Appeals in *Boim v. Holy Land Foundation et al.* has now ruled that those who knowingly give material support to the humanitarian branch of a supposedly "terrorist" organization are just as guilty as if they were supporting terrorists directly. The vexed issue of what counts as affiliation becomes crucial. The minority opinion in this case, expressed by Justice Ilana Rovner, is more sensitive to the realities of humanitarianism.[13]

The case of Jamaat-ud-Dawa in Pakistan raises the issue starkly. In December 2008, after the attacks on Bombay, this self-styled charitable organization was banned by the Pakistani government, being already blacklisted by the United States. But in 2005, after the Kashmir earthquake, Jamaat-ud-Dawa had provided rescue aid with the approval of the Pakistani government and the active cooperation of NATO, the UN, and numerous other external agencies (Ratcliffe 2007). A question of humanitarian ethics arises. After a massive earthquake, is it wrong to work with an effective relief

3. For the pitfalls encountered by some Western NGOs that have set out to promote gender equality in Muslim central Asia, see De Cordier 2009:182–201.

4. Technically Islamic charitable societies and zakat committees in the Palestinian Territories are distinct. The former are for the most part constituted under old laws dating back to the Ottoman Empire. The latter are regulated by the Ministry of Awqaf (Religious Affairs) under a law dating back to the time of the later Jordanian administration.

5. The neologisms "emic" and "etic" derive from an analogy with the terms "phonemic" and "phonetic." The emic perspective focuses on the intrinsic cultural distinctions that are meaningful to the members of a given society, in the same way as phonemic analysis focuses on the intrinsic phonological distinctions that are meaningful to speakers of a given language (for example, whether the "glottal stop" is recognized as an alphabetical letter). The etic perspective relies on extrinsic concepts and categories that have meaning for analytic observers, in the same way as phonetic analysis relies on the extrinsic concepts and categories that are meaningful to linguistic analysts (for example, dental fricatives). "Emic knowledge is essential for an intuitive and empathic understanding of a culture, and is essential for conducting effective ethnographic fieldwork....Etic knowledge, on the other hand, is essential for cross-cultural comparison" (Letts 1996:383).

6. A report on a field research project conducted in May–June 2009 on zakat committees in the West Bank, by Emanuel Schaeublin, of the Graduate Institute of International and Development Studies, Geneva, with my assistance, was published since the drafting of the present chapter (Schaeublin 2009). This substantially confirms my own findings. Schaeublin stresses particularly the virtues of the West Bank zakat committees (before their reorganization) in responding to local priorities rather than being subservient to the agenda of international NGOs. A matching research project by Schaeublin on the zakat committees in Gaza, which are less numerous and hitherto poorly documented, was being undertaken in the summer of 2010.

7. One of the results has been that since 2007 Hamas appears to have forfeited much of its reputation for personal and institutional probity.

8. This is not necessarily the case for many of the Islamic charities based in the petrodollar states, which combine religious and humanitarian aims (as do many important Christian NGOs).

9. To simplify, the "individuo-globalist" model proposes that the cult of individual spirituality and a concern for global issues are not contradictory, but reciprocally reinforcing as part of a movement of ideas that is reaching an increased salience in

advanced industrial societies, a deep structure in which many apparently diverse religious and quasi-religious phenomena converge. For development of this argument, see Benthall 2008b, Chapter 4.

10. The main source for this information is the National Endowment for Democracy's "Democracy Projects Database," accessible through the NED website. For instance, in 1991 the NED awarded $57,068 to the American Friends of Afghanistan to enable the Cultural Council of the Afghan Resistance "to continue publishing the magazine *Afghan Jehad* and to support its Afghan Institute for Policy Studies program."

11. Alison Mitchell, "After Blast: New Interest in Holy-War Recruits in Brooklyn," *New York Times*, 11 April 1993.

12. The Emadeddin Muntasser/Care International case in Worcester, Massachusetts, that came to trial in 2007–08 (no connection with the major American charity CARE) may be an example of this.

13. Some of these issues are explored in *Blocking Faith, Freezing Charity: Chilling Muslim Charitable Giving in the "War on Terrorism Financing,"* American Civil Liberties Union, 2009. As the present book goes to press, an advocacy group based in Washington DC, Charity and Security Network (www.charityandsecurity.org), has become very active. In June 2010, the US Supreme Court decided in a majority holding (*Holder v. Humanitarian Law Project*), much criticized in the American press, that even giving advice to a "terrorist" group on how to achieve its political aims peacefully is a form of material support for terrorism. This confirms an opinion expressed in a recent paper by legal academics that the Supreme Court's reliance on humanitarian law is "often minimal and haphazard" (Weissbrodt and Nesbitt 2010).

14. A similar crisis arose, provoking wide international concern that the "battle for hearts and minds" was being won by Islamists, as a result of the catastrophic floods in Pakistan in the summer of 2010 (Saeed Shah, "Pakistan Floods: Islamic Fundamentalists Fill State Aid Void," *Guardian*, 3 August 2010).

15. In fact, much of the modern Islamist critique of the West is indebted to non-Muslim sources, such as the writings of Edward Said.

16. Judaism, as the matrix of both Christianity and Islam, originally had universalizing aspects but for specific historical reasons became an ethno-religion. Van der Veer argues that the Hindu tradition of "hierarchical relativism" has been obscured by the reputation of modern Hinduism for religious egalitarianism (Van der Veer 1994). In any case, its strong identification with one major country limits its universalistic application.

6

The Value of Orphans

Erica Bornstein

In 2008 a UNICEF donation campaign arrived at my doorstep. An arrow pointed to a bulge in the envelope and explained, "The enclosed nickel could save a child's life!" Inside the plea for funds, addressed "Dear Friend of Children," were free address labels printed with my name. Specific categories of donation, $25, $35, $50, $75, $100, $500, and "other," ran under a banner stating, "I want to do whatever it takes to save children's lives." Like many Americans bombarded with such requests, I usually dismiss them as emotionally manipulative. However, this time I could not shake the feeling that I should not accept anything from the organization. I read the brochure to its end, where it concluded, "Even if you can't make a donation today, please return the enclosed nickel as a sign of your support for children in desperate need around the world." There was something distinctly uncomfortable about receiving money from a charitable organization. Realistically, I thought if I took the time to send back the nickel I would donate additional funds. If I did not respond to this plea I risked becoming a moral spectator. My lack of donation made me complicit in the plight of needy children: my apathy was against humanitarianism. Discomfort at the urge of engagement was itself a predicament, in which inaction made me culpable for a child's suffering.

The children in the UNICEF brochure are alone, without parents, without an explanation of their circumstances, and without context. Without history and orphaned from kin, they are in need of support. Where are their guardians one might ask? Why are they in need? That these questions are neither asked nor required is a particular aspect of humanitarian appeals that focus on children and build on the humanitarian value of orphans. Using this framework as my entry, I examine the ethics and politics of donation as a form of humanitarianism in New Delhi, India, specifically through the relationship of orphans to the gift. I argue that the gift is a form of ethical engagement, a part of humanitarianism, but only if the gift is free from self-interest. When faced with the call to assist an orphan, adoption is one possible alternative, transforming an orphan to kin. Care by NGOs (nongovernmental organizations) and the state is another possible solution, and social sponsorship is yet a third. In India, between these avenues of assistance lies a contentious moral terrain where the secular Indian state (as guardian of its citizens) is a mediating force that limits adoption, protects orphans, and encourages donation as a form of ethical engagement. In addition, the Hindu aspects of this landscape are essential for understanding how the gift becomes a form of humanitarianism. That children are orphaned due to parental abandonment is one part of the picture. That parents see abandonment as a viable alternative when faced with conditions of extreme poverty is another. While anthropological definitions of orphans may draw upon the notion of being bereft of kin, children are also orphaned by poverty: the conditions that make parents unable to care for them.

A PARTICULAR FORM OF GIVING: (DONATION, DĀN) IN INDIA

India, as a nation of poverty and need,[1] is a fertile site for philanthropic activity toward children, and a short search on the Internet yields websites that encourage and facilitate donation to orphans. One Arya Samaj website offers a "Charity for Children" page with profiles of children.[2] As a form of child sponsorship (Bornstein 2001), one can choose a photograph of a particular child, named Ajay, Bharti, or Dharmistha, and donate toward their care. With no more information than an image of a child, their birth date, and the name of their village, one can sponsor an orphan. Another website, http://www.GiveIndia.org, under the category "Child Welfare," offers a list of "Donation Options" that include "subsidize one child's cost for medical assistance," "sponsor a child for a month," "support rehabilitation of a sex worker's child for a year," and "subsidize education, therapy, and rehabilitation," among others. Each donation option is correlated with a particular NGO, costing between Rs. 750 and Rs. 14,800.[3] One can click the "add to cart" icon and purchase the donation.

Juxtaposed with the reality of poverty in India[4] is the other contemporary reality that India is positioning itself as a global superpower: one that is benevolent and offers aid instead of receiving it. It was in this context that in 2004–05[5] I conducted research in New Delhi on donation (or, dān as it is called in Hindi) and giving as an aspect of humanitarianism. My informants included donors and those that encouraged people to give: philanthropists, members of trusts, directors of foundations, individuals, and families that gave dān daily out of their home, *sadhus* (world renouncers or holy men) who received dān, temple workers and pundits who organized the reception of dān, NGO workers that raised money and gave charity, people who gave service (or *seva*) by volunteering their time to charitable institutions, and groups that organized volunteers at orphanages.[6]

While conducting my fieldwork in New Delhi, I read daily newspapers and skimmed the headlines for stories of charitable activity. Rarely was charity a subject of Delhi news until the tsunami hit the Indian coast in December 2004. Suddenly, newspapers questioned India's place in the global context of humanitarian aid. India was vying for a seat on the UN Security Council, and in January 2005, Prime Minister Manmohan Singh refused tsunami-directed aid from the US government. The *Hindustan Times*[7] argued: if India received aid, it would jeopardize its position as a global superpower—one that helped instead of needed assistance. In two weeks, the prime minister's fund for tsunami relief raised Rs. 403 Crore (roughly $90 million).[8] News headlines questioned: "Does Delhi Have a Conscience?"[9] and speculated whether Delhiites would continue to give after the tsunami relief efforts were complete. Yet within national narratives of progressive and benevolent donation practices by Indians for Indians in the larger geopolitical landscape of humanitarian aid, and in the nationalist frame of unity in diversity, which the state has worked hard to politically maintain since Partition, were those who were excluded. Alongside newspapers documenting how Indians were giving to their own were accounts of how they were not. In particular, caste-lines created fissures for the exclusion of aid.[10] The call for aid both unified Indians as "giving" and exacerbated distinctions between Indians. It neither promoted equality nor a more generalized humanitarianism. Competition, scarce resources, and corruption dominated the discourse of national aid.

Scholarship on giving in India has focused on dān, which, as Parry (1986, 1994), Raheja (1988), and Laidlaw (1995, 2000) have shown, is a particular form of donation that does not require a return, at least in this lifetime (there is some debate about this as some people expect *punya*, or merit, from giving dān). It differs from Marcel Mauss's classic treatise, *The Gift* (1990), which examines how giving always requires a reciprocal relation of obligation. In contrast to reciprocal giving, those who give dān strive to release themselves from any future contact with the recipient of their gift. Dān is a "pure" or "free" gift; yet it is not free of danger. In Hindu scripture and some ritual practices, it is through dān that evil, sin, and affliction are ritually transferred from donors to recipients.[11] In the *Bhagavad Gita*, a reference that quite a few informants offered when I asked about dān, it is a gift that is offered through desireless action. The quote below is from a book called *Gita the Mother*:

> There should be no motive in charity and there should be no aim, direct or indirect. Let those, to whom you give, be such, that they cannot make any return to you. Just as, when shouting toward the sky, there is no reply, or nothing can be seen at the back of a mirror, or a ball when thrown on the water does not rebound in one's hand, or just as a wild bull is fed on grass, or an ungrateful person returns no obligation, charity should be without any idea of return. This is the supreme notion of charity.

> The inferior kind is that, in which there is some other intention. It is like feeding a cow with the intention of getting milk, or sowing a seed with the intention of selling corn, or inviting relatives with the intention of getting presents, or sending sweets to friends expecting them to return them, or like working for others after they have paid the fees, or giving medical aid, after charges have been paid. [Maharaj 1972:248]

Thus, with dān, one "gives in order to forget." The "purity of the recipient" is an important scriptural element of dān in ancient texts (Anderson 1997; Heim 2004). There are proper recipients for dān, as well as proper times and places to give dān—religious institutions and holidays being some of the best. Yet this too was being challenged in the course of my research on the contemporary practice of dān. The notion of dān, like all cultural forms, is vibrant and changing. People preferred to give dān to organizations like orphanages where they could "see the results over time" and "make spontaneous visits" instead of giving to a pundit or priest at a temple. People gave dān out of their doorways in urban Delhi to beggars and sadhus (world renouncers; Bornstein 2009). People also considered their donations to schools for the education of impoverished girls to be a form of dān.[12]

Dān is more than a scriptural reference; it is lived practice and a form of donation, like the funding plea marked by the UNICEF nickel. In New Delhi, orphanages have recently emerged as ideal places for people to give dān as donation without any expectation of return. Dān is to be given to strangers, not to kin, and orphanages provide ideal sites for this. At orphanages, New Delhiites gave service (seva) in the form of volunteering; they gave donations of used clothing and made monthly scheduled payments to sponsor children. Some Indians sponsored the weddings of orphans through *kanyā dān*, which in Hinduism means the gift of a virgin. Like *godan*, the gift of a cow, kanyā dān is considered to be one of the most sacred forms of dān. For example, at one orphanage people gave monthly donations to sponsor the education of an orphan, and some Indians paid for the wedding of an orphan if they did not have a daughter of their own to give away in marriage.

HUMANITARIANISM AND ITS ORPHANS

Orphans play a significant part in the discourse of humanitarianism, meriting analysis of the category itself. While the UNICEF plea mentioned at the beginning of this chapter does not specifically refer to orphans, it refers to children who need to be cared for, of which the orphan is the most extreme case. As a social category in the discourse of humanitarianism, orphans are valued—particularly, in the "humanitarianism as a politics of life" that seeks to assist victims of humanity (Fassin 2007a). For UNICEF, orphans fall under a combined category of "orphans and vulnerable children" or OVC. The number of children orphaned globally is astounding. According to UNICEF's *State of the World's Children 2006*, "At the end of 2003, there were an estimated 143 million orphans under the age of 18 in 93 developing countries. More than 16 million children were orphaned in 2003 alone" (UNICEF 2006:39). There are some who argue that the category of the orphan in humanitarian assistance has been overemphasized because of the powerful reaction it inspires from donors (Henderson 2007; Meintjes and Giese 2007). In Africa, for example, where children orphaned by HIV/AIDS have lived in contexts where guardianship has historically been fluid due to labor migration, a statistical overemphasis on orphans is an injustice to the complex experiences and survival strategies of destitute children. Scholars such as Henderson, Meintjes, and Giese (mentioned above), as well as Fassin (2008b), convincingly argue that an orphan's socioeconomic status may not be worse than the status of other children who live under social deprivation and exclusion due to conditions of extreme poverty.[13]

An orphan's status has historically said more about poverty and need than about abandonment. In line with work that explores changing conceptions of children and childhood (Stephens 1995; Zelizer 1985), Lydia Murdoch's (2006) book *Imagined Orphans* explores changing conceptions of orphans in Victorian England. In her case, as well as in my case of orphans in India and other well-documented cases of orphans in southern Africa, most Victorian orphans were not full orphans. They were placed in institutions by parents for periods of time due to life circumstances such as illness, the death of a parent, injury, and poverty. They were not necessarily given up. Although most of the children in state and charitable institutions were not orphaned or deserted, reformers represented them to the public as either parentless or victims of parental abuse. Photography was an important medium for engaging the public in Victorian programs of social welfare, with "before and after" pictures documenting melodramatic transformations of savage waifs transformed into reformed and civilized British citizens. What is salient about this historical case is the disjunction between the popular representation of Victorian poor children as orphans and the ways that families strategically used state and private philanthropic welfare services. While reformers represented poor children as orphaned and endangered by abusive and "demonic" parents, it was the adult poor that were being excluded from the national community. Thus, when one thinks about orphans, one must also consider the parents that are economically excluded through their poverty.

CHILDREN OF THE NATION: ADOPTION AND THE INDIAN STATE

In the spectrum of care for abandoned children, adoption is but one possible outcome. It is not the only solution, and in the section that follows I explore why adoption in India is contested terrain. As mentioned earlier, the orphan, as a social category, represents the destitute, the abandoned, the excluded, and the unwanted. With no one to care for them, orphans are assumed to be free of kin ties. In this manner, they inspire everyone to care for them through the social responsibility of humanitarianism. While some anthropologists no longer consider kinship a useful analytical category, especially after David Schneider's critique (1980, 1984), others have reinvigorated the study of kinship as a social process through an analysis of "cultures of relatedness" (Carsten 2000, 2004) and alternative families (Weston 1991). Some have used the social relationships that emerge via new reproductive technologies (Franklin and Ragoné 1998; Franklin and McKinnon 2001; Konrad 2005; Ragoné and Twine 1994, 2000) or international adoption (Modell 1994, 2002; Bowie and EASA 2004; Volkman 2005; Yngvesson 2002, 2004) to rethink the social categories of kinship. Terrell and Modell (1994) argue that studying adoption as a category of meaning has the potential to shed light on ideas of family, ethnicity, belonging, and citizenship. Adoption is about who belongs and how; it is a social transaction, a "social fiction" as Jack Goody so aptly wrote in 1969, that involves fundamental beliefs about persons. What does this social fiction, legislated by states, say about the value of particular human beings in international context and about kinship in humanitarian assistance? Moreover, how do discourses of humanitarianism that highlight children elude the social conditions of poverty that compel parents to abandon their children and mask existing kin relations?

Although the word *orphan* may imply an unparented and therefore unprotected child, in India the government and NGO-run orphanages have officially taken over the role of guardian so that orphans become children of the nation, with certain rights and responsibilities. In a time when transnational adoption is a common practice for parents in the United States, the status of Indian orphans as children of the nation has precluded parallel adoption practices, which are currently increasing in other parts of the world.[14] Orphans, as children of the nation, are protected, saved, and managed by humanitarian institutions and the state. Transnational adoption, as a transformation of an orphan's status is not the only possible outcome. Some are kept in orphanages where the state becomes legal guardian. Other contexts of orphan care include social adoption where the state remains guardian and an individual (or family) unrelated to the orphan economically supports an orphan's education and care.

In India, it is estimated that there are 44 million destitute children, 12.44 million of whom are orphans. While these statistics might imply a booming national adoption program, the number of annual official adoptions in India is estimated at five thousand.[15] Herein lies a puzzle. Why are there so few children being adopted in India while there are so many children in "need" of adoption? Reflecting the potential "need" for children to be adopted, a CSA (Catalysts for Social Action) case study at http://www.indianNGOs.com documents there are approximately three hundred NGOs (nongovernmental organizations) working on the issue of adoption in India. Adoption in this case becomes a cause for NGO activism. Yet not everyone agrees that this is a worthy cause. When I met with the director of the national agency responsible for coordinating adoptions in India (the Central Adoption

Resource Agency or, CARA, a department of the Ministry of Social Justice and Empowerment), I tried to describe my research interests on charity in India. "What does charity have to do with adoption?" she asked. Our interview was notably brief. I asked why there were difficulties for foreign parents who wanted to adopt children from India and she replied, "They are our children so we give the preference to our people first." I had come to the interview with a friend, an American who was trying to adopt a child from India. The government officer seemed irritated by our presence and referred us to the website for instructions on international adoption. It was not something one could address in that particular office in New Delhi; for foreigners to adopt they had to go through an adoption agency in their country of national origin.

In India's contemporary secular state, different legal procedures must be followed according to one's nationality and religious identity before one adopts an orphan. The Hindu Adoption and Maintenance Act of 1956 (Diwan 2000) governs Indians who identify as Hindu, Buddhist, Jain, Sikh, or atheist. The Guardians and Wards Act of 1890 governs the guardianship of orphans for Muslims, Christians, Parsis, and Jews and foreign adoptions. Despite these legal articulations, an orphan's religious identity is not always clear. As subjects of secular legislation, orphans embody a more generic humanity, which must then be translated for adoption purposes into a particular legal identity. In 2005, when I asked the administrator of an Arya Samaj/Hindu orphanage in an upscale neighborhood of south New Delhi if any of the children were Muslim he replied: "I don't think any Muslim child ever came here but you never know. An orphan is an orphan." Orphans in the humanitarian imagination code as "pure humanity" unmarked by kin relations.

There is an affective dimension to an orphan's exclusion. Orphans arouse a politics of pity (Boltanski 1999; Cartwright 2005). Once abandoned, they present a contrast to the bonds of belonging characterized by kin. Orphans are those who have no one, and in this status, they inspire humanitarian assistance. In adopting a child, the child is totally uprooted from the "natural family" and transplanted into a new family. Like the refugee in the family of nations (Malkki 1995), the orphan is assumed to be exiled from kin. Neither here nor there, the orphan re-enters society as a "member" only after rites of passage, rituals, and ceremonies, such as adoption, have been performed. Both refugees and orphans allude to the temporality of their status: that refugees will be repatriated, for example, and become citizens again or that orphans will be adopted and become kin. However, like refugees in permanent refugee camps, some orphans remain in orphanages, which, as boarding schools, represent a far better alternative to destitution.

In order to understand why and how the Indian state mediates the care and adoption of orphans, it is helpful to know how legislation regarding adoption and the care of orphans in India has changed historically from a focus on the needs of adoptive parents to the needs of adopted children. Before 1956, when the Hindu Adoption and Maintenance Act was passed, adoption was governed by Hindu scripture and colonial legislation. Adoptions in India were of sons and took place between close relations. The 1956 Act allowed for the adoption outside of families, of girls, and of orphans. In order to distinguish this postwar legal context from its historical antecedent, I elaborate a bit upon scriptural practice—especially the ways in which it both informs contemporary legislation and differs from it.

In Hinduism having a son is spiritually and materially important and has historically been an impetus for child adoption.

> According to the Hindu scriptures, a man is born with three debts—debt to *rishis*, debt to gods, and debt to one's ancestors. The debt to *rishis* is paid by studying the *Vedas*, the debt to gods by offering sacrifices and the debt to one's *pitra* or ancestors, by the birth of a male child. The son is required for conducting the last rights of the parent(s) without which it is believed, the soul would not attain *moksha*. The son is also valued for continuing the family line and ensuring perpetuation of the name of one's ancestors. Thus, in the Hindu religion, it is the supreme duty of the son to solemnize the final rites of the parents and ensure continuity of family lineage. Besides this "spiritual" requirement of a male child, there is a secular or social desire to inherit and manage the family property. [Bharat 1993:5]

In her study of sixteen adoption agencies in India, Bharat (cited above) documents how the scriptural bias for sons continues in current practice. This may be due to the fact that in north India, girl children are bigger burdens on parents when they are poor because of dowries. One of the largest contemporary orphanages in New Delhi is called Palna (the cradle). Outside the tall gates of the orphanage is a cradle where babies are placed in the middle of the night. The giving and taking of a child, of adoption in the case of orphans, occurs on sacred territory. This is especially true in Hinduism, where sons are necessary for the spiritual merit of a person— if one does not have a legitimate son one must adopt one.[16] In my fieldwork it was the sons who were adopted first: most of the older children the waiting for adoption at Mother Teresa's home and at Palna, which is the Delhi Council for Child Welfare's home for abandoned children, were girls.

Historically, in ancient Hindu law (see Manu cited in Diwan 2000:87), adoption occurred within families through a ceremony of "giving and taking." The filial relation of an adopted son was created by proper ceremonies of adoption (*dattaka mimansa*), which included (1) acceptance of the child and (2) performance of a ritual called *dattak homa*.[17] The filial relation of the adopted son occurred only by performing the proper ceremonies, of gift, acceptance, and *homa*. The courts viewed the ceremony of giving and taking as mandatory and enough for the validity of adoption. For filial relation, it was necessary that after the adoption the child should be treated as a son (as the law was for males). The mere placing of the registered deed of adoption was not sufficient; the child placed under adoption had to be given and taken.[18] During the British Raj these practices continued. Since only fathers and mothers could give children for adoption, orphans could not be adopted, the adopter had to be Hindu (either male or female), the adoptive parent could not adopt more than one son and one daughter, and only the father or mother could *give* a child in adoption.

In 1956 the Hindu Adoption and Maintenance Act was passed in a postwar international context marked by an increase of displaced, abandoned, and orphaned children and a correlative new humanitarian concern for these children. Only at this point was adoption seen as a humanitarian solution (Bharat 1993). In addition to the social reforms initiated by Indian independence, which included a shift in the language of care of destitute children from "charity" to "welfare," an increase in welfare services for children grew in India. This may have been related to the growth of welfare programs for children in the West and their influence on Indians returning after working abroad. The Hindu Adoption and Maintenance Act made it possible to adopt a female child, for single females to adopt an orphan, and for adoption to take place outside a family-caste group.

Most importantly for the purposes of my argument regarding humanitarianism and orphans, the Hindu Adoption and Maintenance Act transformed adoption from a practice within a related group to a welfare practice among strangers. From the inception of the Hindu Adoption and Maintenance Act, foreigners were adopting the majority of children. This was attributed to cultural factors, primarily the social stigma of adoption in India, which marked couples as infertile (Bharadwaj 2003) and inspired anxiety about the child's past and his or her potential undesirable traits (Bharat 1993).[19] The stipulation regarding persons who may be adopted by the Hindu Adoption and Maintenance Act is simply that they are Hindu, have not already been adopted, have not been married, and are not yet fifteen years of age.[20] While in ancient Hindu law caste was a determinant category in adoption (as in Dharmashastra), in the 1956 Act caste and/or subcaste are no bar. Caste was not discussed in fieldwork although some mentioned that families would try to find a child that phenotypically resembled the adoptive parents—further building a narrative of potential kin and belonging. I observed one Indian family returning to Mother Teresa's orphanage with the child they had adopted, visiting the sisters/nuns who had arranged the adoption. The sisters excitedly exclaimed that the child resembled the parents and that they looked like a family. It was a compliment in an ultimate kinship narrative of success.

The 1956 Act originally stated that a guardian could give a child in adoption only if the parents were dead or had "completely and finally renounced the world" or had been "declared by a Court of competent jurisdiction to be of unsound mind" (Diwan 2000:74). In 1962 this legislation was amended to include children who were abandoned or whose parentage was not known. The 1962 amendment enlarged both the category of possible children who could be adopted and possible guardians to include guardians appointed by courts, such as a manager, secretary, or person in charge of an orphanage. In 1972 there was an attempt to impose uniform adoption law in India with the Adoption of Children Bill of 1972, which was opposed by "minority communities," particularly Muslims (see Bharadwaj 2003; Bharat 1993), and the bill was allowed to lapse in 1976.[21] In 1984 the Supreme Court of India further codified processes for adopting children by creating specific government agencies tasked with oversight of all adoptions. A new requirement was implemented for orphans to be certified abandoned by the state before adoption was considered a possible option. A marked increase in Indian adoptions took place between 1977 and 1987, which corresponded to a decrease in international adoptions. In 1977, 80 percent of adoptions were by foreign parents, and less than 20 percent were by Indian parents. One decade later, adoptions by Indian parents had increased to 50 percent while adoptions by foreign parents decreased to 50 percent (Bharat 1993:119).

However, in this landscape transnational or domestic adoption is not the only possible outcome. Some orphans are kept in orphanages where the state becomes the legal guardian. As mentioned earlier, another method of care for orphans is social adoption where the state remains the legal guardian and an individual (or family) unrelated to the orphan economically supports an orphan's education and care. This is in line with other forms of sponsorship found in programs of economic development and humanitarianism, such as programs in which a donor sponsors a child, or a cow, or a village. What is not often considered, but is extremely important in understanding the figure of the orphan in humanitarian aid, is the relation of orphans to poverty. Many children who are considered orphans are not children who have lost both parents. In Delhi, as elsewhere in India and perhaps in the world more broadly, children are placed in institutions due to the poverty of their parents. Although not the extreme form of abandonment caused by parental death, poverty, too, has the potential to strain ties and create social exclusion. When one looks closely at the orphan, as a figure in humanitarian discourse, one begins to see a symbol of "the excluded," and this is an important part of the pathos of orphans. Some orphans in orphanages may have lost one parent and the other cannot care for the children, or the orphanage may be a temporary home for an orphan while their family weathers difficult economic circumstances. As a stop-gap welfare strategy, an orphan's status may not be a permanent phenomenon (as in Fassin 2008b). Orphans who cannot be adopted—the status of many orphanage-dwellers in Delhi—are children whose parents are destitute but have not abandoned them. A study by Noor Jahan Siddiqui (1997:43–45) on adolescent girls in four orphanages in Delhi documented that 52 percent of the residents were partially orphaned girls. In the case of the remaining girls, the reasons listed for entrance into an orphanage were either that both parents were dead (36 percent), lost, or unknown, or that their parents were extremely poor (26 percent). Mothers brought the girls to the orphanages in 53 percent of the cases, distant relatives in 25 percent of the cases, and the police in 12.73 percent of the cases where children were found abandoned. In India, orphanages are often boarding schools. Fatherless girls are sent to these schools, and the schools arrange for marriages. Relatives may visit on weekends during certain visiting hours.[22] As Siddiqui's study attests, poverty also orphans children.

An Arya Samaj–focused Hindu orphanage in south Delhi was one of my ethnographic sites. Out of the three hundred girls in residence, only fifty to sixty were "full orphans" without any surviving parents. These children had all been socially adopted by Indians who paid for their care and visited them at specific times. The orphanage decided which of the resident girls were most eligible for social adoption, described as the girls who were "intelligent and don't have anybody." Another NGO I studied had socially adopted eighteen of the girls at this orphanage, and at one school in Delhi the teachers were required to socially adopt one child. Hence the state, in partnership with the NGO, became the guardian of its excluded children. I asked the warden of the NGO (which was called a *vidyalaya* or school, not an orphanage) why the institution did not allow formal adoptions. She explained that "people used to adopt children from here but they didn't care for them and brought them back when they had their own [children]." Other staff members told me of children running away from their adoptive parents back to the school. At the time of my research and for the past thirty-five years, the school only permitted social adoption.

ADOPTION SCANDALS IN A TRANSNATIONAL FRAME

At issue in the political economy of humanitarian efforts toward orphans is the calculation of their value. The question of a child's worth is both a rhetorical question and a humanitarian concern. What, for example, is the value of an orphan? The nickel sent by UNICEF almost provokes offense in its paucity. Such questions of value not only garner donations for needy children, they inspire the Indian government to limit transnational adoptions in the face of potential human trafficking.

A celebrity media context sets the backdrop for scandal relating to adoption. On January 1, 2008, the *Times of India* ran a short piece about Madonna vacationing in India. Titled "Madonna in Jodhpur to Ring in the New Year," the five-paragraph article began with a description of Madonna, her family, and five family friends, ringing in the New Year at a "private heritage resort" in Rajasthan. The third paragraph was short and abrupt. "Sources in London have revealed that the 49-year-old singer and her husband Guy Ritchie have sent aides to hunt the Asian country for a new daughter." One can imagine agents scouring India for the predatory and wealthy humanitarian music star. The article continued with a comparison of Madonna and Angelina Jolie (another mother-without-borders) who adopted a son from "the poor country" of Cambodia in 2002 and wanted to adopt from Malawi but had "changed her decision because of the difficult adoption procedures there." The last paragraph described how Madonna had adopted a child from Malawi but that the adoption was not yet formalized. The scandal regarding Madonna's adoption of her Malawian son was made famous when the boy's biological father went to the press and announced that he had not realized the adoption would take his son away forever and that it meant "giving up his son for good."[23] Angelina Jolie is no stranger to adoption scandal either. With children adopted from Cambodia, Ethiopia, and Vietnam, and three biological children of her own, she seems to live the humanitarian ideal she promotes as a UNHCR Goodwill Ambassador (Office of the United Nations High Commissioner for Refugees Goodwill Ambassador). As a cover story for the magazine *In Touch Weekly* (November 26, 2007) titled "Zahara's Family

Wants Her Back," the magazine featured pictures of Zahara, "the woman who claims to be her birth mother," and of Angelina Jolie. The article told the tragic story of how Zahara's biological mother was raped by a stranger who broke into her home. Unable to care for the child while working as a laborer, she ran away from her home and left the child with her mother, who could not afford to keep the child and brought her to an orphanage. Government papers used in the adoption identified the child as being an AIDS orphan. Looking at the narrative of abandonment, it is not only the Ethiopian child who was abandoned. The state of desperate poverty that led Zahara's mother to abandon her child is an instance of abandonment of the mother by society. That a foreign, wealthy movie star could claim the abandoned child as her own is a critical factor in the political economy of orphans and humanitarianism.

In India, one condition of legal adoption and the transformation of an orphan to a member of a particular family—from a member of the family of man, or a generic member of humanity, to a member of a specific constellation of familial relations—is that there can be no payment. This speaks to the ritual purity of the process of adoption and the transformative potential inherent in the change of status from orphan to kin. In India, the court may attach conditions to an adoption order, such as the payment of the upkeep of a child, of the actual cost that a guardian has spent from their own pocket. The 1956 Act stipulates that in adoptions, "the applicant seeking permission has not received or agreed to receive, and that no person has made or given or agreed to make or give to the applicant any payment or reward in consideration of the adoption" (section 9[5] Diwan 2000:75). This requirement provides a clear categorical distinction between "adoption" and "human trafficking," which is illegal (compare to Cohen 2004a on organ trafficking).[24] In profane contrast to the sacred category of the orphan stands the "adoption market."

Two adoption scandals—one broadcast on National Public Radio in 2007[25] for an American audience and the other a cover story in a weekly news magazine in India in 2005—are examples of the profane equation of money and adoption. The first details the experience of the Smolin family, who adopted two adolescent girls from India. When the girls arrived at the airport from India, the adopting parents explained, "they were clearly very upset. They were avoidant of us and then eventually they became very emotionally disturbed....I've never seen anyone—and I hope to never, ever see anyone again—as upset as those girls were in the first nine months that they were in our home." The girls had been described by the adoption agency as children who had been waiting for a long time for a home. The girls, on the other hand, insisted that they had been stolen from their mother. The girls' story was true: their mother had been poor and had placed the children temporarily in an orphanage, which sold them. The girls' biological mother was informed that the girls were being placed temporarily in a boarding school. When she returned to see them, however, she was told the girls were not permitted to see her. The orphanage director was later placed in jail in India on charges of selling babies. Years later, the adoptive parents of the two girls in the United States contacted a social activist in India who, with the name of the biological mother and the name of her village given by the two daughters, tracked her down. The adopted parents arranged a reunion with their biological mother, although by that time the two girls were almost grown. Mr. Smolin recounted: "Yes. It was really one of the most moving things that I've seen. When Manjula returned and met her mom, the mom took her in her arms and she wept. And then she started to chant in her own language the whole story of her life. She said that I bore you, I nursed you, I carried you, I raised you and I lost you. And now, you've been reborn to me. And she said this in this kind of chanting, weeping way as she held her child." The grown children did not return to India permanently. Their mother asked Manjula to live with her, and Manjula told her mother, "No, I can't do that. I want to get a job." Mr. Smolin continued, "And Manjula's trying to explain to her mom why she just doesn't feel comfortable anymore in her own village with her own mother, in her own culture with her own language." The story of loss and reunion is also the story of the permanent transformation of the girls' citizenship from Indian to American. The girls had been orphaned from their native context.

The second example is a cover story in India's national magazine *Frontline* (May 2005), which presented a series of eight articles exposing the underbelly of international adoption. In the details of this exposé are some moral assumptions about the value of humanity, which the Indian adoption laws are set up to protect. The cover story investigated "a multi-billion-dollar, countrywide racket in inter-country adoption of children." It was not focused on adoption within India, but on international adoption, and this is significant not because adoption within India does not exist, but because there is a particular ethical and political economy of adoption that is exposed via international adoption practices. The *Frontline* articles, written after the 2004 tsunami, mention the arrest of kidnappers who "sold over 350 children" and document how "trade in inter-country adoptions... appears to be a roaring business for some unscrupulous agencies." The buying and selling of babies, "the commodification of children," contrasts to the sacred value of attachments, which is symbolically elucidated via orphans unattached to kin.

One article titled "The Adoption Market" detailed how "some unscrupulous agencies made India an international baby shopping centre." I quote from the article: "Papers are forged and guidelines violated as babies are matched rapidly with foreign parents. Touts of private adoption agencies hunt for vulnerable families. Often, the mother has little negotiating power. For as little as Rs. 150 to Rs. 500, a newborn is handed over to touts who are paid about Rs. 6,000 a baby by the agencies. Mothers who go to reclaim their babies are turned away. Some agencies look the other way from the trafficking, stealing, and buying of babies." The adoption market was a moral accounting of purpose that juxtaposed parents from developed nations against those from developing nations. As one article explained, demand grew for children in developed nations due to "fertility declines, the greater availability of contraceptive aids, the legalization of abortion, higher participation of women in the workforce, the rise in the age of marriage, the postponement of childbirth and state support for single mothers." In developing nations like India, supply rose due "to an increasing number of orphaned and abandoned children because of poor and worsening socioeconomic conditions," namely increasing poverty. This socioeconomic inequality between nations reared its head at the convergence of demand and supply: "To cut the going global rate of $22,000–$25,000 per child, international adopters come to India to shop for babies, available at a fourth of this price." And one nation's prosperity was linked to another's decline.

Abuses of corrupt adoption agencies abound in the *Frontline* cover story. They include abducting babies for adoption, identifying vulnerable mothers from poor families and enticing them to give up their babies, falsely informing the mother that her baby was stillborn, buying children from poor families, accepting financial or material rewards for the adoption agency in exchange for children, and offering women financial incentives to conceive a child specifically for adoption abroad. This was particularly the case with girl children, further exaggerating the profanity of trying to calculate the value of a child. Moreover, adoption agencies, since they were forbidden by law from charging fees for adoption greater than a specified amount of "maintenance,"[26] asked for "donations." These donations were crass demands, considered unethical when juxtaposed to the sacred basis of giving and receiving a child and of the purity of orphans. One parent explained: "The agency's staff constantly kept harassing us during the time we were in India asking us if we can pay them more.

The director even asked us to get him a particular brand of whisky."[27] Another parent wrote of an agency director asking for bottles of whisky for his son's and daughter's weddings. Some parents decided to stop dealing with particular agencies because "their dealing was very business oriented," focusing on profit and not persons. In this political economy, adoption became the "privilege of the elite." "In the existing set-up, no ordinary childless working class family can afford to adopt."[28]

In the wake of the tsunami of December 2004, the "risks" for orphaned children and affected communities came to the attention of Indian media. Sixty child-rights organizations called for a yearlong ban on the adoption of children affected by the tsunami.[29] Wealthy and greedy foreign adoptive parents threatened poor, vulnerable Indian children and families. To counteract the potential for clear injustices, the postcolonial Indian state has instituted laws that protect orphans, the poor, and their particular histories. In the ethical political economy of orphan adoption, managed by the nation-state, there emerges a hierarchy of humanity (Fassin 2007a). As mentioned earlier, in 1984 the Indian Supreme Court[30] laid out principles that adoption agencies had to follow when giving a child for adoption to foreign parents. The judgment was the effect of a petition by a lawyer to the Supreme Court "to restrain private Indian agencies from carrying out further activity of routing children for adoption abroad." Although adoptions by foreign parents are governed by the Guardians and Wards Act of 1890, particular components of the Hindu Adoption and Maintenance Act of 1956 pertain to the regulation of foreign adoptions: primarily, that, first, effort is made to find adoptive parents from within India (Diwan 2000:143, as with quotes below). Reasons given for this are issues of establishing membership in a group and safeguarding the adoptees' future sense of belonging "because such adoption would steer clear of any problems of assimilation of the child in the family of the adoptive parents which might arise on account of cultural, racial, or linguistic differences in case of adoption by foreign parents." Thus, if it is not possible to find adoptive parents in the country, then foreign parents may be sought, rather than allowing a child to grow up in an orphanage or institution where there is no "family life, no love, and affection." Most cases of inter-country adoption are of "orphans, destitute, or abandoned children, or those children whose parents have been lured into giving them in adoption" (Diwan 2000:144).

Like dān, the giving and taking of adoption cannot have a return; it must be unfettered. Pure humanitarianism, as with pure philanthropy, can have no ulterior motives. Applications by foreign parents for guardianship are scrutinized and evaluated by distinct bodies, including the Indian

Council of Child Welfare, which conducts home visits and child study reports before children are placed. Clearly, adoption is not humanitarianism because of the self-interested motive of building a family. Adoption agencies and NGOs caring for orphaned children, on the other hand, are humanitarian in their concerns.

The hierarchy of humanity, based on the legislation of placement, has two intersecting components: (1) the hierarchy of desired children based on sex, age, and health and (2) the hierarchy of adoptive parents based on religion and nationality (Lobo and Vasudevan 2002). The most preferred children for adoption are those who are young, male, and healthy, then the female, then older children, and finally those with mental or physical problems. In the hierarchy of prospective parents, the first priority for adoption goes to Indian parents who live in India, next are Indians with non-resident Indian citizenship (NRIs), then mixed couples where one parent is Indian, and finally, foreigners (Apparao 1997). This priority list challenges the egalitarian face of the "family of man" that humanitarianism often promotes. To protect the orphan as a legal category, history is mapped onto the child—of religious identity (Hindu) and of national origin (Indian). Foreigners are given (or take) the less desired specimens of humanity: older babies, unwanted babies, and children with mental or physical impairments. The most extreme cases, of course, are not adopted at all and remain wards of the state.

DONATION AS A FORM OF ETHICAL ENGAGEMENT

What makes orphans good to give to but not good to take? The status of orphans, as a target of humanitarian effort, inspires the possibility of integration. Excluded from kin, orphans are simultaneously the responsibility of no one in particular and everyone in general. "The orphan," as a social category, is structurally analogous to "the world renouncer" or sadhu in Indian society: both exist outside systems of kin-based structures of social responsibility and are, ideally, cared for by society. When confronted by a sadhu or an orphan—although one has renounced the world and the other has been renounced by it—the humanitarian is tested and perhaps compelled toward action to give. With so many children in orphanages who are not adoptable, there is a growing market in both international and Indian humanitarianism focused on children. In Delhi alone at the time of my research in 2005, there were thirty-six "children institutions" registered with the Department of Child Welfare, a few of which were homes for abandoned children while others were homes for children whose parents had not abandoned them but could no longer provide care.

When boundaries of kin are severed by poverty or tragedy, the state steps in to protect its citizens. Orphans considered for adoption in India speak to other categories of destitution and abandonment. Because potential adoptees must be certified abandoned and without family by the state before they are adopted, photographs and advertisements of abandoned and missing children are placed in both English- and Hindi-language newspapers. After a one-month waiting period they may be declared abandoned and become wards of the state, children of the nation (*desh ke bache*) with rights and responsibilities. "Our children go to Indians first," as one welfare agent specified. The nation is, after all, "Mother India."

Prospective adoptive Indian parents who request a child with a particular lightness of skin and desire their adopted children to phenotypically match their own physical attributes may reaffirm the stigma associated with adoption in India. However, these parents also affirm the possibility of transforming a destitute child into a member of one's family. In Delhi, I was told a story of two women, an unwed mother and another woman who was perhaps a friend, a relative, or an acquaintance. The unwed mother gave birth to a baby who was immediately given to the adopting mother. The adopting mother's name was entered onto the birth certificate as if it had been her own biological child. This "systematic misrecognition" of biological kinship (Bharadwaj 2003:1879, Das 1995) does not announce itself. The stigma associated with gifts and self-interest in Hinduism (one of the most sacred forms of dān is anonymous, and is called *gupt dān*) contrasts the potential self-interest of building a family, which may be why the director of CARA I quoted earlier was reluctant to identify adoption with charity. As with other sectors of the Indian economy, there is no reason to expect adoption and humanitarianism to exist in purely formal realms. Some adoption, such as that done within families, is informal and undocumented—something difficult to "prove" statistically but evident ethnographically in rumors, stories, and lives. In my small circle of family and friends in north India I stumbled upon several cases of women who had "adopted" a relative's son because they could not have their own. This was so commonplace that it was neither something to speak about nor to register as a legal issue.

Yet, when one embraces a stranger and makes them one's own, the act of adopting an orphan has the potential to become either humanitarian or an act of predatory geopolitics of desire, in which wealthy women from foreign nations consume poor children in India. Despite the anxiety in India over foreign adoptions, the most dramatic stories of social transformation occur in the context of foreign adoptions. And this, I believe, speaks to the value of orphans in humanitarian discourse more broadly as symbols of how "the excluded" can be embraced. Stories of abandonment that turn into miracles are, of course, the marketing material for NGOs involved in child welfare. I hesitate to repeat these stories for fear that I reinforce such disaster pornography (Benthall 2010). Yet the stories are haunting. I was told of a girl found abandoned on the side of the road in Noida, a suburb of Delhi, in a polyethylene bag, her face half-eaten by rats and dogs, who had four plastic surgeries donated and was then adopted by a family in Spain. This story had a happy ending, although I never had the opportunity to meet the girl. One may assume that the girl's life continues happily in Spain, and this continuation is a transformed status, from being painfully and tragically excluded to becoming a member of a new family. This is the powerful conclusion that "the orphan" in humanitarianism has to offer: orphans can be cared for. Exclusions of poverty, on the other hand, are much more difficult problems to solve.

I was told another story of a boy taken to a government hospital and abandoned by his impoverished mother—he was sick, one eye was shut; he was near death. When his mother found out he had a heart condition and needed emergency surgery that she could not afford, she abandoned him at the hospital where she left a false name and address. He was subsequently given to a child placement orphanage, where the director scrambled to arrange payment for the heart surgery. She had to do it in one day or the boy would die, and she raised the money in a heroic act. As she told the story she seemed exhausted by it and said she did not know how she managed to raise the money, something she accomplished by convincing a friend who was a cardiologist to do the surgeries at a reduced rate. At the time the NGO director was telling me this story, the boy was about to be adopted by a family in Europe. To me he was a story, a phantom, yet a powerful one. The director showed me a book of photos pasted on graph paper with a narrative of the boy's recovery. It was painful for me to look at the book, his sickly beginnings and subsequent transformation. I realized the adopted family would probably treasure the book and perhaps the boy would too, one day. Stories such as these disturb, but how does one write about them without becoming a "moral spectator" (Boltanski 1999; Cartwright 2005)? Or worse, complicit in the suffering (Sontag 2003)?

CONCLUSION

If not adoption, then what is the humanitarian alternative? In India, orphans are good to give to because they require no return, no relation, and no self-interest. When a gift has the expectation of a return, in the form of interest or social debt for example, it is no longer a gift. Instead, it becomes exchange, commerce, or a right. As Derrida (1992) has argued while critiquing Mauss's classic work for mistaking exchange for the gift, when law regulates a gift it is bound by obligation and becomes part of economy or exchange (not gifts). Pure gifts are gracious; they do not expect a return. To translate this to orphans in India, giving to orphans through dān is a sacred gift. Giving time to orphans, by volunteering at an orphanage for example, also requires that there is not an expectation of a return. Yet adoption, which enters into an economy and involves self-interest, is not a gift. Orphans must stay orphans to represent, symbolically, the non-economy of humanitarianism. When humanitarianism becomes part of an economy, it loses its sacred standing and is corrupted by interests. In order to circumvent the dangerous terrain of the "adoption market" where orphans are potentially bought and sold, volunteers give their time, presence, and experience at orphanages. These efforts also circumvent the fraught moral terrain of humanitarianism in the contemporary political economy of poverty and the excluded in India. Like the plea for a nickel from UNICEF without any expectation of return, donation is a form of ethical engagement in which one is interpolated and urged to question whether one is giving enough.

Notes

1. India is also a nation of wealth and greed, but for the purposes of this chapter I focus on how it is constructed as a site for philanthropic effort.

2. See website: http://www.aryagan.org/aryasamaj/profile.php, accessed February 8, 2008.

3. At the time of writing, the conversion rate was roughly US$1= INR 40.

4. The World Bank estimates that 29 percent of the population of India is below the poverty line as of 2006 (see http://devdata.worldbank.org/AAG/ind_aag.pdf, accessed December 10, 2009).

5. Research for this chapter was made possible through a generous grant from the American Institute of Indian Studies and the National Endowment for the Humanities. A Social Science Research Council resident scholarship at the School of American Research offered a serene environment to start writing some of these ideas.

6. I did not set out to study orphans, and in fact I did not end up doing any deep ethnographic "hanging out" with orphans at all. I spent time in orphanages and interviewed those who came to donate goods or their time, as well as those who managed, directed, and facilitated the daily operations of the orphanages. I was a participant observer at three orphanages, but I did not have the sense that I got to know

the orphans at all. This was partly due to my interest in humanitarianism and giving, and partly due to the approach I took to dwelling in the field (Bornstein 2007b). I did not live at the orphanages and did not confine my research to one particular institution. With my ethnographic attention diffuse, my presence was always novel, and I never became "part of the group." I was perhaps seen to be a foreign donor, certainly a foreign researcher. Sometimes I came with a research assistant, sometimes I came alone. In all cases, when I spoke with children residing in the orphanages about their lives, they were reluctant to talk about the past. In one case I was told by one of the wardens of the orphanage not to ask questions about either the orphans' pasts or the women's pasts who worked there since my questions might be upsetting. Many women who worked in the orphanages were themselves destitute, or had been abandoned by families. I listened to the directive, perhaps too carefully. When I asked the children about their lives they gave me simple answers in both English and Hindi that really said nothing. Sentences like "everything is fine here" or "we like it here very much" raise a methodological point about the difficulty of studying recipients of humanitarian aid ethnographically. Because there is a danger of "looking a gift horse in the mouth," or "biting the hand that feeds you," how does one obtain "reliable" information about humanitarian aid from those who may be critical of it, but at the same time depend on it and do not want to jeopardize its continuation? While the institutional nature of the orphanages—some were gated, all were highly monitored—made for some very deep hanging out once I entered, they did not allow for objectification. I was not permitted to take pictures, for example, and this I believe is an important part of the ethnography of humanitarianism that may require anthropologists to rethink what it means to study a group partially, as part of a larger group more fully, over time.

7. January 4, 2005, page 4, author Saroj Nagi.

8. Note: one crore = Rs. 10 million, or 10 lakhs, so Rs. 403 Crore is roughly US$90 million. Exchange rate on January 9, 2005, was US$1 = 43.75 rupees; 403 crores/4.375 = US$92.114 million. Source: http://www.kshitij.com/utilities/LnCtoMnB.shtml for conversion.

9. *Sunday Hindustan Times*, New Delhi, January 9, 2005, page 2.

10. Several articles ran in local Delhi newspapers documenting caste-based discrimination regarding the allocation of tsunami relief. See "Even Government Divides Survivors on Caste, Says It's Practical," *Indian Express*, January 7, 2005. "Tsunami Can't Wash This Away: Hatred for Dalits: In Ground Zero, Dalits Thrown Out of Relief Camps, Cut Out of Food, Water Supplies, Toilets, NGOs Say They Will Start Separate Facilities," *Indian Express*, January 6, 2005. "Waves Failed to Crack Caste Wall," *Hindustan Times*, January 8, 2005.

11. Purity and the gift have been a dominant trope in the anthropology of South Asia, and many scholars have addressed it; see Parry 1994 in the context of Benares priests, Raheja 1988 on the jajmani system of a rural north Indian village.

12. In Delhi, one of the primary organizations conducting research on philanthropy is called Sampradaan Indian Centre for Philanthropy (see Sundar 1997, 2000; Kapoor and Sharma 2000).

13. In UNICEF's subsequent annual reports on the state of the world's children, titles shift from a focus on orphans and vulnerable children, "Excluded and Invisible" (2006), to "Women and the Double Dividend of Gender Equality" (2007), and "Child Survival" (2008).

14. At the time of this writing, there was a global trend against international adoption. In the past five years China has added more stringent guidelines in terms of age and income for prospective adoptive parents. Skepticism has grown in places like Guatemala due to the influx of foreign parents wanting to adopt (see Marc Lacey, 2006, "Guatemala System Is Scrutinized as Americans Rush In to Adopt" in *the New York Times*).

15. Statistics are from an adoption advocacy organization called Catalysts for Social Action (CSA), see www.csa.in.org as well as IndianNGOs.com, http://www .indianngos.com/issue/child/adoption/statistics/index.html, accessed December 6, 2006.

16. There is an additional distinction between the adoption of a son and the appointment of an heir who does not have kin relations.

17. In old Hindu law, the Shastras prescribed two sets of ceremonies: one religious and the other secular. Religious ceremonies included the recital of certain prayers and Vedic hymns (dattak homa, or the oblation of fire). This involved ceremonies of gift and acceptance and burnt sacrifice. It was done to procure good fortune for the adoptee. Caste had its place in the scriptural hierarchy of humanity: in the case of Sudras (the lowest of the four varnas), neither dattak homa nor any religious ceremony was essential. In the Shastras, the secular ceremony of giving and taking was a mandatory ceremony for the validity of adoption. The performance of the ceremony made the transfer of the child complete, final, and irrevocable. "The ceremony of giving and taking has to be performed by the person who gives the child in adoption, whether he is father, mother, or guardian, and by the person who takes the child in adoption. According to Baudhayana: 'One should go to the giver of the child, and ask him saying 'Give me thy son!' The other answers 'I give him!' He receives him with these words: 'I take these for the fulfillment of my religious duties; I take these to continue the line of my ancestors'" (Manu cited in Diwan 2000:89).

18. The Hindi word for orphan is *anāth*, which translates literally as "without

lord, without God, or without protector." Hindu conversion is one of acceptance into a community. It is not a product of individual choice or being "born again" as it is in Christianity. There is no formal ceremony of purification or expiation to *effectuate* conversion. Conversion, in other words, is a matter of belonging. The bare declaration of Hinduism is not enough to convert. One must be accepted by members of the community as such and recognized socially.

19. In contemporary postcolonial, secular India, each community has its own family law. While Hindu and Muslim law is claimed to be of divine origin, no such claim is made by the other communities. Some communities are governed by custom. For example, Jewish family law in India is "customary law." Ancestral and customary law is relevant to the legislation of joint property in some places. "Scheduled tribes" are governed by "custom" and Hindu law does not apply; thus there are many exceptions to instances where Hindu family law is applied to family disputes. In addition, personal law differs from state to state within India. Each community is governed by a single system of law, yet within the community (for example along divisions of caste, subcaste, subsect) there are regional particularities. Different "schools" of Hindu and Muslim law are also regionally specific. However, all adoptions are governed by the codified law of the Hindu Adoption and Maintenance Act of 1956. Only Hindu law recognizes adoption. Adoption is not recognized under any other Indian personal law with the exception of Parsi personal law, which has two forms of recognized adoption.

20. There are many other specific conditions that must be present for a valid adoption. (1) If adoption is of a son, the adoptive parents must not have a son, son's son, or son's son's son; (2) if it is of a daughter, then parents must not have a Hindu daughter or son's daughter. (3) If adoption is by a male and the person to be adopted is a female then the adoptive father must be at least twenty-one years older than the person to be adopted. (4) If adoption is by a female and the child is male then the mother must be twenty-one years older than the boy she is adopting. (5) The same child cannot be adopted simultaneously by two or more persons. (6) The child to be adopted must be given and taken by parents or guardians to be adopting. Before the 1956 law, the ceremony of giving and taking was mandatory and considered enough for a valid adoption.

21. There are two definitions to which the current law (1956) applies: creedal and secular. The creedal definition is based on religion—defined by the religion of the parents. If both parents are of a religion, the child is of the religion. It also applies to any child abandoned by parents and brought up in that religion and to converts and "reconverts" to that religion. Note: nothing contained in the act pertains to "scheduled tribes." The secular definition of who is a Hindu is "persons who are not Christians, Parsis, Muslims, or Jews." It includes atheists.

22. Caste does not seem be a significant aspect in Siddiqui's study. She notes that out of her 157 respondents, 72 percent belonged to the upper or middle caste of Hindus, Jains, and Sikhs. Only 2 percent of the girls belonged to scheduled castes. The rest of the girls (41 percent) belonged to the Muslim community. There was only one girl who was Christian (Siddiqui 1997:43).

23. "Father Questions Madonna Adoption," BBC News online, http://news.bbc .co.uk/2/hi/entertainment/6075476.stm, accessed October 22, 2006.

24. "A 2004 law limits organ donation and transplantation in India to blood relatives and close family friends. No money may exchange hands." CNN, "Police Parade Kidney-snatching 'Mastermind,'" http://articles.cnn.com/2008-02-08/world/ kidney.arrest_1_kidney-transplant-transplant-law-police-station?_s=PM:WORLD, accessed February 8, 2008.

25. "An Adoption Gone Wrong," July 24, 2007. Morning Edition, Steve Inskeep, editor.

26. "Maintenance" includes (1) "provision for food, clothing, residence, education and medical attendance and treatment"; (2) in the case of an unmarried daughter, the reasonable expense of her marriage (Diwan 2000:23).

27. *Frontline*, May 2005, "Complaints from Foreign Adopters."

28. *Frontline*, May 2005, "The Adoption Market."

29. See http://www.indianngos.com, accessed December 6, 2006.

30. *Laxmikant Pandey v. Union of India*, 1984.

PART III

Humanitarian Bodies

The third part of this volume focuses on medical aspects of humanitarianism that map onto human subjects and bodies in particularly charged transnational settings. For all that the aid world may have defined humanitarian action around emergency response (Calhoun 2008), that institutional definition proves porous in practice, as a concern for suffering migrates back into a variety of venues and inspires a wider field of efforts to ameliorate the human condition. Building on the long association that humanitarianism has had with the politics of life, and with saving lives through medical practice, Sandra Hyde's chapter explores Sunlight-International, an American, Christian self-help program for heroin addicts transplanted to China. This "traveling therapeutic" substitutes for earlier efforts to control drug addicts in China through state prisons and labor camps, producing an altered regime of knowledge and a new type of surveillance. By seeking to reform a population it suggests a mobile and transnational form of governance, even amid challenges of cultural and political translation. In Hyde's chapter we see the influence of an NGO in post-Maoist China, mapping new humanitarian terrain. Here a foreign humanitarian aid organization trains Chinese drug specialists in intensive group and family-centered residential therapy, even as local NGOs in

China serve as the transmitters of this form of humanitarian aid. Her chapter thus not only builds on the broader theme of the centrality of medical care to contemporary inflections of humanitarianism (Fassin, Redfield, Ticktin), but picks up the thread of religion (Benthall, Bornstein). She discovers that new forms of religious belief and capitalist practice syncretically merge in the post-socialist Chinese clinic and residential treatment center. The philosophy (or theology) of Sunlight may rely upon salvation from outside and is similar in structure to twelve-step programs, yet it manifests an amalgam of influences rather than a simple religious genealogy. While therapies travel—as in the case of Sunlight—they are not immutable. Sunlight, we learn, was created by a Roman Catholic from New York, but in China its practitioners are Buddhists. In its Pentecostal-style Christian Bible study for residents (which 20 percent of residents attend), Sunlight uses the therapeutic community model of residential psychiatry toward reforming drug addicts. In China, it also integrates previous models, including a Maoist labor model of drug treatment that "forges a kind of bodily exorcism," since drug addiction is a behavioral matter and requires the treatment of the whole person. Thus what we find in the Chinese residential treatment center is the reformation of post-socialist bodies, in which good patients become good citizens through an intervention that exceeds both frames of ideology and nation-state. As treatment facilities are no longer funded by the state, the task falls upon the therapeutic governance of international NGOs like Sunlight-International. Hyde concludes that such traveling therapeutics signal a new norm of humanitarian governance—a "new kind of humanitarian aid that stays put once it arrives."

Tracing a different vector of international connection, Miriam Ticktin examines the increasing importance of medical status in migration from the global South to the global North. With ethnographic examples from medical clinics in France and the United States, her chapter documents how illness can sometimes cross borders even when poverty cannot. As bodies come to tell the truth of suffering, humanitarian doctors and nurses seek illness as evidence to help claimants pursue their cases. In this manner, illness becomes a distinctly political—if also exceptional and liminal—condition. Focusing on legal claims of asylum seekers in France, Ticktin exposes an economy of hope centered on bodily suffering and the means to certify exceptional status in order to remain in the country. Examining the expanded role of medicine in providing evidence for human rights claims, she further suggests a form of "biological involution," where the success of rendering one's body as truly needy comes at a price of dwindling returns, in the form of continued suffering and even death. Seeking evidence of clear symptoms, medical examiners look for scars, marks of ill-ness, or signs of post-traumatic stress disorder (as with Hyde's addicts, a condition that sits at the intersection of the psyche and the body). Since "biology stands in for the self," humanitarian doctors produce and repro-duce truth claims in the medical-legal context of the clinic, where, in effect, would-be immigrants and refugees must "highlight their pathologies in order to access basic rights." The chapter thus continues a thread in the volume underscoring humanitarianism's medical lineage (Fassin, Redfield, Hyde), while also recalling its fluid boundary with human rights (Englund). In what Ticktin describes as a "dual regime of truth," those from the global South must increasingly present a fixed image of their own nature, even as members of the global North increasingly consider biology as a fluid matter of choice. For this surplus humanity, biology becomes one of the few sources of potential value, a resource to mobilize strategically in human rights and immigration claims. Yet it is a dangerous resource, for to sacrifice biology for hope is to place oneself at risk of death.

Together, both contributions emphasize how humanitarian need maps onto bodies and how subjects reshape themselves to meet the way that need is defined. Recipients thus join states and NGOs as strategic actors in humanitarianism, if hardly in equal positions. As therapeutic techniques migrate between contexts and humans escape misery across national boundaries, we find echoes of religious influence emerging in formally atheist states and see humanitarian organizations taking on new legal roles. In the name of humane treatment, biomedicine looms ever larger in national and international governance.

7

Screams, Cries, and Whispers

Traveling Heroin Therapeutics and Humanitarian Aid in Post-socialist China

Sandra Teresa Hyde

INTRODUCTION

History illustrates that opiate addiction in China can be traced from its popularity in the late Qing dynasty (1644–1911), to the founding of the People's Republic in 1949, to its eradication in the mid-1950s, and to its ultimate reemergence as refined heroin in the late 1980s due to the open-door economic reforms, the relaxation of border controls, and the rise in global drug trafficking. Although Chinese socialists in the late 1950s eradicated opiate addiction, in the reform era market socialism has served as a catalyst for the reemergence of illegal drug use and trafficking.[1] As of June 2009, "official statistics show that registered drug users in China total 1.22 million," and unofficial estimates range as high as 14 million (*China Daily* 2009; Chu and Levy 2005; Sullivan and Wu 2007:120).

Until the late 1990s, all Chinese drug addicts[2] were treated as criminals and placed either in the justice system's drug prisons or in labor camps. China has over seven hundred compulsory rehabilitation prisons; Yunnan Province alone has two hundred that incarcerate injection drug users without trial or due process (Bartlett 2006). Of all registered drug users, 85 percent are male and 74 percent are under the age of thirty-five (*China Daily* 2009). Today, while the drug prison and the labor camp still exist, there is a small group of psychiatrists who want to embrace what Foucault (1988) labeled the "humanism of the asylum" and provide clinical residential care to allow drug addicts to heal their addictions. As such there are two competing ideologies on controlling drug epidemics in China, one punitive and the other therapeutic, and within these two ideological positions, there remains a massive disjuncture between the reality of everyday life and official policy (Biehl 2006; Fassin 2007b; Hyde 2007; Nguyen 2005).

What is at stake is no less than a reversal of the drug prison model that is characterized by high rates of recidivism, upward of 90 percent (Malinowska-Sempruch and Bartlett 2006:27). In its mandate to reduce Asian drug trafficking in the early 1990s, the US government teamed up with the American humanitarian aid organization Sunlight-International in order to train Chinese drug specialists in intensive group and family-centered residential therapy. Beginning in 1999, drug addicts from throughout China voluntarily came to Sunlight-Yunnan in order to kick their addictions and attempt to become what the Chinese state demands: productive and drug-free citizens. Sunlight-Yunnan helped establish two other centers, one in central China in the city of Wuhan and another in the capital, Beijing. Both of these centers are independent of Sunlight-International.

In rethinking the global politics of humanitarian aid, this chapter focuses on one new humanitarian project at the limits of what is thought of as humanitarian aid, a local NGO that provides medical therapeutic care for injection drug users. In this chapter, I ask how do new citizen-subjects emerge with respect to recent medical therapeutics? How do Chinese drug addicts learn to perform their emotions as part of the Western narratives of Narcotics Anonymous and self-healing? What lies beneath the therapeutic desire to pull people apart both physically and psychologically and then build them back up again? What sort of humanitarian aid travels between the United States and China, and what forms does it take?

The difference between this kind of humanitarian medical aid and others mentioned in this volume (Feldman, Redfield, Bornstein) is that Sunlight's sort of aid is here to stay as it has been incorporated into state mental health functions. New therapies for drug addicts have both replaced the former functions of the state's Institute on Drug Abuse and, at the same time, provided new avenues for the Institute on Drug Abuse to give care in more *humane* ways. In the attempt to create healthy post-socialist citizens that rely on themselves, one of the tenets of the Sunlight philosophy, there is a fine line between salvation from outside, via a Christian God and therapeutics, and self-regulation and empowerment from within. By thinking through these configurations of therapy, addiction, humanitarian intervention, personal affect, subjectivity, and power relations, I narrow my focus in this chapter to two themes: (1) the movement of one form of humanitarian aid across nation-state lines; and (2) tracing what happens when we wed a former atheist state with Western Christian therapies. Here new aggregates of religious beliefs and capitalist practices find interesting bedfellows in the space of the post-socialist clinic and residential treatment center.

SUNLIGHT

During my search for a new research project in China, which had roots in my earlier HIV research, a psychiatrist and director of the Yunnan Institute of Drug Abuse, Yang Maobin, invited me to conduct an ethnography of his first residential drug treatment center, when the center was in its infancy (Hyde 2007 and 2008). It was not until 2006 that I seriously entertained studying drug treatment. During the summers of 2006, 2007, and 2008, I spent a total of three months at the Sunlight residential treatment center (TC), officially as an anthropologist, and informally as an English teacher, art therapist, and yoga instructor. In this larger fieldwork project, I wanted to focus on the therapists, peer-educators, clients, aid workers, and NGO sponsors as they navigated their relationships within a powerful set of party-state institutions (the Ministries of Public Security, Health, and Justice) that organized health care and social control around drug addiction.

Sunlight, as a residential therapeutic community and refuge, fosters a sense of liminality, neither here nor there, neither at work nor at rest, and neither addicted nor free from addiction. As addiction specialists note, residential treatment for drug addiction is never easy: in North America a figure of 15 percent is often repeated for rates of recovery. In contrast, Sunlight-China claims a 35 percent recovery rate, which is a 100 percent improvement over similar methods used in Europe and America (from conversations with staff). Now let me take you to Sunlight-Yunnan.

Sunlight

As the bell sounds at 7:30 in the morning, all rise, get dressed, and face the first inspection of the day. Rooms contain eight bunk beds, one desk, and two freestanding closets and are to be immaculate at all times. Demerit points in the form of black X's, versus praise as red flags, are posted on a bulletin board. Black X's three days in a row results in extra housework for all roommates—scrubbing bathrooms, doing piles of dirty dishes, and cleaning filthy grills. Other residents, who have worked their way up in the rehabilitation hierarchy, earn the right to police others and conduct these inspections. After a breakfast of spicy noodles, everyone, all thirty of us, gather in the common room, and with hands linked in a circle and voices raised, recite the Sunlight motto (*xintiao*), a direct translation from the American version:

> I am here because there is no refuge, finally from myself until I confront myself in the eyes and hearts of others. I am running until I suffer them to share my secrets. I have no safety from them. Afraid to be known, I can know neither any other, nor myself, I will be alone. Where else but in our common ground can I find such a mirror? Here, together I can at least appear clearly to myself, not as the giant of my dreams or the dwarf of my fears, but as a person, part of the whole, with my share in its purpose. In this ground we can take root and grow, not alone any more as in death but alive to myself and to others.

Embedded in this motto is the entire Sunlight universe that encompasses the following: the goals of individual self-care mastery within a tightly knit community, the need to rebuild the self in order to create a new persona, socially dependent on a group but wholly accountable only to one's self, to move beyond suffering, to reveal one's innermost fears and secrets, and to learn how to express a full range of emotions—anger, sadness, and joy. In many ways there is a symbolic Geiger counter measuring semantic fairness, where addicts' linguistic failures mean that their secrets keep them sick, and their verbal emotional revelations allow them to heal. The Sunlight motto was verbally recited each day before morning therapy and immediately followed by what I call a series of criticism–self-criticism encounters where residents are urged to verbally attack one another for their behavior during the previous day, as the octaves of their voices rise into harsh screams. Behavior is measured by work, and work means running the center, from repairing the solar water heaters to cleaning the bathrooms and preparing three meals a day for a community of up to eighty people. At Sunlight there are four cardinal rules: no drugs, no stealing, no intimate contact with the opposite sex, and no physical violence toward self or others, but verbal critiques are highly encouraged.

At Sunlight, psychological therapeutic notions of being cultured and taking care of oneself pepper almost all discussions of treatment. A key component of the Sunlight philosophy is the notion of salvation from outside in contrast to adhering to self-regulation from within. This notion comes almost straight from the neoliberal humanitarian aid organization that helped fund this center and their undying belief in the healing powers of therapy introduced by peer-counselors who are former addicts, the wounded healers of twelve-step recovery models (Jackson 2001). In the Chinese post-socialist context, most religious belief systems remain muted—atheism is still the state religion—but not entirely ignored. As one therapist said: "How can we ignore Christianity when it is an American Christian organization that gave us the money to start this center?" A nurse said that her Buddhist beliefs keep her working in an environment that she finds difficult. When there are many patients and they are screaming at her for more methadone, she finds strength in her religious convictions.

Sunlight originally was the brainchild of a Roman Catholic monsignor from New York State, as a broadly defined humanitarian NGO. While Sunlight-New York provides residents access to religious communities and services within the geographic vicinity of their center, only in China does Bible study come to the TC one afternoon a week as a voluntary therapy. As the director of the center himself is Christian, and as the residential treatment programs in Hong Kong are Christian based, there has been an effort to provide Christian Bible study for the residents. This is a stark contrast to the Maoist atheist past, and with this history in mind, only 20 percent of the residents attend these sessions. During my three summers there, only four confessed to be true converts. However, many residents would attend the Bible study sessions. There in the church-like structure attached to the residence hall, former female and male drug users cum evangelical converts (by American missionaries) pray, sing, and place their hands on a resident's shoulders. But this is no ordinary prayer; it is done in a Pentecostal format. Residents are asked to physically kneel on the floor, as former drug users stand above them and place their hands just above the residents' shoulders but never quite touching them. These Christian converts then ask Jesus to take away the addictions of their charges and replace them with faith in him and his teachings. All the while these former users are whispering or hissing in the hushed voices that one reserves for intimates. The former users implore everyone present to take in Jesus as their savior from drugs. Christianity, though, is only one form of belief system that travels.

IMMOBILE THERAPIES AND MOBILE ADDICTS

In 1990 the United States Department of Law and Drug Enforcement, in conjunction with the NGO Sunlight-International, arranged to bring six Chinese psychiatrists who specialized in drug addiction to Sunlight-New York for six months' training in what is known as the therapeutic community model (the family-centered residential care unit based on intensive group therapy). In 1987 Sunlight-International received consultative status with the Economic and Social Council of the United Nations as their work had spread to sixty-six countries, casting a wide net across Asia—from Indonesia, Malaysia, and Thailand to Kazakhstan, Tajikistan, and Hong Kong. Sunlight's goals are a drug-free world achieved by providing training, technical assistance, and support to develop competency in self-help social-learning drug treatment models and to foster a global network of addiction treatment specialists. After many years of bureaucratic setbacks, Dr. Yang Maobin, one of the original psychiatrists trained in New York Sunlight, convinced Yunnanese health officials in 1997 that this American model for dealing with addiction could work in China.

Injection drug users (hereafter referred to as IDUs) are the second largest documented risk group for HIV, accounting for 45 percent of all Chinese infections. By 2005, drug transmission trailed sexual transmission by just 2 percent (Qian, Vermund, and Wang 2005:442; Watts 2008:103). AIDS researchers demonstrate that patterns of drug trafficking have spread the unusual recombinant HIV subtypes first seen in Yunnan to far-flung regions of China and Southeast Asia (Xiao et al. 2007). While drug users are predominantly male, the HIV infection rates among women have increased over time due to sexual transmission. The male to female ratio of HIV infection has dropped from 40 to 1 in 1990 to close to 2 to 1 by late 2006 (Bartlett 2006; Lu et al. 2005; Xiao et al. 2007). Drug trafficking enters China primarily through three points: (1) through Yunnan Province from Burma, (2) into Guangxi Province through Vietnam, and (3) into Xinjiang from the "golden crescent" countries of Afghanistan, Pakistan, and Iran (Qian, Vermund, and Wang 2005). These drug routes also grow and spread out through the southwestern provinces of Yunnan, Guangxi, Guizhou, Guangdong, and Sichuan and in the northwest, through Gansu and Xinjiang.

Compared to twelve years ago when I first began working on HIV, there is a stark contrast between the older model of the Ministry of Public Security's compulsory detoxification centers, the Justice Department's reeducation through labor camps, and this new kind of therapeutic community that embraces global treatment modalities of harm reduction in a residential care setting. In an effort to restructure drug treatment in China, a new drug law went into effect in 2006 that has outwardly erased the labor camps and renamed the detoxification centers as "compulsory drug rehabilitation centers" (geli qiangzhi jiedusuo). Nonetheless, while the names have changed, reality is far more complex. All drug use remains illegal, and punishment for breaking the drug laws, over the past half century, still involves compulsory hard labor, even if it is now combined with some form of treatment. The idea in the 1950s was that through physical labor, addicts would reform themselves, just as counter-revolutionaries during the Cultural Revolution were put to work. In the case of addicts, heavy labor is intended to reinforce their allegiance to the socialist worker state. Thus, labor is thought to solve all their physical, emotional, and material crises. This Maoist labor model of drug treatment forges a kind of bodily exorcism. In many ways, there are also threads of this bodily exorcism that wind through these new therapeutic behavioral treatment models. When drug users become convicted addicts, they must compulsorily shed their old dysfunctional selves in exchange for a new more regulated, familial self-actualized and responsible self. Here it is not the Communist self of the 1950s, but the new post-socialist self of the millennium.

In Kunming city, Yunnan's provincial capital and a city with a high number of international NGOs, public health notions of harm reduction strongly influenced the psychiatrist who began to treat heroin addicts in the late 1980s and early 1990s (Wu et al. 2007). After becoming frustrated with working in the government-run detoxification prisons, psychiatrist Dr. Yang founded Sunlight, the first of a new type of treatment center with funding from the China–United Kingdom HIV/AIDS Prevention and Care Project, the original Sunlight in upstate New York, the Yunnan Institute of Drug Abuse, and nominal fees from residents. Dr. Yang said the government detoxification centers were just placing people in prisons and not treating them. Later, when he treated patients in the mental health hospital, he said: "I treated the addict like a doctor would treat a patient. I'm ill, so cure me; but I now know it is behavioral. It is a disorder of the whole person."[3]

In Kunming the major drugs of choice are heroin and, in growing demand, club drugs, amphetamine-type stimulants (*anfeitaming*, 安非他命), and MDMA (commonly known as "ecstasy," or in Chinese, "head-rocking pills," *yaotou pian*, 搖頭片). Heroin and methamphetamines have taken hold in China, particularly in the south and northwest, due to what Chinese psychiatrists and sociologists label as frustration with high rates of unemployment and emotional problems associated with rapid industrial development and the disrupting influences of massive rural to urban migration. Both the disaffected rural youth, who are unemployed when they migrate to the city, and, on the other end of the socioeconomic spectrum, the rising middle classes, who frequent nightclubs and ingest illegal mind-altering drugs, do what one psychiatrist labeled as "deadening their feelings, to numb themselves." Illegal drugs are read as a means to erase the body as an emotional and sensual container, precisely because deadening one's feelings can have deadly consequences. Sharing heroin needles, syringes, and cookers transmits the HIV virus into one's bloodstream. Current prevalence rates of needle sharing among injection drug users are 45 percent, and rates of HIV are as high as 85 percent among IDUs (Qian, Vermund, and Wang 2005:442–443).

TRAVELING THERAPEUTICS

Wang Xiaoguan, the former vice director of Sunlight states, "We need to do away with the compulsory camps, as they are jails." For him, the Sunlight model of harm reduction through participation in a therapeutic community works. It got him off heroin. According to Sunlight-Yunnan, hundreds of people have passed through their programs, and 35 percent have remained off drugs, which if accurate is one of the highest rates in the world. Ideally, completing the entire program means beginning in the residential thera- peutic community for one month of bed rest and drug detoxification, then moving upstairs to the therapeutic residential center for at least one year, and finally working at the reentry center and learning new skills for approximately another year for a total of two years in treatment. The skills developed through Sunlight's programs vary in vocation from becoming a counselor at the treatment center, to an HIV/AIDS or drug peer educator, to a car mechanic, car washer, restaurant worker, or hair stylist.

Medical anthropologist Anne Lovell (2006) points out that addiction sci- ence is evolving in biomedicine and that addictions, categorized as public health scourges, are becoming one of the prototypical diseases of modernity. Lovell (2006:2) further argues that through the discourse of harm reduc- tion, treatment options such as methadone substitution have fit into a highly individualized set of bodily practices and meanings. These treatments then translate addiction into purely individual lifestyle decision-making models in much of Europe and America. In reconfiguring opiate addictions from acute illness states and delinquent practices to chronic diseases, collective or com- munal options for treatment have often been replaced by pharmaceutical solutions that do not get at the root of psycho-social problems, nor do they affect the proliferation in local youth drug cultures. Most studies of addic- tion pharmaceuticals do not tease out what Philippe Bourgois (Bourgois 1995, 2000; Bourgois and Schonberg 2009) calls the power relationships between drug users and the society they live in. Interestingly enough, phar- maceutical solutions are frowned on at Sunlight, at least beyond the two- to three- week detoxification period. I want to further tease out these power relations, but before I do that, I first will provide what I call "a vertical slice of life" at Sunlight and explain what sort of institution it is and how it works.

The Sunlight treatment model is an amalgamation of twelve-step

Narcotics Anonymous programs, Maoist Speak Bitterness (a technique from the Cultural Revolution that uses criticism–self-criticism), Christian confessionals, and a program of psychological behavioral reconditioning embedded in a military-like, rigorously structured regime. With the increase in Western therapies in China comes a globally supported revolution in drug rehabilitation inclusive of residential treatment centers, employment-generating businesses for graduates of the program, methadone clinics, and needle exchange programs on the streets of Kunming. According to Sunlight's promotional literature, a therapeutic community is a drug-free self-help group program whose primary goal is the cessation of substance abuse behaviors and encouragement toward personal growth. In Sunlight's language on their own literature, "the therapeutic community model incorporates social learning theory that utilizes a community approach to fostering behavioral and attitudinal change, to be absolutely drug free." In many ways the TC model initiates certain processes to reappropriate the post-socialist body. Bodies here are balanced between what the community demands (well connected and cared for by their families) and what the state wants (a healthy hard-working citizenry).

The Sunlight TC model provides a family-like atmosphere and a haven for those addicted to drugs, replete with a small pharmacy staffed by a doctor and a nurse who supervise methadone-maintenance treatment (MMT) that will ease the horrors of withdrawal. This idea of the therapeutic community (hereafter referred to as TC) for drug addicts originated in 1957 in a Californian utopian community called Synanon. Synanon started out as a social movement to promote a better world based on the values of honesty, creativity, enthusiasm, and respect and with the goal of changing the substance abuser from "dope fiend" or "emotional child" into a "self-developing person" aware of his or her own potential (Kaplan and Broekaert 2003:204).[4] In order to accomplish this, Synanon required disciplined behavioral change and growth of self-awareness through what was called "the game" in order to learn to express one's full range of emotions and to "act as if" one were addiction free so that the reality of everyday life would prevail (Soyez and Broekaert 2005:306).[5] The psychologist Abraham Maslow described Synanon as the best example of "Eupsychia," but Synanon, like many projects of the human potential movement of the early 1960s, became a cult and was dismantled by 1991. While Synanon went the way of many 1960s self-help movements, other therapeutic communities have made inroads in drug-addiction treatment the world over.

Ever since Sunlight-New York helped Yunnan establish its center, three or four employees from Sunlight-Yunnan travel every year to upstate New

York for a three-month training in the American TC model. Once there they attempt to learn new techniques based on the merits of behavior malleability. As Bruno Latour (1987) argues, treatment modalities of scientific rationality are rhetorically treated as if they were immutable mobiles when they are not. Once transported to the rural United States, Chinese participants and therapists could not understand most of the therapy sessions, due to what they called the local dialect. They could not eat the bland American food and most of all could not understand why the residents were so angry and so down and out in one of the richest countries in the world. They observed many differences between the two centers and the two cultures. Therefore, while therapies and therapists may travel, as Latour points out they both are transformed once they move—they are not entirely immutable.

HARM REDUCTION AND PUBLIC HEALTH PATHOLOGIES

While the residential center in rural Yunnan was built around the TC model, the Chinese psychiatrists did not adopt all programs and facets of the American treatment paradigm. They incorporated programs that are not traditionally part of a TC, namely harm reduction[6] practices associated with needle exchange and methadone substitution treatment. Since this was the first center in China, it could not rely on one method alone, nor was the American model perfectly suited for the situation. According to Dr. Yang, they lacked trained personnel, legal resources, rehabilitation facilities, and employment options for recovering drug users.

Heroin addicts arrived from many places in China, mainly the southwestern provinces of Guangdong, Guangxi, and Yunnan, as both low-income residents sent by local health and police authorities and as high-income residents with families exasperated by their self-destruction. They were all paying residents, although charges were nominal and reduced each month as an incentive to stay at the center for at least one year (approximately US$1,000 per year). Despite the moderate fees and recent government scholarships, the center continued to struggle both financially and politically. In 2006 it faced accusations of corruption from foreign NGOs and the threat of closure from local public security officials who denied that therapy was better than imprisonment. In 2008 the provincial government repossessed the land under the treatment center, and Sunlight moved its residential treatment program back to their headquarters in Kunming in early 2009.

In presenting my narratives, I seek to illuminate personal struggles as they are subjectively experienced and politically managed through the structure of the TC to point out how humanitarian care works. In the summers of 2006, 2007, and 2008, there were twenty to forty men and women aged eighteen to forty-six, mainly from the Han Chinese majority with a small minority of Bai, Hui, and Tibetan ethnicities. They were former college students, surgeons, businessmen, prostitutes, athletes, diamond sellers, unemployed youth, fathers, and mothers. The residents who live at Sunlight are subjects who move from the periphery as imprisoned drug criminals among the rising middle classes to the center of what it means to be a good patient and thus a good citizen: free from HIV, free from drugs, and free from uncivil, uncultured, and unproductive behavior. All the lay therapists that work at Sunlight are former addicts, as is the case in most drug TCs the world over. The exception to this practice is the presence of a doctor and nurse team that arrives every three days for a seventy-two-hour shift and the farmers who tend the fields surrounding the center. Every new staff member or visitor, such as myself, must participate in a one-month practicum that requires him or her to be part of therapeutic sessions and live in accordance with the center's rules, including being subject to critique.

SCREAMS

The center's therapeutic focus is on intensive group therapy embedded within a militarized regime of family-like care. This regime of care combines intensive group-therapy sessions, criticisms sessions, and also forms of catharsis such as soccer, yoga, karaoke contests, field trips, and morning games. While harsh criticism sessions pepper the Sunlight therapeutic regimen, there are many scheduled opportunities to reach catharsis, to develop ways to heal the criticisms, to create group bonding, and generally to encourage a wider range of emotions that include laughter and smiles. Every morning after the session, there is time for play and recuperation. Tasks are divided up so that everyone in attendance will perform by presenting a weather report, a news report, and a personal philosophical motto for the day, or, if they join forces, two or three people can be in charge of a daily game. In one of my first weeks at the center, I was asked to sing the weather report as an American rap song. My weather report was a rap version of what I assumed would be the weather, although we had no newspapers and I was told I could just look at the sky and guess what the weather might be.

The games vary from performing on the spot in contact improvisation; dancing; singing anything from Western rock and rap to traditional Chinese folk songs; performing skits, mini-plays, and karaoke contests; or just mercilessly teasing the youngest member of the group. Xiao Guang was the least theatrical of the residents and thus brought endless rounds of laughter when asked to perform. Although everyone was supposed to take a turn, Xiao Guang was called upon almost every morning because of his innocence, his cuteness, and because of, as one resident explained, his age. He was only eighteen years old. There is nothing at Sunlight that forces anyone to do anything including performing at these sessions. However, there are consequences for violating the collective agreement that everyone must abide by: the four cardinal rules of no drugs, stealing, intimate contact, or physical violence.

One of the stark contrasts with Sunlight-New York[7] is that men and women live together, albeit on opposite ends of the hallway, and thus work, clean, attend intensive group therapy sessions, and pray together. In the American model, the sexual division of residents is de rigueur in order to maintain the rule of not fraternizing with the opposite sex. Since Sunlight-Yunnan only had a limited amount of funding, they decided to just keep women and men on separate ends of the hall rather than follow the American model. According to the counselors and medical staff this caused a lot of problems. A core belief at Sunlight is that it is too easy to fall in love with another former drug user and then, once you are both back on the streets, to start using drugs again. Following the American TC model, the Sunlight philosophy espouses the idea that you are sick and that for medical and personal rehabilitation you are not to seek love or a partner. Treatment and love are mutually exclusive.

The most disturbing event that occurred during my research was not witnessing the residents, who brought in drugs, alcohol, or violated smoking bans in the building or maintained unsanitary or dangerous practices. The most disturbing event did not occur around those who smoked around oxygen tanks, handed lit cigarettes to the only infant as toys, or inhaled carbon monoxide from poorly ventilated stoves. The most disturbing event during my fieldwork resulted from the simple act of carrying a love letter between two residents. This was viewed as a grave violation of the community's trust. In assessing this action, the three parties who were involved had to sit on small stools in the upstairs corridor during the early morning work period, and in the evening they were subject to criticism sessions for hours at a time. These were euphemistically called "*titou*" or getting a haircut, in other words, to bring someone down to size. The following is a summary of one such session.

CRIES

A knock at the common room door.
"Who is there?"

A small voice calls out, "It is Xiao An."[8]

Again, in a louder voice, "Who knocks at the door?"

"Xiao An."

Screaming now, counselor Wang says, "Come in."

Xiao An sits down and hangs her head low. Her eyes and face are red and swollen from crying. She is weeping quietly. The head therapist, a former addict who has been clean for eleven years, begins to scream at the top of his lungs. "How dare you do this to your sisters and brothers. How dare you begin to violate our trust, to do this to your sisters and brothers? How could you be so stupid, so disrespectful, so lacking in love, in care?" he screams. There are eight of us in the room and everyone, except me, offers criticisms. They would have welcomed my critiques as well. Most of them address breaking trust, not honoring conduct codes, and, most of all, leading her fellow residents down the path back to drug use.

During this event some people spoke in tones that were polite. Others screamed so loud I thought I heard the windows shake. The most vociferous critique was from my roommate Xiao Su, a former heroin user and the newest member of the staff. She was screaming in such a shrill voice that, combined with her Yunnanese dialect, I could barely make out what she was saying, but her affect was certainly unmistakable.

When I returned to our room that night, I jokingly told her I wasn't sure I wanted to share our room. She was so ferocious. She explained that violating one of the cardinal rules is taken very seriously and requires absolute attention to detail. In order for everyone to take her seriously, as a woman, she had to be fierce. Fierceness earned her both fear and respect, the perfect balance for a lay counselor. She explained that in purposefully passing the letter, Xiao An was the worst culprit because she violated the group's trust and also the trust of two people involved. Thus, she furthered their own conspiracy to break Sunlight's behavioral codes. I told her that I thought there were far worse violations that were actually harmful to the community. I asked why this was seen as so severe. Again, she explained that to keep people off drugs meant sticking strictly to the rules. Therefore, to prevent former users like her from using again meant preventing clients from getting romantically involved. If drug users are involved romantically when in residence, they will certainly be involved when they leave. In the past, love has only ended in sorrow. Xiao Su had seen several couples keep clean for a while, and then go back to using heroin. Sunlight's goal is to keep people off drugs for life, to allow the residents to refashion their lives, to see another way of acting, seeing, feeling, and believing, which means breaking with all old habits and behaviors, including romantic liaisons.

Romance, like drinking alcohol, could wait until they were clean, until they were healthy citizens again.

In this ménage à trois, Xiao An, the letter courier, was most severely criticized, even though it was Xiao Bin, the short, funny guy from central China, who wrote the letter and was in love. He convinced Xiao An to send it to Xiao Cao, a young woman from northern Yunnan, who was playful, pretty, and always so full of laughter, except during the past few days when her eyes were swollen from crying so hard. Xiao Bin seemed to receive the lightest sentence, the most lenient treatment, and was able to keep his emotions in check during his own screaming interrogations. I could not help but imagine the Cultural Revolution in these sessions, recounting what I had seen on film or read in books about Red Guard interrogations for members of the wrong class. Why such verbal violence toward two women and one man?

When I approached the head counselor, he almost died of laughter when I invoked the Cultural Revolution. He said, "We learned these techniques from Sunlight-New York, from psychologists and drug treatment specialists. It has nothing to do with the Cultural Revolution. In fact, we are much less harsh than you Americans are. You should see how strict they are in New York Sunlight."

WHISPERS

Many of the residents had been in and out of drug prisons several times. Several had been in and out of Sunlight several times, and recidivism rates were so high that a project was initiated in the summer of 2008 to study why residents were reluctant to stay for the full yearlong course. While Sunlight should be commended for its unique and innovative programs, there were almost no efforts to redress gender differences in treatment, care, or rehabilitation, other than making women do a larger share of the household cleaning and cooking—a typically gendered division of labor.

One of the most striking aspects of the Sunlight treatment philosophy, as in that of all TCs, is the idea of breaking down old patterns of behavior and replacing them with new ones. In the process, violations of the Sunlight code are severely punished with restrictions on privileges; for example, not being allowed to visit sick relatives or go on group outings. Instead, one is subject to lengthy group criticism sessions.

When I interviewed the director of Sunlight-International's programs, Dr. Lowe, he laughed and said that these criticism sessions were something that both the US State Department and Sunlight-International were very concerned about. The idea that family therapy involved verbal violence was a puzzle to Dr. Lowe. In my conversations with him, I suggested it was perhaps a leftover from the Cultural Revolution. In the stories that friends and colleagues have told me, criticism–self-criticism sessions targeted the "wrong" classes (intellectuals, business people, the bourgeoisie). In these sessions the "right" classes (workers, peasants, and soldiers) were allowed to scream, throw things, and belittle those from the "wrong," or unhealthy, classes. Dr. Yang, the therapeutic director at the Sunlight-Yunnan TC, laughed when I mentioned the Cultural Revolution connection, in contrast to the American director at Sunlight-International, who said that my theory made a lot of sense. As stories of physical abuse had come out of many of the residents' narratives on trauma, I questioned whether this method only reinforced the violence done to those in abusive relationships. I also questioned whether the therapeutic sessions should not also take into consideration the differential power relationships among the staff, clients, and former addicts who were now lay therapists. There were very clear class divisions among the residents—those who were university educated and those who had barely graduated from middle school, those who had held respectable jobs and those who had been marginally employed before entering Sunlight. These questions remain unanswered.

One hot July afternoon, Xiao Wen, a Han woman of thirty-eight with short cropped black hair arrived with her parents and other relatives, carrying only the clothes on her back, stylish army pants, a long-sleeved t-shirt, nylon socks, and brown sandals, and her weary, worn self. She stayed two days and left, and then was coaxed back by her family. Xiao Wen graduated from college in Shanghai and married a Japanese businessman. When she was in her twenties, she had a child, moved to Tokyo, and then realized she hated both her marriage and Japan. She came back to Shanghai, leaving her child behind with her husband and his new wife. She worked as a teacher in Shanghai and then returned home to Yunnan and her parents. Afterward she moved south with a boyfriend to create a successful tourist transit enterprise. Through her business relationships, she began hanging out with her boyfriend and his friends, who used drugs for fun, and then her boyfriend became addicted to heroin. She then began using heroin and lost everything: her partner, her business, and her life. Hers was a tale of loss and recovery that I was to hear over and over again.

Xiao Wen often sat outside in the sun to talk with me during the breaks between therapy sessions and work. She found me to be simpatico as we both had university educations, both had learned difficult Asian languages, both had lived in another part of the world than our natal homes, and most of all we had both worked in southern Yunnan in the late 1990s. When Xiao Wen left the center after two days she was not forced to return to the TC—it is not a prison—but her parents persuaded her that this was the best thing for her, that addiction had ruined her life and that this could be a new start. Xiao Wen would often take a long drag of her cigarette and lament her previous life and the fact that her son was far away. But then she would say he is far better off, Japan is a more advanced country, and he is in good schools and loves his stepmother. While Xiao Wen was shy, she had to perform her emotions just like the rest of us. On her return to Sunlight, she was subject to a special criticism session, where one has to bow one's head in shame as three or four other counselors yell at the top of their lungs for periods of up to one or two hours. In these sessions there are the ever-present neon overhead lights and the often scared and new resident, who is subjected to a barrage of verbal humiliations in what the staff described to me as their attempts to keep the former addict at the center, to keep him or her on the therapeutic path. Xiao Wen was devastated, but like all the others, when she finally asked for forgiveness, she said, in almost a whisper, "Rescue me, please rescue me, please rescue me." It is only then that the session stopped and she was allowed to join the rest of the group, albeit on a stool at the back of the room for her first day back with the group.

SUNLIGHT AND TRAVELING THERAPIES

In focusing on the introduction of the Sunlight therapeutic approach in China, I want to highlight two processes. One, the rise in humanitarian aid organizations from the early 1990s onward inside the former closed doors of the Communist state. Here drug treatment facilities are no longer funded by the state, but by what Vanessa Pupavac (2004) calls the therapeutic governance of international humanitarian NGOs. And two, the absolute warp speed in the rise of new forms of post-socialist and Chinese authoritarianism accompanied by new forms of biosociality and social distress (Rabinow 1996). Extending Foucault's insights, to function in post-socialist China is to sit at the table and behave like a healthy citizen (1988: 254–255). Not like the asylums of 150 years ago, which Michel Foucault (1988) described in *Madness and Civilization* through the legends of Pinel and Tuke, people have moved from the prisons to the tea party.

In drawing on Foucault's (1986, 2003) notion of biopower and the care of the self, I argue that modern power operates productively when individual citizens learn to internalize self-regulation and self-empowerment in the name of self-discipline. But as Nikolas Rose (1996) points out, self-regulating and self-actualizing human beings do not emerge out of nowhere, they become self-actualizing through what Foucault understood as an amalgamation of forces, discourses, and interests that framed them and, in this case, frames new forms of therapeutic treatment. Another way of explaining what is happening in terms of humanitarian aid efforts is Aihwa Ong and Stephen Collier's (2005) notion of the global assemblage. China itself is *the* prime example of a global assemblage writ large. Within its borders and territories are the world's largest factory workshops, the world's largest trash and recycling bins for highly toxic industrial and cyber waste, and, at the same time, it is developing at warp speeds.[9] China is experiencing one of the greatest upheavals of the twenty-first century; 35 percent of the population have left their natal homes in search of work. The country is one large construction site where building cranes have jokingly become the new national bird. It is also experiencing what many call the second industrial revolution, rapid cultural change, and new forms of sociability that are accompanied by rising social problems as well as new solutions that are often mediated through humanitarian interventions like those of Sunlight-International.[10]

At Sunlight-Yunnan, we find strange global assemblages and citizen-subjects: monsignors from upstate New York, heroin addicts who are diamond sellers from Guangdong, bus drivers from Sipsongpanna via Japan, women from a village with one of the highest rates of heroin use in China, lay counselors who are former addicts, psychiatrists, and traditional Chinese medical doctors, who all converge at the rural outskirts of an unsightly industrial city. Ethnography here offers a critical vantage point for exploring global circuits of medical knowledge and humanitarian aid to readdress personal suffering by creating patients out of prisoners and healthy citizen-subjects out of former addicts who will neither rely on the state, nor live outside it.

While there is a burgeoning literature on humanitarian governance around the world, much of that work has been specifically targeted at large humanitarian aid organizations that follow wars such as Médicins Sans Frontières and Care International (Bornstein 2005; Pandolfi 2003; Redfield 2006). The former have carried out missions that *never* formally become part of state modernizing projects. In other words, MSF carries out a series of missions but never becomes embedded into local institutional structures. On the other hand, Sunlight has become a model program for all of China. Simultaneously, humanitarian NGOs are beginning to replace some former state institutions through newly emerging religious and secular projects designed to improve the quality of China's citizens (Adams and Pigg 2005; Greenhalgh 2005; Kipnis 2006; Yan 2003). In anthropology there has been a renewed interest in studies of personhood, subjectivity, and affect as socially productive sites for ethnographic investigation and theoretical analysis (Good et al. 2008). The disease concept of addiction is a liberal invention, linked to behavioral ideals of self-independence and economic productivity (Levine 1978). Governance here is in the interest of humanitarianism and economic conceptions of the self, where developing China means creating the most economically productive human beings possible.

CONCLUSION

In order to make sense of all these particular forces, discourses, and interests, I rest with the idea that traveling therapeutics has become the norm of humanitarian governance. In a manner similar to Anthony Giddens, Aihwa Ong and Stephen Collier (2005:9) argue that global assemblages are sites where we find "the displacement and reappropriation of expertise to a range of non-expert sites" and, more important for my argument, the penetration of modern institutions that travel. Sunlight's promoters parallel nineteenth-century French and English missionaries who spread Enlightenment ideas to Yunnan through the Christian medical missions that set out to erase the health scourges of the day: leprosy, plague, and malaria.

In the post-socialist era, therapeutic humanitarian aid organizations now spread out across China to further neoliberalism through building global medical humanitarian civil society. In doing so, they provide a new kind of humanitarian aid; one that stays put once it arrives. In anthropology today, there are many discussions about the relevance, messy power relations, and cultural politics of aid (see this volume Redfield, Bornstein, Fassin, Pandolfi). For example, in discussing how humanitarian NGOs move from one war zone to the next to dispense medical and humanitarian aid, anthropologist Mariella Pandolfi (2003, 2008a) argues there is always a strong trace of old-fashioned imperialism, as humanitarian aid often trails military incursions. For my purposes, Pandolfi's term *mobile sovereignty* suggests that sovereignty has been unhinged from the state and is now running amok in war theaters around the globe. In China it is not the war theaters, but the drug theaters of the world where Sunlight was originally brought in to stave off the American drug market, to reduce those trafficking across national borders, and, at the same time, to address the psychosocial problems associated with global drug use.

In this chapter, I have tried to show how multiple regimes of knowledge, medical treatment and surveillance, religious ideas, and therapeutic governance operate in the world of drug-use treatment and how, in turn, these knowledge regimes become internalized and reconfigured by Chinese therapists and former drug addicts alike. Sunlight, however, emerges as one new norm for traveling humanitarian aid. Rather than just outsourcing medical care and aid to another mobile sovereignty, China incorporates the NGO model into its own medical and regional centers of care. In the process we begin to see new patterns of therapeutic governance and citizenship the world over. But this form of governance is not the same in every site, thus focusing on traveling therapeutics is a way to understand how mobile global therapeutic practices, like the TC treatment model, transform Chinese heroin addicts and how the Chinese model is transformed at the same time.

What counts is how these knowledge regimes become internalized, thus begging the question, what exactly is the responsibility of the Chinese and American NGOs that fund Sunlight, evaluate its effectiveness, and give carte blanche to its internal operations? In recent work done by anthropologists on global humanitarianism, Peter Redfield (2006:18) and Didier Fassin and Paula Vasquez (2005) remind us "that the results of any humanitarianism are not simply salutary or redeeming," that there are benefits and costs to rethinking the prison yard and labor camp. The only way to really understand these is to turn to the ethnographic particular to imagine and problematize the alternatives.[11]

Notes

1. There is some debate over the use of the term *post-socialism*, versus *late socialism*, or *authoritarian socialism*. I have specifically chosen the term *post-socialism* as the work of humanitarian NGOs in China has brought in a new era of neoliberal organization as a neoliberal civil society model. However, this neoliberal model is different from many other developing countries because while many social services are no longer regulated nor provided by state institutions, they almost all have clear attachments to the Communist state, as does the hybrid organization Sunlight-Yunnan, which employs both state workers from the Yunnan Institute of Drug Abuse and independent staff hired from NGOs' moneys. While I recognize that *post-socialism* is not a precise term, it is the best term I can find for this current period of history that is changing as I write this piece (Fisher 1997; Zhang 2007; Zhang 2001).

2. I am using the terms *addict* and *user* interchangeably. I am aware that this creates some confusion in terms of who is speaking. Many therapists, former users, and NGO staff use the term *addict*, rather than *user*, as there is a very limited awareness in China of people being functional drug users rather than engaging in illegal drug practices.

3. Conducting research on HIV and sex work in the late 1990s, I visited an older drug prison. High above the prefectural capital of Jinghong are rubber farms, rock quarries, and a high-security drug prison. Vines cover the high red brick walls, an old Beijing jeep lays in a heap, mangy mongrel dogs bark, and inmates and guards squat in the noonday sun, smoking tobacco from long water pipes. It was here that I was first introduced to Lao Yan, one of the prison guards, who gave representatives from the NGO Save the Children–Hong Kong a tour. The buildings, all in disrepair, were organized according to three levels of security: (1) the high-security cells where inmates were first assigned; (2) the medium-security rooms where inmates shared bunk beds and a courtyard; and (3) unlocked rooms, above the prison cells, where female inmates were in rehabilitation. Inmates reached the prison through police raids on drug addict hangouts or neighborhood arrests. Inmates spent their days smoking cigarettes, chopping wood, and working at the prison. Lao Yan said there was no money to pay the resident nurse let alone even to consider the idea of drug rehabilitation; these were merely holding pens, literally cages, where inmates passed the time working in the prison until their sentences were completed. The recidivism rates were high, and many inmates returned until they exhausted their sentences and were then sent to labor camps elsewhere. Most of the guards, while amiable in appearance and demeanor, were more concerned with their salaries, rather than their drug-using charges. In Yunnan, like elsewhere, many believe the way out of the high rates of HIV transmission is simply to eradicate drugs as they did in the 1950s (Hyde 2007:94–95).

4. I am quite aware that the notions of the TC go back much further historically than just California in the 1960s and 1970s. Given the nature of this piece, I have not explored that literature here. I am in the process of completing a manuscript on this project and in my historical chapters will explain the transformation of the TC and how it moved from Europe in the early twentieth century to California and how it was incorporated into current therapies in behavioral medicine.

5. According to historian Eric Broekaert, the rise of Synanon came out of the massive social movements that characterized California after World War II. Synanon's philosophy was grounded in Christianity and Zen Buddhism, the ideas of the Oxford group, Alcoholics Anonymous, and the Human Potential Movement, as well as Skinner's *Walden Two* and the utopian community described in the book (Soyez and Broekaert 2005:306–307).

6. Harm reduction is a philosophy in public health that provides an alternative to outright prohibition of certain illegal risky behaviors. It takes as its premise that certain people will always use drugs, and thus harm reduction policies and practices aim to mitigate the dangers and health risks associated with injection drug use. For injection drug users, harm reduction usually stands for safe injection practices, like the

Vancouver Insite project, which provides safe spaces for injection drug users to use drugs and insists on clean needles to prevent the spread of HIV/AIDS.

7. In my first two summers at Sunlight, I made no headway in gaining access to Sunlight-New York. However, in summer 2008, the director of Sunlight-International came to Yunnan.

8. With the exception of the director, and those few staff quoted in news articles, all my informants' names are pseudonyms, including the name of the organization itself.

9. However, given the recent economic world downturn and global economic recession, China's supercharged growth is also slowing down as it "begins to feel the effects of the global financial crisis." Its growth in the last ten years has averaged above 10 percent and has now slowed to 9 percent and appears to be dropping (Barboza 2008:13).

10. In the future development of this work, I explore the implications of personal suffering and injury through psychoanalytic interpretation, but that is not the focus of this essay.

11. This chapter has traveled many miles to its current incarnation. For this version, I am extremely grateful to Ralph Litzinger and Dominic Sachsenmaier for Duke University's Mellon Seminar on India and China; Michelle Rivkin-Fish and UNC–Chapel Hill Speaker's Series; Joe Dumit, João Biehl, Aihwa Ong, Sean Brotherton, Kelly McKinney, and Elizabeth Roberts for their comments on two AAA panels; Mary-Jo DelVecchio Good and the Harvard conference on "Affect, Power and Subjectivity"; Cornelius Borck and Andrea Tone for the McGill WIPS seminar; the graduate students in my ethnographic writing course; and, most of all, Peter Redfield, Erica Bornstein, and the participants of the School for Advanced Research Advanced Seminar on Humanitarian Aid in March 2008. And most of all, I dearly thank all those at Sunlight-Yunnan who shared their precious stories and their lives with me.

8

From Redundancy to Recognition

*Transnational Humanitarianism
and the Production of Nonmoderns*

Miriam Ticktin

The primary domestic program of HealthRight International (formerly Doctors of the World-USA)[1]—their "Human Rights Clinic"—works to help refugees and immigrants attain legal status. The project started in 1993 by supporting cases of torture survivors and providing written affidavits by doctors for use in asylum proceedings. I spoke with Dr. Taylor in the spring of 2004. She volunteered her time with both HealthRight International (formerly Doctors of the World-USA) and Physicians for Human Rights. As part of HealthRight International's human rights clinic, Dr. Taylor told me that she had spent a number of years going into detention centers to evaluate refugee claimants, evidence she subsequently used to write affidavits on the basis of her medical expertise. Having attended a training session and several follow-up discussions, I know that she, like other doctors, is trained to look for clear, delineated symptoms, forensic evidence, and "not to believe the patients." She looks for scars or incompletely healed bones, altered vision or amputated body parts. She looks for inconsistencies in their accounts, intrusive memories, detachment—signs of post-traumatic stress disorder, or PTSD. The training sessions teach doctors, psychologists, and social workers to read the body—to see the body as a site of truth and authentication, one that, while it may not tell the whole truth, has the power to legitimate or undermine the larger narrative constructed by both refugee claimant and lawyer.[2]

On one of her visits to a detention center, Dr. Taylor told me that she had evaluated a woman who was claiming asylum. She had visited the asylum seeker—whom I will call Fatou—once before. When she arrived, Fatou said that she was not quite ready to be seen. Once in the examination, Dr. Taylor saw that the woman in front of her had undergone FGC, or female genital cutting. But Dr. Taylor gradually realized that she was not examining the same person she had seen before—but rather, an acquaintance of Fatou's. It was unclear whether Fatou herself had also undergone the genital surgery.

While this story about Fatou remains but a fragment—it was all I was able to learn about her—it nevertheless reveals the encounter between humanitarian doctor and asylum seeker as a space shaped by expectations, desires, and a contested notion of what counts as truth—the truth of persecution. Such a space forces us to look beyond the question of fraud and focus instead on the interaction, and the game of truth and counter-truth. Indeed, I want to suggest that looking at this as an issue of fraud leaves unexamined the logic on which it turns, namely, the way that the body is the main source of truth for asylum claimants like Fatou. Many people have participated in producing and reproducing this truth, Fatou and Dr. Taylor just two among them. In this logic, while she may be able to speak, her body is both the origin of and the necessary supplement for her account—it is what makes her account legible.[3] More precisely, according to this scene, it is not just her body, but a specific *part* of her body: at issue were her genitals. Her exchange of bodies with her friend reveals an implicit acknowledgment of biology as that which matters; body parts disembodied, disaggregated, although not entirely abstracted from selves, as the biology that matters is determined by gendered and racialized perceptions. Fatou got caught in the messy space of the relationship between biologies and identities: it is not clear when biology renders identity irrelevant and when biology *stands in* for the self—when does it become identical with her as a person? To be sure, biology is a resource that must be used strategically in this messy space; Fatou traded on the popular knowledge that her biology—as a refugee—was also her locus of ultimate truth. Humanitarians are not just observers in this matter, but they participate in shaping this regime. As another member of HealthRight International (formerly Doctors of the World-USA) said to me when talking about cases of so-called fraud, "One cannot deny that with these kinds of programs, immigrants or refugees have to highlight their pathologies in order to access basic rights; this is the unfortunate fallout of the structural reality." In other words, for immigrants, biology is becoming more central in the recognition of political worth, and humanitarians are key players in producing this reality.

In this essay, I want to explore how biology allows for and fuels a form of hope: how it provides a hope for a better life. And in particular, I am going to focus on the role biology plays in the politics of immigration. I am interested in how biology has become a central tool in the ability to travel, while labor power is rendered a liability—a threat, even. Here, I use "biology" to focus on the materiality of the life processes of human beings, from the molecular to the species level, emphasizing biology as a signifier within the larger fields of biomedicine, biotechnology, and genomics, one which is constantly being negotiated. In other words, this comes from the recognition that bodies are increasingly understood in biological terms: whether it be through biometrics or genetic testing. Here, I combine one part of my previous ethnographic research with undocumented immigrants in Paris (2005, 2006a, and 2006b) with comparative research in the United States, which has included interviews and participant observation with members and volunteers of HealthRight International (formerly Doctors of the World-USA), the New York chapter of Doctors Without Borders, New York immigration and asylum lawyers and activists, and some participant observation of clinics for refugees in the Detroit area. In other words, this essay brings my earlier arguments about the politics of immigration in France into a larger, transnational framework.

To be sure, there is a vibrant ongoing debate about how biological understandings of human beings relate to notions of political belonging such as citizenship and projects of citizen-building. Adriana Petryna first coined the term "biological citizenship" in her ethnography *Life Exposed: Biological Citizens after Chernobyl* (2002), and of this literature, I engage most directly with this notion of biological citizenship as articulated by both Petryna and by Nikolas Rose and Carlos Novas in their article by the same name.[4] In a broad sense, each of these analyses builds on a Foucaultian notion of *biopower*, where discipline of the body and regulation of the population constitute the two poles around which the power over life is now deployed (Foucault 1978). In this essay, I emphasize the biopolitics of immigration, where both human life and biology have new potential value to be negotiated through a range of novel and often counter-intuitive practices.

In exploring the biopolitics of immigration, and the hope linked to biology in this arena, I make two specific interventions. First, I want to suggest that while everyone is subject to what Rose and Novas call "a new political economy of hope" (2005:442; Rose 2007) created by the notion of biology as manipulable, one's corporeality is subject to different types of manipulation and choice, depending on one's positioning; in other words, there is always hope, but this hope takes on different meanings and exhibits different constraints, depending on whether one is a subject of the global North or South, elite or underclass, whether one is black, brown, or white, a man or a woman. In a situation where biology is a primary resource, I ask whether the hope connected to it might need to be qualified by what I call "biological involution"—the way that the manipulation of one's biology can come with limited returns, even to the point of death.

Second, I argue that while immigrants—often coming from the global South—make use of their biology in the process of immigration, participating in this political economy of hope whatever the form or constraint, they are often subject to a different regime than those already a part of the privileged classes of the global North, who are seen as increasingly able to manipulate their biology due to new forms of biotechnology. For the modern neoliberal subject, biology is increasingly fluid, open to choice; biological norms can be created and manipulated. In contrast, this regime sees immigrants from the global South and anyone else not yet counted as a modern liberal subject as biologically determined, and I relate this to government in the form of humanitarianism. Thus, more specifically, I am describing a *dual regime of truth*—where different epistemologies and disciplinary practices are used to both produce and govern different populations. As I will argue, immigrants are governed increasingly by humanitarian practices and by the humanitarian industry, not by immigration laws and policies. And because humanitarianism works largely on the basis of biomedical intervention, biology plays a more central role in claims to recognition in ways that both include and go beyond the commodification of body parts. What I am suggesting, then, is that while biology fuels hope for a better life whatever the context, because of the mediating influence of humanitarianism and the way that it replaces other means of entry, biology simultaneously provides a means for stratifying populations and maintaining discriminations that derive from colonial and imperial histories, by rendering those histories invisible.

I want to point out that the biopolitics of immigration brings into relief not only the hierarchies created by external borders, but the role biology increasingly plays in structuring all kinds of borders—external and internal—obfuscating inequalities in race, class, gender, and sexuality. These borders and hierarchies are at play for everyone: indeed, who gets to be a full-fledged neoliberal subject or "citizen" is often negotiated and renegotiated through biology and whether one is seen as properly "responsible" for one's health. While not treated in depth in this essay, these "internal" borders are nonetheless an integral part of this dual regime of truth.

In order to think about both the political economy of biology and of hope I am going to follow what I see as the trajectory from a "redundant" humanity to a "nonmodern" humanity.

FROM A REDUNDANT HUMANITY...

As I have been suggesting, in their discussion of "biological citizenship" Rose and Novas (2005) raise the idea of a "political economy of hope" created by a notion of biology as manipulable. In this logic, life is open to shaping and reshaping, even at the molecular level. As Rose writes, "natural" life is no longer "the ground or norm against which a politics of life may be judged": the "natural" must be produced through labor on the self (Rose 2001:17). This sense of hope or optimism grounds their notion of biological citizenship, which is shaped by technological and biomedical changes as well as a sense of responsibility, vis-à-vis one's biology, to make the right choices. In this logic, bodies are all open to alteration and modification: it is not the exception to be treated with Prozac, Viagra, and plastic surgery, but the routine—it is almost expected. Indeed, in this moral economy, ignorance and resignation in the face of the future are denigrated. I want to suggest that this logic of alteration and modification of one's biology must be seen through another lens. Indeed, depending on one's location, this regime of citizenship can be seen as a part of a larger, more drastic reduction in choice and possibility. In order to understand how a similar political economy of hope can result in such a different form of biopolitics, I think it is critical to look to the global political economy.

Thus, even as we all become potential sources of "biovalue"[5] (Rose and Novas 2005:454), and part of a market economy of health more broadly, we cannot lose sight of the fact that the context for this form of biopolitics is one of deepening inequality between the global North and South, with growing urbanization and poverty. This shapes the contours of the political economy of hope for those who choose to migrate and the biopolitical form it takes. Mike Davis calls those produced by these changes "the New Wretched of the Earth" (2004a:11). He describes a situation where the developing world is increasingly a universe of urban slums and shantytowns and where 90 percent of the increase in world population over the next generation will be accommodated in urban areas of the developing world (2004a:11). Davis draws on reports produced by UN researchers to suggest that this urban population will be almost completely removed or "disincorporated" from industrial growth and the supply of formal jobs

(2004a:11)—according to a document produced by the United Nations Human Settlements Programme, nearly two-fifths of the economically active population of the developing world are so-called informal workers (Davis 2004b:24). This has resulted in people fitting themselves into further subdivided economic niches such as casual labor, street-vending, begging, and crime.

There are different ways of naming and hence thinking about the people engaged in these types of temporary, physically dangerous, and socially degrading forms of work, whose everyday life is dominated by risk; for instance, Sandeep Pendse (1995) calls the poorest of the poor in Mumbai "toilers," distinguishing them from the working or laboring classes. Zygmunt Bauman speaks of the production of "wasted humans" or those he defines as "excessive" or "redundant" as an inevitable outcome of modernization and now globalization, where the modern form of life creates greater and greater numbers of "human beings bereaved of their heretofore adequate ways and means of survival in both the biological and social/cultural sense of that notion" (2004:7). He likens a state of redundancy to that of being disposable, like a plastic bottle or syringe, the destination of which is the garbage heap; he is careful to distinguish this state from what it meant earlier to be unemployed, that is, part of the reserve army of labor (2004:12). A critical difference here is that this redundant or excess group is excluded from the realm of social communication—they are unable to speak and be heard. Perhaps most damningly, Bauman reminds us that to be modern, each of us requires the production of excess, the production of human waste and wasted humans—we need them to become our modern selves.

In a similar manner, Davis calls this group the "outcaste proletariat" and states that it is both the fastest growing social class on the planet and yet also the most novel, in the sense that this urban informal working class is not a more traditional labor reserve army with the strategic economic power of socialized labor, but rather, "a mass of humanity structurally and biologically redundant to global accumulation and the corporate matrix" (2004a:11). For this "surplus humanity," informal survivalism is the new primary mode of livelihood in a majority of Third World cities (2004b:26). Ultimately, Davis is interested in the sorts of historical subjects that emerge from these circumstances; he does not assume that this "surplus humanity" is passive and points to the way they tap into historical and cultural traditions of resistance. However, as part of this process, he nevertheless argues that there are vicious networks of microexploitation with poor exploiting the poor and, indeed, "ever more heroic feats of self-exploitation," what Davis, adapting Geertz, calls "involution": "a spiraling labour self-exploitation...which continues, despite rapidly diminishing returns, as long as any return or increment is produced"(2004b:27).[6]

I suggest that it is this condition of a "redundant" portion of humanity, existing outside formal relations of production and channels of social communication, which must be placed alongside the new citizenship that Rose and Novas speak of, where biology is no longer seen as destiny. Biology becomes one of the few sources of value for those who exist outside the socialized collectivity of labor. The global economy has produced a set of circuits of capital and people that move, as Nancy Scheper-Hughes has written, from South to North, Third World to First, poor to rich, black and brown to white, and female to male (2000:193). I do not mean to suggest that biology is the *only* resource available to the poorest of the poor; as Appadurai suggests in his essay "Deep Democracy," there are those who engage in what he calls "the politics of patience" by opting for various sorts of partnerships with other more powerful actors, including the state, to achieve their goals (2002:27). What I am arguing is that for those moving from the South into the North or, more broadly, from what Bauman calls the "social homelessness" of the redundant into social recognition, biology is clearly a *central* field of action, as it is for those designated "modern."

My point here is that this choice about biology must be placed in a context in which those migrating—whether to the United States, France, or elsewhere—may be part of networks that make biological trades more thinkable than selling one's labor power, which has become difficult in any formal manner. For instance, Cohen writes that in a Chennai slum, just outside the real "kidney belts" of southern India, kidneys have become a "normal" way for the poor to pay off their debts. However, he makes clear that kidney zones are not simply the result of a naturalized state of poverty. Rather, they emerge at the intersection of poverty and established networks for trafficking in kidneys—moneylenders lend more to those who live near kidney zones, creating greater debt crises than might have otherwise occurred. Knowing that one can sell one's organs provides a sense of hope and a way to imagine a different kind of future. That said, if one sells one's organs for a passport—as depicted in Stephen Frears's 2002 film *Dirty Pretty Things*—or perhaps just for money, it carries with it immediate and future health risk, as well as the risk of getting caught and losing all. In other words, in looking at how "operability" (Cohen 1999:139, 2004a) becomes a central modality of citizenship and of hope, we must not neglect the "second order phenomena" in such transactions. In the case of the kidney trade that Cohen writes about, this means looking beyond the dyadic relationship between buyer and seller, or donor and recipient, to look at everyday phenomena such as the debt bondage of those who decide to sell their organs, which does not go away with the sale of the organ (Cohen 1999:148). Those who sell do get money: "life for life." However, it rarely lifts them out of poverty. This is not always part of discussions of organ sales. Perhaps, as Cohen has written (2004a), the wish to sell one's organs is actually just a form of sacrifice that stands in for hope. Here, we must ask whether "involution" can also become *biological involution*; in other words, we must ask how and under what conditions the exploitation of one's biology can potentially become a losing proposition, the biggest risk of course being death.

...TO A NONMODERN HUMANITY

Shifting now to the context of the West, or the global North—the destination point of many of these circuits of capital and people I have just described, often to escape a type of "redundancy"—we see that borders are formally closed to immigrants and refugees in the majority of these nation-states. With temporary protection rather than permanent settlement being the order of the day, there are fewer and fewer ways in which immigrants can enter and claim basic rights.[7] Indeed, the larger context is one in which increasingly restrictive legislation has forced borders closed, while black market and informal economies have grown, and labor conditions have otherwise changed to favor insecure forms of labor with no legal protection. While certain immigrants are still explicitly courted, such as those who are highly technically qualified, and those who are wealthy, these make up a small proportion of the global flow of immigrants. For the most part, those who migrate must enter or gain legal status in countries of the global North through other means, despite being important to the larger economy.

To reiterate, I am suggesting that these means are not guided by immigration laws or policies, but rather by humanitarian or exceptional clauses, and often mediated by medical humanitarian organizations. For instance, the increasing transnational importance of humanitarianism in regulating immigration is revealed by MSF-Europe's growing number of programs that deal explicitly with issues related to immigration—they have focused programs in Italy, Spain, France, Belgium, and Sweden, providing blankets and food when boatloads of immigrants arrive on the shores of Europe, monitoring health conditions at detention centers, and setting up at airports for potential deportation problems when those who are too sick to be deported are forced onto planes. The membership immigrants claim is thus based on what Pandolfi calls a "mobile sovereignty" where politics is displaced from the state onto a "humanitarian apparatus" of transnational processes and NGOs (2003:371). And again, because humanitarianism is most significantly focused on health issues, and the lives and well-being of populations, biology plays a more central role in claims to political recognition.

France

I look to France for my first example of how biology plays in the politics of immigration and to the "illness clause."[8] I am referring to the 1998 amendment to the Edict (Ordonnance) of November 2, 1945, no. 45–2658 on Conditions of Entry and Residence of Foreigners. Article 12b is the right to "private and family life," which is itself a direct reference to Article 8 of the European Convention on Human Rights (CEDH). There are eleven categories, of which the "Autorisation Provisoire pour Soins" or "APS" (temporary authorization for medical care) is the eleventh. This 1998 provision to French immigration law grants legal permits to undocumented immigrants or "*les sans papiers*" already living in France with pathologies that entail life-threatening consequences if they are declared unable to receive proper treatment in their home countries; the goal was to permit them to receive treatment in France. The logic behind this was humanitarian and exceptional; the French state felt it could not deport people if such a deportation had consequences of exceptional gravity, such as their death. It was the lobbying of medical humanitarian groups such as Médecins Sans Frontières or "Doctors Without Borders" and Médecins du Monde or "Doctors of the World" that helped institute the illness clause in France.

During the primary period of my field research in France (1999–2001), this illness clause became one of the most promising avenues of legal entry into France, despite the significant political struggle by and for undocumented immigrants. The local statistics from the state medical office (DDASS)[9] where I did my research show that applications for the "illness residency permit" increased seven times over the course of the 1990s, three quarters of which were given positive responses. Indeed, the most recent statistics are even more striking: from 194 patients treated in 1993, the number of those treated rose to 4,000 in 2003. Similarly, as Didier Fassin (2001a) has noted, the increase in numbers admitted for the illness clause is directly correlated with a decrease in number of refugees accepted. With illness one of the only clear means by which to apply for papers, I watched as social workers in hospital clinics for the underprivileged and excluded asked if their undocumented clients were sick, suggesting it implicitly as a means of entry, and this was happening increasingly in the NGOs I worked with. A woman from an immigrant-rights association confirmed this practice at a workshop for sans papiers and HIV/AIDS, stating, "Isn't it terrible? We almost wish for illness when we talk to sans papiers." This wish for illness, of course, was not out of malice, but in order to better help them.

This said, we must certainly inquire how the French state reconciles the denial of papers to immigrants because they are perceived to be criminal or economically burdensome with the decision to give papers and social services to immigrants who are sick. Stated otherwise, why is it that illness is allowed to travel across borders, while poverty cannot?

I suggest that those entering under the illness clause do so—and are permitted to do so—*only* when they appear as apolitical, suffering bodies. This is the face of the population required for humanitarian intervention. As Liisa Malkki first argued in 1996, the refugee as a universal humanitarian subject is one whose corporeal wounds speak louder than words; political history is rendered irrelevant (Malkki 1996). What mobilizes action is the ahistorical victim, the suffering body. Indeed, the same logic holds for immigrants trying to claim legal status through the illness clause. While immigrants and refugees have been recast as suspicious—and Western nation-states consistently function on the basis of a belief that immigrants lie and cheat—insofar as sick immigrants present themselves as "bare" biological life, they are seen as legitimate (Fassin 2001a; Ticktin 2005, 2006a; Agamben 1998). Their biological bodies tell the truth; biology cannot dupe the system. Indeed, this humanitarian clause presumes that biology is the domain of the incontestable; it derives legitimacy from the belief in biology's fixity. Scars in the right place attest to torture, and immunity levels cannot lie about one's HIV status. This reveals that a *dual regime of truth* is at work. For the modern neoliberal subject, biology is fluid, open to choice; biological norms can be created and manipulated. In fact, they must be, to be a responsible citizen. Yet for immigrants, particularly those from former colonies or from the global South, biology is seen as their very essence. While biology may be one of their few resources, they are seen, paradoxically, as unable to work on themselves, to be subjects or agents: they are perceived as victims of their environment, of war, of larger struggles. In fact, there is another aspect to this dual regime of truth: immigrants or refugees only become visible en masse, as an undifferentiated group of suffering or dying bodies—we are rarely allowed to notice individuals, except as those generic specimens whose stories are used for NGO fund-raising purposes. Here, biology serves as a resource only in the form of mass; this is in stark contrast to the individualized biology of the modern liberal subject.

Of course, biology is in fact *not* incontestable, even *en masse*, as we have seen, for the new "wretched of the earth" biology can be the quintessential domain of action. Biology is the domain of possibility and of hope, just as it is for the privileged citizen-subjects of the global North. In this vein, I came across examples of immigrants not treating their illnesses in order to keep their papers. Indeed, there was a huge range of creative ways in which undocumented immigrants worked with and on their biology to obtain papers (Ticktin 2006a). Through the illness clause, legal papers are initially granted as temporary permits, which can be renewed if the medical condition persists. Here, "papers" can mean anything from three-month to six-month to one-year to ten-year permits, none of which automatically leads to citizenship. In other words, papers certainly give hope of a different or better life, but this is not necessarily the equivalent of citizenship. I encountered perhaps the most extreme example of manipulation of biology near the end of my fieldwork—one which could be an example of this idea of biological involution, where the hope held out by biology could lead to a quicker demise than without it: the former president of Act Up-Paris told me that he had received calls from people inquiring how they could infect themselves with HIV in order to obtain legal status in France. I should not have been surprised because it was the logical end-result of the tendency I had been witnessing, where one must remain diseased to *remain* in France and to eventually claim citizenship. While this particular account is anecdotal—I have no way of knowing if such self-infections occurred—it is the *rhetoric* of willed self-infection that is important, as it must be located in the larger reality I observed, which was the turn to physical injury or infection to claim the basic rights supposedly granted to all human beings, illustrating the fact that biology is one of the only resources left to many.

Biology thus becomes the domain of strategy, by transforming it into a resource, whether as a market commodity or as part of a humanitarian regime. But contrary to commodification, humanitarianism serves to regulate and govern bodies directly, without the market as intermediary—or perhaps, more precisely, with its own parallel market (Dezalay and Garth 1998); this is what shapes the dual regime of truth that governs immigrant bodies. One can become a subject of humanitarian clauses by either directly transforming the materiality of one's biology or by discursively redefining it, foregrounding it—I suggest these are part of the same continuum. To illustrate this, I want to turn to an example from my research in the Paris suburbs. One day in the state public health office where I sat with nurses and doctors as they received undocumented immigrants in their quest for papers, Felicia, the nurse on duty, received a phone call from an official at the *préfecture* (immigration office). She was very wary at first, because the préfecture focused primarily on reducing the numbers of people let in, working at cross-purposes with the nurses and doctors whose goal was to help heal people, regardless of status or circumstance. The official spoke of a young man named Boris who had tried to claim refugee status but had been refused by the préfecture because this official's boss would not acknowledge the claim that the young man made: that he had been forced into a prostitution ring, one that was linked to drug smuggling. The boss refused to acknowledge that there were links between these two types of activities.

The official had clearly been moved by the story of Boris, who had come from Eastern Europe. The official was calling confidentially to ask if the medical office could help him and suggested that the young man might have hepatitis. Felicia, the nurse, was excited and intrigued but nervous that it was a trap designed to catch her in creating pathologies for papers. She said, "No problem, we'll take care of it." Whatever this young man had in the way of pathology, it was clear they would find a way to help him. We waited and waited for him to show up with his file; I was there with the nurses when he did. He was a young blond man who appeared very nervous and uncomfortable. One nurse asked him a few questions in a kind voice, trying to draw him out; she was hoping to hear his full story, but he revealed only the minimum and left as quickly as he could. The nurses translated stories into pathologies, trauma narratives into biologically based injury; this translation between regimes of truth was in many ways their job and what they themselves saw as their moral calling. Even the short version of his story sufficed; they let Boris use his biology to tell a truth that otherwise would remain unheard.

Like many sans papiers, Boris experienced his illness as a *political condition.*[10] In other words, for him, he experienced his illness first and foremost as a way to get papers, establishing his relationship to the French state. He seemed less concerned with treating his illness—it was incidental, in some sense, that he had hepatitis and likely other illnesses. He had fallen ill through his forced participation in a prostitution ring—for him, *that* was the problem. His condition was at once political, social, and biological but understood primarily for him through a political and social lens—he wanted to escape the prostitution ring. Yet he was granted papers for "humanitarian reasons," that is, on the basis of the illness clause. Ultimately, his biological condition determined his social condition—that is, insofar as he proved he was life-threateningly sick, he was granted social and legal status in France. Of course, because the illness clause requires a life-threatening condition, it is in fact his physical life that he trades in for social recognition—the prospect of his death is what ensures his social life. He has to remain ill to keep his papers—belonging is limited by the fact that he needs to be officially recognized as sick or disabled; this usually precludes a work permit. Being part of the formal economy of illness requires that he remain part of the informal labor economy. In this sense, biology allows for the political claim while revealing the impossibility of any substantive belonging. This forces us, again, to face how biology can offer hope while also keeping strict limits on the actualization of these hopes; the danger, in Boris's case, is that it could leave him even worse off.

While in Western liberal democracies—or rather, in a privileged sector of these societies—biology may no longer be imagined as destiny, being bound up with general norms of enterprising, self-actualizing, and responsible personhood, those who belong are now distinguished from those who do not by a different imagined relationship to their biology. As I suggested, the illness clause is based on an imagined notion of the biological fixity of immigrants. And this takes on added significance as a postcolonial condition when it is noted that those who come in for papers are primarily from former French colonies. In the time I was doing research, the largest group of claimants came from Algeria, then from Mali, Morocco, and Congo-Zaire.[11] Here—rather than grapple with colonial histories—racial, political, and economic inequalities are mapped onto the body, enabling what Ann Stoler (2001) has called "colonial aphasia"—an occlusion of knowledge about the relationship between empire and immigration, race and nation. Indeed, because many immigrants confront a regime of truth that understands them as simply immutable biological bodies, and hence essentially "other," they enter into the strange situation of being exemplary liberal individuals, but with essentially illiberal choices. Insofar as most strands of liberalism find the idea of willed maiming abhorrent or aberrant (Breckenridge and Vogler 2001), examples such as willed infection, which take advantage of biology as a resource to be manipulated, are labeled "uncivilized," rather than being seen as enterprising. And in this manner, immigrants are categorized as "other."

The United States

As we have seen, the links between humanitarianism, biology, and immigration are not limited to the French situation: humanitarian NGOs in the United States also work in this nexus. The United States clearly has a different relationship to health and to biology than does France, which has a history of mixing the social and medical, from ancien régime hospitals to contemporary universal health care. In the United States, migrants have consistently been desired as laborers but largely excluded from public benefits, especially health benefits, which have been either contradictory or nonexistent (Hoffman 2006). For instance, California Proposition 187, proposed in 1994, required doctors to report suspected aliens rather than to treat them. Strikingly, in the French case, an immigrant can have the right to health, without the right to work; in the United States, an immigrant may have the right to work without the right to health. Up until January 4, 2010, in the United States, HIV-positive immigrants were excluded or deported rather than taken care of. That is, so-called aliens infected with HIV/AIDS were prohibited from entering the United States.[12] Even low-income, unemployed, or marginally housed citizens who are HIV-positive cannot get assistance with housing or social services unless their T-cell count goes below 200, which means five to ten years after infection. In the American context, it is easy to see how immigrants and those considered second-class citizens blend into a global underclass, governed by a logic by which biology is their key resource, one which is increasingly commodified.[13]

The United States and France also have different histories of incorporating immigrants into their fold. The French hold on to the idea of republican citizenship—a particular incarnation of universalism, sees that everyone has the potential to be equal, to be assimilated as citizens of the Republic. Yet what is now termed "the immigrant question" in France, which puts immigration at the center of political debate, is grounded in post–World War II migrations from the French colonial empire. France's relationship to its immigrants is shaped in large part by the tension between its republican ideas of universal equality and inclusion and the bitter legacy of French colonialism. Jean-Marie Le Pen, leader of the extreme right-wing party, le Front National, who came in second in the 2002 presidential elections, has successfully mobilized the hatred and bitterness from this colonial history to push for "zero-immigration" policies. With Sarkozy's entry into power in 2007, this trend has been furthered in the language of "law and order." Yet there is still an underlying ideological commitment to universal equality. In this sense, contemporary medical humanitarianism continues in the footsteps of one of its predecessors—colonial humanitarianism—in fixing the problems caused by the deferral of the application of universal ideals. Medical humanitarianism has particular appeal in France even in the realm of immigration insofar as it is a revamped universalist project, grounded in the idea that all people have equal dignity by virtue of their membership in humanity.

The United States, on the other hand, is not haunted by this history of universalism; rather, a model of pluralism has shaped its relationship to immigrants and immigration. The United States is considered a nation of immigrants, yet there is a complex relationship with migrants who enter its territory—they are simultaneously celebrated and denigrated, desired and yet excluded by forms of nativism (Coutin 2003). And rather than colonialism, the history of the post–World War II, Cold-War era national security state sets the stage for contemporary immigration policies, that is, where national security and imperialist ventures get conflated and the protection of borders simultaneously requires proactive containment. This has now been renovated for a post–September 11 world into what De Genova calls "the Homeland Security State" (2007:422), with its focus on the "securitization of immigration" as Bigo notes (De Genova 2007:423). The context for the current relationship between biology and immigration in the United States includes increasingly restrictive standards for welfare eligibility and a restrictive immigration act passed in 1996 that was subsequently reinforced by September 11, 2001. Here, a politics of immigration has in many ways been replaced by a regime of security that puts immigrants and asylum seekers straight into detention centers. Studies in the New York City area have shown that 75 percent of asylum seekers are hand-cuffed upon arrival,[14] and because detention centers are overflowing, asylum seekers are held in county jails, alongside convicted criminals. It is in this context in the United States that humanitarian organizations—which also have an increasingly global presence, including greater numbers of operational offices in Western nation-states, such as the MSF-USA office, which has changed from a fund-raising to an operative office—have started to play a more important role in the government of immigrants and refugees, seeing the increased need for emergency health measures.

Obviously, humanitarianism is not a blueprint form of intervention imposed identically in each context; it takes shape in the intersection of global, national, and local discourses and practices. For instance, particularly since the dismantling of welfare in the United States in the 1980s and 1990s, charity plays a much more important role in governing those who are marginalized or disenfranchised; as part of this, religious organizations—charities, social service organizations, and congregations—have been critical players in the nongovernmental management of both immigrants and citizens.[15] The role played by biology for immigrants is inevitably different then, since charities are not simply focused on medicine or health. In this sense, the humanitarian organizations I made contact with in the United States focused more on asylum seekers and detention centers and less on regular health care, since of course lack of health insurance is an issue for so many millions of Americans. Thus, in an interview with a representative from MSF-USA (US section of Doctors Without Borders), I was told that while perhaps concerned about the working poor, MSF could not intervene to help them, as this would entail a political program, not an exclusively medical one. A possible project, however, might involve setting up water tanks for those sitting on the US-Mexico border—this is a critical health issue. Similarly, while being more explicit about feeling that immigration policies are unjust, HealthRight International (formerly Doctors of the World-USA) also shies away from any explicitly political action, feeling that if they did not do so, they would risk their access to detention centers where they are able to intervene on the issue of basic health conditions. Yet, the growing part HealthRight International plays in regulating immigrant and asylum status in the United States is revealed by the fact that they have had to massively expand the program since its inception in 1993. In addition, they have expanded the number of categories for which they can write medical affidavits (for trafficking, domestic violence, forced abortion, rape, FGM, and so forth), revealing that they are increasingly medicalizing—or perhaps humanitarianizing—the field of asylum.

Humanitarian organizations never govern explicitly; they act on the level of the everyday, prioritizing emergency or crisis situations. However, what is considered to be a "crisis" changes according to the context. Thus while immigrant bodies may be read differently in the United States—illness evoking less compassion than in France—my research shows that they are still governed by the same humanitarian regime in which biology reveals a truth that words cannot. In both cases, this truth is revealed using the techniques of biomedicine, despite the fact that different manifestations of biology are drawn on as evidence: rather than as pathology or as illness, as in the French case of immigration, anatomical evidence is what is significant in claims for asylum in the United States. Several different pamphlets advertising the Human Rights Clinic of HealthRight International exemplify this logic: one photo from the cover of one of their pamphlets features the scars on a man's back, obscuring his face, while two female health professionals—one white, one of Asian origin—are pictured head-on. He is a person of color, but he is faceless, his origins unclear; his scars are what count, not who he is, nor where he comes from (see Figure 8.1). Nothing further about him is mentioned in the pamphlet itself. Similarly, we see another man of color featured on the cover of *field notes*

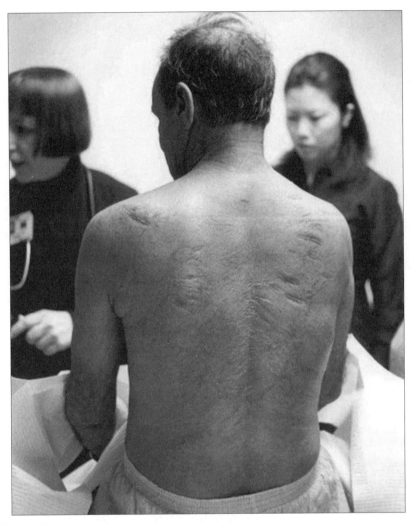

FIGURE 8.1.

Image from the cover of a HealthRight International pamphlet, advertising the Human Rights Clinic. Photo courtesy of HealthRight International (formerly Doctors of the World-USA).

newsletter published by HealthRight International (when it was still Doctors of the World-USA) in 2003; this time he is shown head-on, but he is pulling up his sleeve to reveal his arm—the focus is on his body, on what it can tell us. The racial distinctions between refugee and volunteer are marked. Here, while illness may not count in the same way, disfigured anatomy certainly does.

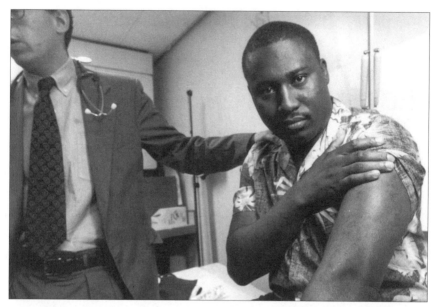

FIGURE 8.2.

Image from the cover of field notes *newsletter published in 2003 by HealthRight International, advertising the Human Rights Clinic. Photo courtesy of HealthRight International (formerly Doctors of the World-USA).*

As a lesson in keeping to this logic, I attended a training session given by HealthRight International (formerly Doctors of the World-USA) that involved a doctor describing a situation in which he examined an asylum seeker who claimed to have been tortured. The asylum seeker, whom the doctor described as from somewhere in Africa, had scars on his chest that he claimed were the result of torture by acid burn. The doctor explained to us that on closer examination, he wondered about the symmetry of the marks; he did some research and found that, in fact, the scars were tribal markings. He told the story to explain that one cannot rely on the narratives of asylum seekers but must follow medical science if doctors are to keep their legitimacy, examining the body to support or falsify the story. In the same vein, a carefully documented article by three doctors who volunteer for HealthRight International (formerly Doctors of the World-USA) explains how to best read and mobilize clinical forensic evidence such as scars in medical evaluations for asylum seekers; their goal is to help refugees.[16] I want to make clear here that my purpose here is not to pass judgment on the claim, or any of these claims, but to point to and examine the larger field that produces such actions on the part of the doctor

—who is interpellated as gatekeeper or guard—and the asylum seeker, who must play the role of impersonator or imposter. Again, as with Fatou, the case is one in which the idea of fraud does not explain all elements of the story. Here, the asylum seeker could still have been tortured, but he acted according to a logic that assumed his story would be much more likely to be believed if it was inscribed on his body. He made use of scars to reveal this truth. The doctor, for his part, patrolled this notion of truth and trained his counterparts to do the same.

This regime of truth recalls the relationship between slaves' bodies and torture, as described by Page duBois in her book on fifth-century Athens. The slave's body is constructed as a site of truth, according to Aristotelian logic: "Truth is constituted as residing in the body of the slave; because he can apprehend reason, without possessing reason" (1991:68). The body is a source of authentication in situations where the subject is conceived of as unable to provide a reasoned, spoken truth. In his analysis of trauma and memory in the context of South Africa, Allen Feldman places duBois's text in a longer line of analyses of slavery in the United States, where he suggests there is a cultural logic of testimonial authentication in the body; for instance, he looks at the famous "Ain't I a Woman" speech given by Sojourner Truth, who also resorts to a testimony of the body (2004:189). Similarly, I am suggesting that truth for immigrants and refugees, as members of an underclass, is found in "the primordial landscape of the racialized body" (Feldman 2004:190), both designating and producing them as "other," as beyond and outside reason.

Following this logic, in the contemporary American context, medical affidavits are increasingly important—according to an immigration lawyer in New York City, one almost needs to have physical evidence or a doctor's testimony in order to get one's claim accepted.[17] The lawyer told me that now that immigrants and refugees have access to medical services through humanitarian NGOs, judges expect "richer evidence." Indeed, humanitarian organizations have systematized the ability to access medical evidence; before, this lawyer said he had difficulty getting physicians to write affadavits and would turn to university psychology or psychiatry departments. Of cases with a HealthRight International Human Rights Clinic affadavit, 85 percent are granted immigration relief, as compared to the national average of 23 percent (Stadtmauer, Singer, and Metalios 2010). It raises the bar for everyone. This reveals, therefore, how humanitarianism has changed the way that refugees are understood, and regulated. While citizenship is the goal here, unlike the French case, it implies that in both places there is little room for the immigrant or refugee to be anything other than a non-Enlightenment, premodern subject, whose body—not words—is legible.

CONCLUSION

Now I want to bring these pieces together. With the entry of a right-wing government in France in 2002, the illness clause came under attack by then–interior minister (now president) Nicolas Sarkozy and his new "*loi sécuritaire*" (security law).[18] Increasing numbers of claims led to suggestions that both immigrants and doctors were acting fraudulently; those getting papers were not seen as valid humanitarian subjects, but rather as politically motivated actors. This reveals that humanitarian subjects cannot be seen to be modern liberal individuals; they cannot appear to be enterprising, nor politically embedded.[19] They cannot engage in corporeal self-fashioning in the way that citizens do in the regime of biological citizenship depicted by Rose and Novas. Interestingly, while modern liberal sensibilities still recoil from willing engagement with suffering, as Talal Asad (2003:121) has noted, in this case, it is not clear that the state is recoiling from cases of willed infection or purposefully prolonged illness; what seems most problematic for the state is that these people are manipulating their own biology, so that their bodies are no longer legible. In other words, the disruption is epistemological: the regime of truth has been disturbed, and the state no longer knows how to recognize and understand the "other" in its midst.

The relationship between the political economy of hope and biology for immigrants cannot be separated from the fact that government in the form of humanitarianism works primarily in the idiom of health; it seeks to isolate and address threats to lives and well-being. Doctors Without Borders/MSF, HealthRight International (formerly Doctors of the World–USA), and other humanitarian organizations do this by focusing on biology in a minimal sense—they often focus on survival, but without its social component.[20] Yet in so doing, they never isolate or protect this minimal or "bare" life (Agamben 1998); rather they serve to produce a particular form of political or governable humanity. The result is often diseased, disabled, or biologically compromised citizen-subjects and a continued racialized division between the humanity of the elite and that of the underclass couched in biological terms.

Let me sum up. I have argued here that we are all subject to a new political economy of hope linked to biology and to new biotechnologies. However, by broadening the context to think about what this political economy means, and the different circuits of capital and labor it is connected to,

I have suggested that we need to understand that the stakes can be higher and the picture perhaps starker depending on one's positioning. In this sense, while the hope might remain the same, there is nonetheless a distinction between those whose biology is their primary resource and those for whom biology is still one of *many* potential arenas in which one's recognition—as a legal, moral, cultural, social, and economic actor—can be enacted and claimed. Or, in Lawrence Cohen's (2004a) terms, people must be understood as differently "bioavailable," a term he uses to describe the likelihood for a person or population that its tissues may be disaggregated and transferred to some other entity or process. We can broaden this term to mean the likelihood that one needs to use biology as a primary resource. Hope takes shape in the space of these material realities. Indeed, by looking at this regime of biopolitics, we see that the will to health must be distinguished from the will to biological integrity; the will to health embraces an overall well-being that may not be identical with—and may even be in opposition to—the will to biological integrity. This is particularly true if we follow Bauman's argument that the modern liberal subjects that Rose and Novas describe require the production of excess, surplus, "wasted humans." Well-being for one inevitably circumscribes the well-being of the other.

Circuits of migration from the global South to the global North—or from the underclass to positions of privilege—might then predictably involve biology, seeing as it may be one of the few resources available; yet insofar as humanitarianism increasingly performs the techniques of government, targeting certain disenfranchised populations including immigrants, humanitarianism manages the ways that biology is leveraged. And as humanitarian subjects, immigrants' biology only has value when it is perceived as pure, untouched; it gives them access to the circuits of wealth and privilege only insofar as it does not reveal them as modern political subjects. Biology therefore plays a fundamentally different role in their relationship to the nation-state, due to the mediating influence of humanitarianism. And here, I think, biological involution could take on a different, more powerful meaning, related not only to the individual physical returns, but to the spiraling effect on the host societies of the global North; while biology provides hope for a better life, this biopolitics of immigration refuses inclusion or recognition under conditions of equality, which in this case would mean recognizing that immigrants are also self-enterprising subjects, able to engage and fashion themselves and to actualize their aspirations and desires. Recognition is given instead to subjects of humanitarian regimes as victims, as nonmoderns. This can only have diminishing returns, both in terms of future possibilities and sense of self for immigrants and for a society built on the principles of equality for all. And while immigrants may have escaped the redundancy of the new "wretched of the earth," recognition only comes as the necessary "other" against which the privileged of the West, or the global North, may continue to define themselves.

Notes

1. HealthRight International (formerly Doctors of the World-USA) was "Doctors of the World-USA" when I conducted most of the research for this essay. It changed its name in 2009. In the rest of the essay, I refer to it in its present incarnation, as HealthRight International (formerly Doctors of the World-USA), as requested by the organization itself.

2. See, for instance, "An Analytical Approach to Clinical Forensic Evaluations of Asylum Seekers: The HealthRight International Human Rights Clinic," by Gary J. Stadtmauer, MD, Elizabeth Singer, MD, Eva Metalios, MD. The article is also available on the HealthRight website: http://www.healthright.org/news/feature-stories/detail/hrc-study-10, accessed February 13, 2010.

3. For other work on how the body functions as a site of truth, particularly in the case of asylum seekers or refugees, see Fassin and D'Halluin 2005; Malkki 1996.

4. Unfortunately, in the limited space I have here I cannot do justice to these various insightful and distinctive approaches to the relationship between biology and citizenship: in addition to Petryna and Rose and Novas, Vinh-Kim Nguyen describes what he calls "therapeutic citizenship," which he defines as "claims made on global social order on the basis of a therapeutic predicament" (2005:126), while Deborah Heath, Rayna Rapp, and Karen-Sue Taussig (2007) describe "genetic citizenship"—a new form of technosocial engagement where emergent forms of public discourse take place related to identities and subjectivities inscribed at the molecular level. Nancy Scheper-Hughes (2002) has talked about "medical citizenship" while João Biehl has written about "biomedical citizenship" (2001) and "patient citizenship" (2007) in the context of AIDS in Brazil. Didier Fassin (2001a) provides an analysis of the links between biology and citizenship in France using a slightly different concept, "biolegitimacy." Finally, Stephen Collier and Andy Lakoff (2005) describe the relationship between citizenship and biology as "a counter politics of sheer life."

5. Rose and Novas take this term from Catherine Waldby in her study of the "Visible Human Project," where it refers to the ways that bodies and tissues derived from the dead are redeployed for the preservation and enhancement of the health of the living (2000:30).

6. Geertz's original notion of involution referred to "an overdriving of an

established form in such a way that it becomes rigid through an inward over-elaboration of detail" (1963:82).

7. This has been dubbed "Fortress Europe" in the European context, where there is a growing number of viable groups on the far right who ground their political platforms on an anti-immigrant rhetoric. This phenomenon began well before Le Pen's second place finish in the French elections of 2002: Austria's Jörg Haider led the way by creating a right-wing coalition in February 2000, with Italian Silvio Berlusconi following suit not long after. The murder of far-right anti-immigrant candidate Pim Fortuyn in the Netherlands on May 6, 2002, did not deter Dutch voters from voting for Party Pim Fortuyn. Denmark, Spain, Portugal, Switzerland, Belgium, and Germany all have substantive extreme-right xenophobic parties that threaten to enter into coalition governments, if they haven't already. "Immigration, asylum seekers, crime and security" have together become a mantra that accompanies talk by and about the far right, touted as the cause of the political shift.

8. See Didier Fassin (2001a and 2001b) for work on this topic; I thank him for bringing the illness clause to my attention. For a more explicit analysis of the illness clause, see also Ticktin 2005, 2006a.

9. Direction Départementale des Affaires Sanitaires et Sociales or Departmental Directorate of Social and Health Welfare.

10. See Didier Fassin's (2001b) article about immigrants with HIV/AIDS, where he describes how HIV/AIDS can function as a political condition before it is experienced as an illness.

11. This list comes from the regional state medical office with the largest number of claims for papers. The statistics from the year 2000 showed the Ivory Coast as next on the list, followed by Cameroon, Tunisia, and China; Pakistan, Haiti, and Yugoslavia; and finally, Senegal. French colonies made up well over 80 percent of claimants.

12. This changed when the Centers for Disease Control and Prevention (CDC), within the United States Department of Health and Human Services (HHS), amended its regulations to remove "Human Immunodeficiency Virus (HIV) infection" from the definition of "communicable disease of public health significance." Those requesting papers no longer have to undergo a medical examination testing for HIV. Prior to this final rule, "aliens" with HIV infection were considered to have a "communicable disease of public health significance" and were thus inadmissible to the United States according to the Immigration and Nationality Act (INA). See Federal Register/Vol. 74, No. 210/Monday, November 2, 2009/Rules and Regulations. http://www.immigrationequality.org/uploadedfiles/E9-26337.pdf, accessed February 20, 2010.

13. See, for instance, "'Come back when you're dying': The Commodification of AIDS among California's Urban Poor" by Crane, Quirk, and Van der Straten

(2002), which discusses how for low-income, marginally housed, and former or active substance users, a diagnosis of HIV-positive or of AIDS could result in improved quality of life by allowing access to subsidized housing, food, and services. In this case, they argue that an HIV/AIDS diagnosis operated as a commodity.

14. See "From Persecution to Prison: The Health Consequences of Detention for Asylum Seekers," a report by Physicians for Human Rights and the Bellevue/NYU Program for Survivors of Torture, Boston and New York, June 2003.

15. For the management of immigrants and asylum seekers, see, for instance, Susan Coutin (1993) on the Sanctuary movement and the role churches played in helping undocumented immigrants. See also Omri Elisha (2008) on evangelical faith-based activism.

16. See "An Analytical Approach to Clinical Forensic Evaluations of Asylum Seekers: The HealthRight International Human Rights Clinic," Gary J. Stadtmauer, MD, Elizabeth Singer, MD, Eva Metalios, MD (2010).

17. Interestingly, and perhaps as evidence of a transnational logic, Fassin and D'Halluin write that the same goes for asylum claims in France: the number of medical certificates issued as part of applications for asylum doubled from 1990 to 2000, as recorded by the institution the Comède (2005:599).

18. See the published circular of May 7, 2003, which adapts the previous immigration law; in particular, see Section 2.2.3 on "The Case of Sick Foreigners" (La situation des étrangers malades).

19. As Dr. James Orbinski, who accepted the prize for MSF, stated in his Nobel lecture, "For MSF, this is the humanitarian act: to seek to relieve suffering….We affirm the independence of the humanitarian from the political."

20. This has recently changed at HealthRight International (formerly Doctors of the World-USA); as part of their new identity adopted in 2009, they focus on sustainable forms of development and engagement with local people.

PART IV

Political Limits and Stakes

The last part of this volume begins with Ilana Feldman's chapter, which provides a historical perspective on the liminal boundaries between humanitarian relief and development initiatives. Focusing on responses to the 1948 displacement of Palestinians in the Gaza Strip, a key early (and long-lasting) case of contemporary humanitarianism, she concentrates on the organization CARE and its operations in Palestine between 1955 and 1967. Feldman traces what she calls the "humanitarian circuit"—relations between donors, relief organizations, and recipients of aid through the medium of assistance technologies—and analyzes the nodes formed by a particular form of giving. We learn that as CARE's work in Gaza continued, its focus shifted from emergency relief to a self-help model of development, resolving problems of governance into those of fostering a properly self-fashioning subject (parallel with Hyde's chapter in this volume). Feldman's particular case provokes a critical temporal question: What does it mean when a humanitarian crisis extends into a more permanent condition, as in the case of Palestinian refugees in Gaza? Here, the temporary strategy of relief encounters longer-term questions of development. Debates at the inception of CARE's work in Gaza about the terms of its engagement held implications for the future, defining who constituted an appropriate recipient of aid amid the continuing deferral of a political settlement. As CARE transitioned from relief to development in Gaza, its care packages were translated into an array of humanitarian kits (educational, medical, carpentry, midwifery, fisherman's, recreation, shoemaker's, dental, agricultural) that both expressed the specificity of purpose for gifts in order to ensure results and concretized compassion. For CARE, founded on a business model involving the selling of food packages (care packages), donors were customers. The transmittal of care packages in relief settings involved the tracking of donations and provision of receipts. The promise of a guarantee in exchange for the gift was a central part of CARE's strategy of relief provision. In the context of the 1950s, fresh from the triumph of the Second World War, CARE saw giving as both a natural American desire and an essential responsibility of post-war American citizenship. CARE sought to foster international civic responsibility by encouraging Americans to take up the mantle of global citizenship through donation. This particular conception of the gift involved a strong sense of return in the form of moral and fiscal responsibility: donors gave to CARE with specific intents for their gifts and with the expectation of accountability from the organization and from its beneficiaries. Feldman's chapter thus brings us back not only to the relationship between development and relief (Englund) but also to the fraught topic of gifts, echoing the question of what it means to be a proper donor (Benthall, Bornstein) and a proper recipient (Ticktin, Hyde).

Mariella Pandolfi explores another key liminal boundary of humanitarinism: the "gray zone" between violence and humanitarian response. Examining the blurring of humanitarianism and war amid NATO action in Kosovo, she argues that a perennial state of exception has emerged through the militarization of humanitarian aid, enforcing the reliance on national and international armed forces in post conflict zones. The "haze of humanitarianism" serves as moral camouflage to hide the implications of actions. How is it, Pandolfi wonders, that military humanitarianism through NATO both bombs Serbia and Kosovo and offers humanitarian aid to the resulting massive influx of refugees? In this deterritorialized managerial space of military humanitarianism marked by badges and professional accreditation, membership in an international organization becomes the most crucial operative identity. The mobility of humanitarian personnel accelerates during states of emergency even as the mobility of citizens, civilians, and refugees faces roadblocks and restrictions. Only by paying close attention to the bureaucratic apparatus of humanitarianism in war zones, Pandolfi suggests, can one see past its rationalization. She finds herself a witness to small acts that victims of catastrophes display for humanitarian workers in the international circuit, asserting history, memory, and continuity in the extreme circumstances of war. Pandolfi contrasts such small acts of dignity to the assertions of moral political authority by the international community, where humanitarian programs mask their own unlimited duration and justify military presence—a condition Pandolfi describes as migrant, or mobile, sovereignty. Pandolfi (like Fassin, this volume) recognizes that the humanitarian actors in this apparatus are not simply uncritical but rather offer their own self-critiques. Pandolfi's ethnographic account, however, adds a critical self-reflexive dimension. Her research in Kosovo triggered childhood memories of post–World War II militarized Naples, Italy, distorting the certainty of the present through the return of earlier category confusions and causing her to reflect, "How does one analytically interpret one's surroundings when the frame is one of disorientation?" Pandolfi suggests that this is a methodological question for ethnographers as well as a moral one for humanitarians. Evoking a longer, unsettling trajectory of the liberator who simultaneously occupies, she calls for an "ethnography of disorientation" to counter the relentless logic of military humanitarianism.

Both chapters in this part emphasize interstices and links between relief, development, war, and humanitarianism. By examining this greater architecture we begin to glimpse how aid-world humanitarianism can work to reiterate itself, ever temporarily, into something like a state of permanence and a natural response. As signaled at the outset of the volume, the questions it raises are rarely reducible to false intentions, poor techniques, or lack of accountability. Rather, the border zone humanitarianism straddles between ethics and politics poses less comfortable figures: aporia, Faustian bargains, and shades of gray. Thus it is only fitting to close on a note of disorientation.

9

The Humanitarian Circuit

Relief Work, Development Assistance,
and CARE in Gaza, 1955–67

Ilana Feldman

There are fierce debates among humanitarian practitioners about how
to define the boundaries of this form of action. The field is broadly characterized by a desire to "do good," a vision of intervention driven by ethical imperatives of human connection, and concern about the conditions in
which other people are living (Feldman 2007b; Li 2007; Fassin 2010b).
Beyond these commonalities there are tremendous disagreements about
whether humanitarian actors should seek to transform—to develop—the
places where they work or whether they should restrict their work to crisis
management (Redfield 2005; Slim 2000) as well as whether such work
should engage political questions and rights-based language (Rieff 2002).
As a way, not to adjudicate these disagreements, but to understand more
clearly the forms humanitarianism takes, I turn attention to a relatively
early moment in the elaboration of post–World War II humanitarianism. I
take as my site the Gaza Strip in the aftermath of the 1948 displacement of
Palestinians (known in Arabic as the *nakba* [catastrophe]) and as an organizational apparatus, CARE (Cooperative for Assistance and Relief
Everywhere), now a large and international development organization,
then a specifically American relief group. I highlight Gaza in part because

this is where I have long been engaged in research, but also because its particularly difficult conditions shed light on the challenges that face humanitarian actors more generally. CARE's history illuminates an especially broad swath of the humanitarian spectrum and therefore serves as a helpful entry point for exploring the difficulties involved in navigating this terrain.

CARE—originally the Cooperative for American Remittances to Europe—was founded to facilitate the delivery of food packages to Europeans in the aftermath of World War II and later transformed into a permanent body with the mandate to offer development assistance as well as emergency relief (and in the process becoming the Cooperative for Assistance and Relief Everywhere). CARE's work in Gaza in the years between 1955 (when it began its first project there) and 1967 (when the Israeli occupation of the Strip changed the dynamics quite significantly) provides an opportunity to explore—not the very first incarnations of postwar humanitarianism—but the shape that this field was beginning to take over time: both as it became clear that the Palestinian refugee problem would not be solved quickly and as CARE reconfigured itself into a permanent organization from its roots in crisis response. These transformations from "crisis" to "condition" and from "relief" to "development" shed light on the evolution of postwar humanitarianism and clarify some of what Didier Fassin (this volume) calls the aporias of humanitarian action.

In other writing on humanitarian aid to Palestinians I have examined both the wide-ranging effects of such aid on political community and social relations (Feldman 2007a) and the tremendous ethical dilemmas this work created for some providers (Feldman 2007b). Here, I further consider a third party in the aid dynamic: the donors—in this instance the American public as donors. Just as important as these assorted actors are changing technologies of assistance—technologies that serve as the conduit for relations among these parties. Mechanisms of assistance—which for CARE began first with the CARE food package and developed through to "self-help" projects and their related kits—not only reflect changing humanitarian goals, they create new demands on such organizations and therefore help shape them. Thinking about the humanitarian circuit—relations among donors, relief organizations, and recipients of aid, through the medium of assistance technologies—sheds light both on how humanitarianism was defining itself in the years after World War II and on how the differently located subjects of this form of action were shaped in this process of definition and transformation.

Exploring these transformations on the ground in Gaza shows a process that is crucially connected to the places and conditions within which humanitarianism takes shape, but which also has difficulty adequately incorporating or addressing these conditions in its practice. Although examining the nodes along this humanitarian circuit can clarify what is absent or unaccounted for within humanitarian practice, my primary purpose here is not to judge these projects to be successes or failures (though these were often the terms of the participants). Rather, I seek to understand more clearly how an international circuit of relations is produced through particular forms of giving, as well as what the consequences are for the participants. As CARE's trajectory makes clear, the humanitarian circuit is tremendously dynamic. Changing organizational goals demand and produce corresponding shifts in how the various parties to this network of relations are understood. Development assistance requires different kinds of knowledge and forms of distinction about the recipient population than does relief work. The latter asks about status (refugee or not? needy or not?), the former also about capacity (in CARE's terms: victims or indolent?). Similar differences can be found in regard to donors and providers. CARE's move from relief to development transformed not only what the organization did, but who the parties to its work were understood to be. Even as CARE felt strongly that it was a distinct kind of agency within the humanitarian field, its experiences reflect, and illuminate, broader trends in postwar humanitarianism.

As CARE developed, and as the displacement of Palestinians continued, the idea of self-help came to be a central feature of its humanitarian circuit. It became an important technique of intervention, a frame through which to evaluate Gazans and their governors and a key selling point for donors. The self-help of humanitarianism (or humanitarian development) was not quite the same as the self-help of social reform movements targeted at poor citizens in other places (Cruikshank 1999). It was not just subjects, but governments (in this case the Egyptian administration and local municipalities) that were its targets and which were judged in its terms. CARE's experiences with deploying self-help in Gaza indicate that finding "good" targets for such interventions cannot guarantee their success.

FROM CRISIS TO CONDITION: THE SPACE OF RELIEF

In 1948 approximately 750,000 Palestinians were displaced from their homes and an additional number were dispossessed of their lands even as they were not displaced. In the course of the war around the establishment of the State of Israel, many refugees fled to neighboring countries—most to Lebanon, Syria, and Jordan, some to Iraq and Egypt. Others sought refuge in parts of Mandate Palestine that were not incorporated into Israel:

the West Bank (shortly thereafter annexed to Jordan) and the Gaza Strip (administered, but not annexed, by Egypt). Faced with a widespread humanitarian crisis and acknowledging at least some degree of responsibility for the fate of Palestinians, the United Nations initially commissioned outside organizations to manage the delivery of UN-provided relief (the American Friends Service Committee in Gaza [AFSC], the League of Red Cross Societies, and the International Committee of the Red Cross in other places). As it became clear that an immediate resolution was not at hand, in 1950 the UN established its own organization to provide relief and (it was hoped) assistance toward resettlement: the UN Relief and Works Agency for Palestine Refugees in the Near East (UNRWA). Since then UNRWA has been the most significant source of humanitarian assistance for Palestinian refugees, but it has never occupied this field alone. Not only have the various "host countries" where refugees live provided support, numerous organizations—international, regional, and local—have contributed to the humanitarian field.

Gaza is a distinct space within the landscape of Palestinian displacement in a number of ways. It is part of historic Palestine—the only part not absorbed into another state after 1948. Consequently, its entire population is Palestinian—meaning that the negotiations between native populations and incoming refugees that are part of any displacement scenario were quite distinctive. Further, not only did refugees (200,000 to 250,000 people) and natives (80,000) share national identity, they shared the experience of loss, both in the sense that all lost their country and in the sense that much of the native population was dispossessed of their lands (which were in territory that became Israel), even as they were not displaced. These dynamics had important consequences for the aid regime that developed in this particular locale and were one source of the tremendous anguish that Quaker volunteers felt as they were mandated to assist only refugees and not the equally needy natives (Feldman 2007b).

However inadequate to the full scope of need, the work of the AFSC, and that of UNRWA which followed, helped transform conditions in the Strip from acute crisis to a more endemic condition. The provision of rations, housing, health care, and education (all part of UNRWA's mission) kept the refugee population alive, both physically and socially. At the same time, there was widespread recognition that this assistance was inadequate to enable people to lead full lives. Rations were insufficient; UNRWA regularly commented that it was unable to provide as many calories as would be ideal. A CARE report from 1959 notes that "of the 315,000 people now living in the Gaza Strip only about 40,000 have employment enough to support themselves."[1] Education without employment opportunities could only produce unfilled potential and social frustration. These conditions—in which almost the entire population was surviving on relief and "lack cash because...[they] get no money assistance from the United Nations [but rather] food enough to keep them alive (1500 calories daily) from UNRWA"—suggested that it was imperative to begin thinking beyond simple relief to more significant transformation of the economic environment. As UNRWA had already discovered, large-scale development projects were impossible in Gaza, due to both the massive overcrowding of the territory and the population's concern that such projects might be part of an effort at resettlement (*tawtin*) rather than return (Husseini 2000). It was in these circumstances that CARE began working in Gaza in 1955—first providing food assistance to natives who did not qualify for UN rations and later expanding into self-help projects that sought to promote some kind of development in the Strip.

FROM RELIEF TO DEVELOPMENT: THE CHANGING FACE OF CARE

At its creation CARE was a new sort of organization within the humanitarian landscape. It was a cooperative, composed of a variety of other organizations that continued to pursue their own work. It was organized along a business model, with a profit margin built into the cost of each package to be delivered—this margin was used to fund operations. Even as there were many religiously defined organizations in the cooperative, CARE came to see itself as part of an emerging secular humanitarianism, one that drew more centrally on a sense of the obligations of citizens than on religious commitments.[2] Indeed, in the early years it was a specifically American organization, one that saw its mission as connected to the position of the United States in the postwar world. So even as its initial mandate was carefully circumscribed—facilitating the delivery of person-to-person food aid—the implications of this new organizational style were potentially far-reaching.

According to a history of the early years of the organization written by a CARE employee (Charles Bromstein), the business model was a key part of its distinctiveness. Bromstein compared CARE to what he described as a typical kind of relief agency, which raises funds and uses whatever money is available after covering expenses to deliver relief—and therefore "takes no risk and has no possibility of loss."[3] In contrast, CARE sold packages with specific contents and with guaranteed delivery to the recipients or the money would be returned. The margin above cost would fund the organization's operations, but if volume was low or delivery unsuccessful, it risked bankruptcy: "CARE was completely new in that it had to operate as a business organization, although with a relief purpose. Its success or failure had significance beyond the immediate, since a totally new form of enterprise was involved."[4] Distinctive as it may have been at the time, the professionalization of relief work that this business style represented is where humanitarianism has gone in the years since (Barnett 2005).[5]

CARE's distinctiveness was sometimes a source of internal disagreement about the agency's purpose. Because CARE was a cooperative made up of a number of preexisting organizations, each brought a particular set of expectations to the arrangement. The major disagreement was about whether CARE should be a strictly short-term operation with the purpose of managing the delivery of package remittances only. Even though its charter envisioned the possibility of something more, including "rehabilitation and reconstruction,"[6] a number of its member organizations rejected this approach. As early as 1947, disagreement about the future of CARE created a crisis for the organization. In a meeting of the cooperative's members, a proposal that CARE move to a more general relief model (away from individually designated packages) was strongly contested:

> Charges were made that it did not indicate any understanding of the basic religious motivation of relief work; that CARE's overseas personnel were ill-equipped for such operations, having been selected on the basis of their training in the movement of merchandise and in administration rather than in the selection of needy individuals; that CARE, as a child of the member agencies, should not presume to compete with its own parents in activities in which they had a long and honorable record.[7]

These arguments indicate not only that there were deep divisions among the member agencies about what CARE could accomplish, but also that not every group that had signed on to become part of the cooperative accepted the new direction in humanitarianism that CARE represented. In contrast to the faith-based understanding of humanitarian motives expressed by some member agencies, CARE defined itself in secular, civic terms. Criticism of CARE for operating as a "business activity, paying high salaries and not drawing on those people who entered the field because of their own inner dedication" proved to be at odds with the emerging professionalization model in humanitarianism, which presumed that "doing good" requires efficient, effective delivery—skills that became in some ways more important than "inner dedication."

Despite these deep-seated disagreements, which meant that no decision was reached in 1947, the move toward general relief proved inexorable. From 1951 until 1956 a standing "Committee on the Future of CARE" provided a space for debate. The views expressed to the committee included: "I have always felt that CARE should serve for one specific function…the sale of relief packages" (from the War Relief Services division of the National Catholic Welfare Conference) and "CARE…should in all appropriate ways capitalize the good will that has been developed in meeting emergency relief needs and develop its potential in the field of rehabilitation" (from the Advisory Committee on Voluntary Foreign Aid, State Department).[8] In 1951 Paul French, CARE's director, commented that "since CARE was organized, world needs have changed. Initially, the individual package served a basic purpose and it still does at many points. The rehabilitation is becoming of increasing importance. We have tried to meet some of these needs with our Book Program, tools, plows and seeds."[9]

In 1955 the organization found itself in serious financial difficulties as a result of having grown more quickly than its fund-raising could handle. Given its business model and emphasis on nonprofit profitability, Paul French responded to this crisis by suggesting that it wind down operations. The board, however, rejected this proposal. After this point, it was clear that CARE intended to be a permanent agency with the mission of both general relief and "promoting self-help development in the Third World" (Campbell 1990:72). As it did so, it relied on both individual contributions and US government resources. The 1954 US Public Law 480, which provided government surplus food free of charge (Campbell 1990:69), was part of what made it possible for general relief to become a large part of CARE's operations. Those agencies that disapproved left the organization. As training materials produced in 1965 described CARE's transformation, the move from Europe to other parts of the world meant "the major shift from relief for war ravaged peoples to development assistance for peoples whose backwardness and poverty is oppressively general and perennial."[10] Much of CARE's development work was pursued under the banner of self-help projects—supplying equipment and materials to support initiatives that were indigenously run and staffed.[11] In becoming permanent, CARE became a new sort of organization.

"A GIFT FROM AMERICA": CUSTOMERS, CITIZENS, AND DONORS

The intersection of CARE and Gaza provides an opportunity to consider further the particular claims made by this organization and its style of aid delivery, not only on recipients, but on both potential and actual donors. It further illuminates what sort of return such donors may have received, or anticipated, from their gift. Humanitarian organizations provide a mechanism for people to concretize and channel compassion; they also make a demand that people feel such compassion, seeking to create it where it may not already exist. In order to compel care, organizations need to think carefully about how they address their audience. CARE addressed its contributors in three different registers: as customers, citizens, and donors.

Because the cooperative was founded on a business model that involved selling food packages (with profit required and loss possible), donors were always also customers. CARE's initial intention was to facilitate assistance between known individuals. An American would buy a CARE package to be sent to someone they knew in Europe. Central to its "customer service" was guaranteed delivery of these packages. As Wallace Campbell described in his personal history of the organization, each package was accompanied by an assortment of documents to track its movement, which "meant that Americans who sent CARE packages were getting documents to demonstrate that their gifts were being delivered" (Campbell 1990:111). The first innovation in CARE's procedure was to permit the purchase of "undesignated packages"—to be sent to anyone who was hungry, but the promise of the guarantee remained. The importance of the customer relationship was underscored in the response to a proposal to eliminate the signed receipt from general relief delivery. A CARE official suggested that this proposal had to consider very carefully the impact on "costs, public relations, our basic contract with the donor, and in fact the signed receipt, the very thing which made CARE different from all other agencies."[12] He further commented that this distinctive feature was a clear "selling point" and that the savings from streamlined operations might not match the "loss in business if the receipt were eliminated." As customers, people who gave to CARE needed to be satisfied by the relationship; as citizens they needed to feel responsibility for it.

In addressing the American public as citizens, CARE described giving as (1) a natural American desire, (2) an essential responsibility of postwar American citizenship, and (3) a tool that could help teach Americans how to occupy their new position on the global stage. As a retrospective on the organization's first fifty years put it: "CARE, which emerged in response to World War II, became the humanitarian manifestation of America's leadership role in the postwar world. If the conflict and its aftermath convinced Americans that the world needed their help, then CARE gave them a way to act on that belief" (Morris 1996:vii). In support of the idea that CARE should become a permanent body, the executive director of the Advisory Committee on Voluntary Foreign Aid (a presidentially appointed committee) suggested that "there are many ways in which CARE can be an expression of the desire of the American people to share with the people of other countries in the development of more orderly society."[13]

In 1953 Paul French highlighted the ways that giving could help teach international civic responsibility: "There is a basic function that is essential if the American people are to mature in their responsibility as citizens of one of the major world powers. CARE is in a unique position to be useful in meeting this problem because it is the only nonsectarian agency that can reach into communities across racial and religious lines and enlist real community support."[14] CARE could speak to Americans as citizens— regardless of individual background—and therefore could, it was hoped, speak more broadly to "the world" than could organizations that were explicitly tied to religious traditions. As training materials developed later put it, CARE provided "the chance to demonstrate outside the inhibitions of official channels, the very real concern of American people for the welfare of others less fortunate."[15]

In order for CARE to serve as an expression of American civic responsibility, it was of course necessary that Americans become donors—first in the form of buying packages and later in donation to either specific projects or to general relief. Wallace Campbell describes how, as the organization moved toward undesignated relief, "we made sure that when the package went out it included the name and address of the person who had made the contribution. The recipient...often sent a letter of thanks. This helped persuade a lot of donors to keep giving" (Campbell 1990:118). The records of CARE's work in Gaza show a significant degree of specificity in donor intentions—and a high degree of willingness on the part of CARE to keep the donor relationship personal even when people were not purchasing individual packages. Among the internal guidelines for determining which projects to pursue was that they should have donor interest: "Lack of donor appeal will not necessarily deny funds to an otherwise acceptable project, but mission personnel must be aware of the practical necessities of securing and maintaining the support of American and Canadian donors."[16]

As a regular matter, CARE sent letters to donors thanking them for their donations and describing in considerable detail the projects their contributions supported. When donors gave with a particular project in mind, CARE often involved them along the way. In 1961, for instance, a donor gave $100 with the expressed desire that it be used "to help provide Self-Help packages to Arab Refugee Camps in Gaza."[17] After some discussion it was decided there was no easy way to help the camps per se, but that the money could be effectively used to purchase several shoe-maker kits for donation to UNRWA: "This kind of help is one of the best ways that CARE, through UNRWA, can improve the refugees' situation."[18] Correspondence in reference to another donation shows just how closely donors were kept abreast of the dispersal of their funds. In this case, a donor gave $250 to support a citrus growing project—choosing this project from a list provided in a CARE appeal. When the vagaries of seed avail-ability caused a delay in the project, CARE asked the donor whether she minded waiting to have her gift applied or if they should redirect it to another purpose. She stuck with citrus. When the seeds were purchased for a cheaper price than anticipated, CARE sent her a receipt for the $180 pur-chase and noted that "we are holding the additional $70.00 for use in something that might complement the project as it develops. Should we find that additional money is not necessary, I would like to suggest another project to you at that time."[19]

In a more highly charged instance of accountability to donors, CARE felt compelled to offer the Illinois Lions group an opportunity to back out of their commitment to provide $4,000 for an eye clinic when it learned that—owing to Egypt's disavowal of Lionism once a branch was established in Israel—it would not be able to offer the customary public recognition (generally in the form of a plaque) of the donation. In the end, the Lions agreed to be anonymous donors, deciding that "the people that it was intended for will receive the benefits and after all we know who made it possible."[20]

Each of these ways of understanding who the people were who were giving to CARE and what the organization's responsibility was to them—as customers, citizens, and donors—speak to changing understandings of what CARE's guarantee meant, as well as what would constitute successful delivery. In order to clarify both these understandings and what was chang-ing, it is necessary to say more about how the recipients of CARE assistance were understood, as well as about the changing nature of CARE's inter-ventions. Among the questions for CARE and its donors were, what does it mean to be an American in the world? And, what sorts of obligations did that position entail? There was also a related set of questions at the other end of the circuit of giving: who were the proper subjects of assistance? (This question had been an especially charged part of the Quaker aid pro-ject [Feldman 2007a and 2007b].) And what were the obligations of receipt of such aid?

CARE IN GAZA: WHO WERE THE RECIPIENTS?

To explore the question of what it meant to receive, I turn directly to CARE's work in Gaza—where determinations about who to aid both highlight CARE's distinctiveness within the humanitarian field and illuminate the process of defining what it meant to be a recipient of assistance. Both relief and development required such definition, and the criteria were not the same. The United Nations aid apparatus, which was the largest humanitarian operation on the ground—not only in Gaza, but for displaced Palestinian populations more generally—was directed specifically at refugees. Native Gazans were not eligible for rations (though a small number did find their way onto the rolls), with the consequence that the aid regime had a deleterious effect on this population (Feldman 2007a). When, in 1955, the UN General Assembly confirmed that it would not expand UNRWA's mission to include the broader array of people who had been made destitute by 1948, other means to get aid to these people were sought. The Egyptian government had provided help without distinction in Gaza from the outset, though its resources were limited. In 1955 it requested CARE's involvement in a native assistance project. Using US surplus food, CARE began provisioning sixty thousand people from among the approximately eighty thousand-person native population.[21] This initial program was interrupted by the 1956 Israeli invasion and occupation of Gaza, though the Israeli government quickly turned to CARE for help in meeting the population's needs. After the Egyptian administration returned, the agricultural surplus program for Gaza was reinstated. CARE was proud of its efforts to feed "these often forgotten Palestinians"[22] and reported that because of this work, "CARE is regarded as the patron of the 'residents.'"

The kinds of distinctions that the UN made in regard to Palestinians were part of a broader trend in postwar humanitarian law, which developed a universalist refugee definition for the first time (Takkenberg 1998; Hathaway 1984) and which later proliferated additional categories—such as internally displaced persons (IDPs)—to account for those who did not fit into the first category but who were clearly in need of international assistance (Cohen 2006; Hyndman 2000). Those nongovernmental organizations that worked under the auspices of the UN, or with UN-supplied relief, were compelled to work within the confines of this emerging legal order. Other organizations, particularly those with financial independence, were able to pursue relief policies that followed more closely the principle of aiding those in need, without consideration for kind or category.

In a report on its work that CARE produced for "World Refugee Year"—a UN-sponsored effort in 1959 to call attention to the plight of refugees—it noted that the situation in Gaza challenged an easy definition of refugee. In a section entitled "Who Is a Refugee?" CARE addressed the problem that had confronted all aid agencies working with Palestinians:

> What about the people of Gaza who made their living there before 1948? They have not moved geographically, but in their position they require relief and rehabilitation no less than the Gaza refugee who formerly made his home in Palestine....Over the years various agencies dealing with these problems have worked out legalistic answers to them. But CARE, whose aim is to give aid whenever possible wherever it is needed, has never felt itself bound by these definitions. And so it may be that some of the people aided by programs which CARE has undertaken with displaced persons (and included in this report) would not all qualify as refugees.[23]

Indeed, the Gaza programs that the report highlighted were its efforts to improve water and electric power throughout the Strip, programs that would benefit the entire population. In a letter that accompanied this report, the director of CARE noted that the organization "has not been thought of as a 'refugee agency'" precisely because

> we are not restricted by legal definitions which often are so important in this work, we find that both refugees and non-refugees alike benefit from CARE's assistance, very frequently in the same program operation. Our agency does not "specialize" in any one segment of the population of stricken areas; its mandate is built upon meeting serious human need regardless of classifications.[24]

CARE touted its provision of assistance across a spectrum of need—from food to equipment—as well as the fact that "every contribution voluntarily made to CARE supplied a known specific item to a specific beneficiary." In describing the ways that its work could be particularly helpful to refugees, even if not directed specifically at them, it further stressed: "For those who have been forced to live for years in the hopeless setting of refugee camps, hope for the future must most often be based on the availability of tools and equipment for resettlement and training for economic self-sufficiency."[25]

This mention of economic self-sufficiency references the second major component of its projects—the development assistance that the organization referred to as self-help. Just as providing rations required a determination of who would receive such aid, so too did self-help. In this case, the determination had a great deal to do with perceptions of the capacity of the population to make use of the assistance. According to the guidelines that CARE developed for its self-help initiatives: "There is, first of all, the belief that many people in the underprivileged areas of the world are victims of circumstance rather than indolence, and that given the proper impetus, they are eager to improve their economic situation through their own efforts. Secondly, it is felt, the proper impetus to stimulate greater productivity is effective programming of necessary tools and equipment."[26] The guidelines further delineated the criteria for taking on a self-help project. The most crucial was need, and in responding to need, "emphasis should be on stimulating permanent improvement as against temporary relief."[27] CARE projects were also meant to be supplemental and should "strengthen existing programs of host governments and private agencies."[28] Equally important was ensuring both that the target populations were able to utilize the tools and that they should be required to contribute to the programs themselves. They had to have, that is, the "will to improve" (Li 2007).

Gaza was a difficult place in which to do development work. Certainly, it was impossible to imagine—as development projects frequently have (Ferguson 1990; Mitchell 2002)—that the problems which faced Gaza were nonpolitical or amenable to a simply technical solution.[29] The presence of more than two hundred thousand refugees in a sliver of land that had been home to eighty thousand people overwhelmed the resources of the area and was simply untenable. The problem was not only the influx of people, but the constriction of space. The Gaza Strip, it should be remembered, was a by-product of the 1948 war, before which this area was part of the much larger Gaza district of Palestine. Its economy was dependent on both the agricultural land that now lay outside of the Strip and on the trade relations with other populations and parts of Palestine. In large part due to this constriction of space, a CARE report noted, "Even if the 230,000 refugees leave, the strip can no longer support its own regular residents."[30] The report went on to suggest that "the alternative is migration to the less developed but rich Middle East countries that need qualified young people." Such migration did indeed become a central part of the Gazan economic landscape.

Despite all of the difficulties in doing development in Gaza, there were reasons that CARE thought this was a good place to try the self-help approach. Particularly, people in the organization seemed to hold the population in high regard, clearly viewing them as among the "victims" rather than the "indolent." As one report described: "In this backwater of humanity, the once proud and advanced Arabs of Palestine are caught, victims of circumstances they weren't able to control or even, in many cases, to understand."[31] Although this is clearly a somewhat tempered compliment, it does reflect a tendency in the reports from CARE's work in Gaza to see the population as somewhat more advanced than other "underdeveloped" peoples. A proposal to provide education kits and sewing machines for the Gaza municipal girls school noted that "Palestinian women are among the most intelligent and emancipated in the tradition gripped Middle East" and that "the awareness of the values of education that is found among Palestinian youth is impressive. It is a pity that these fine people have to suffer in their quest for betterment from the tense conditions which have clouded their lives for many years."[32] Another proposal contrasted this desire for education with other places: "In contrast to some other underdeveloped countries, there is no problem getting Gaza parents to send their children to school. In fact, they fight to get as much schooling as possible for their children."[33] This strong desire to improve their conditions, along with their already "advanced" status, would seem to make Gazans the perfect population for self-help initiatives. And indeed, the challenges of self-help projects in Gaza were not with the population's ability to utilize the assistance, but rather in the structural conditions that severely constrained the possibilities for significant development.

"RESULTS, NOT RECEIPTS": TECHNOLOGIES OF ASSISTANCE AND EVALUATION

The transformation in CARE's work from direct relief to more development-oriented work necessitated some changes in the mechanisms of assistance. Even as new products were introduced, CARE maintained its package style of aid delivery. CARE saw the "known specific item to a specific beneficiary" model as central to its success and sought to maintain this style even as it moved into more complicated programming. As its ambitions grew more expansive, however, measuring success became more challenging. In the early days, when CARE concentrated on the delivery of food packages, it was in fact the physical receipt of the package—documented by the paper receipt that returned to the donor—that marked the successful conclusion of the aid circuit. As the organization moved into self-help, the measurement became more difficult. To deem a project successful required not only that the aid arrive to the recipients, but that it have the desired effect.

In developing its self-help products CARE built on its experience with CARE packages—clearly defined products with known contents—to develop a series of standardized self-help kits that included the basic items needed to launch various projects. There were, for example, carpentry, educational, midwives', and fishermen's kits. Not only were these kits designed to meet specific programmatic needs, they helped donors continue to feel the direct and individual connection to the act of giving—not any longer through the personal identification of the recipient, but through the detailed knowledge of the particular implements that a gift might purchase. Among the materials CARE produced to advertise its programs was a booklet with pictures of various self-help kits, with a description of the contents and purpose of each kit and with the prices for each. Of the "elementary students kit," for example, it said: "The possession of the Kits, which are distributed in individual carrying cases to the children, swells the youngsters' pride in what they are doing and helps maintain and increase school attendance."[34]

As a technology of assistance, standardized kits have tremendous logistical value. As Peter Redfield describes in the context of MSF's increasing use of kits, they are versatile and facilitate rapid response to crisis. MSF's kits, he notes, "were designed to respond to situations of *crisis*…[and were not] part of an effort to reshape or capture economic terrain" (Redfield 2008c:162). CARE's kits, on the other hand, were precisely intended to provide tools to assist in such a transformation. Further, CARE's kits seem designed as much to speak to donors—providing a visual on the help they would be giving—as to assist the providers. The kits both concretized compassion—a feature of the CARE packages before them—and pointed toward the new kinds of measurements of success that were required in the move to development.

Recognition of the complexities of moving from relief to development is evident throughout the documentary record of CARE's work from this period. The concerns were acutely described in an internal report (undated, but apparently from 1965) on "giving for growth." The report tracks the changes in CARE's mission and suggests:

> In each phase of CARE's evolution there has been a demand for specific organizational competence. Designated food packages required a competence primarily relating to delivery; central

concern was given to accounting and receipting measures. The creation of non-designated standard hand tool kits required an additional concern for selection of recipients, and for training. The inclusion of the more complicated equipment into more involved projects placed a new emphasis on a new thoroughness and competence.[35]

The necessity for new kinds of competence did not arise simply from the increasing technical complexity of the projects, but from their aim to transform the quality and character of people's lives—that they were development, not simply relief. As the report argued:

By accepting the challenge of development, implicit in its major actions for more than a decade now, CARE also assumed new ground rules to measure its service. Effectiveness could no longer be measured merely by delivery and receipt. Since the act of giving can be definitely harmful in some situations, the need to maximize experience, to make critical evaluations and to incorporate these into organizational practices becomes highly important.

In what way did the report suggest giving could be harmful? If recipients did not understand the motives of the givers, resentment could arise. If ownership of the gift was not clarified in advance, conflict could develop. If the groundwork for the gift was not properly prepared, recipients might not see it as opportunity to innovate. The report argued that the systematic and careful evaluation of projects that was necessary to avoid these potential pitfalls was not yet in place:

The difficult task of administering private giving overseas for permanent improvement must be a hard-hitting, self-improving, professional enterprise. Compassion it must certainly have; self-immolating handouts it must avoid. CARE has a magnificent potential for the best of American giving abroad. That potential is not yet being fulfilled. The true value of assistance can only be measured in results, not receipts.

In an earlier stage the multiple pieces of paper that tracked every package from purchase to receipt distinguished CARE as an organization. In its new incarnation as a development organization it had to find other mechanisms for the CARE guarantee. Responding to these concerns, the program department designed elaborate guidelines for self-help projects, intended to ensure that such "results" would be forthcoming from these projects. Program design, implementation, and evaluation were each addressed.[36] To understand more clearly how evaluation evolved as CARE moved into the development arena, I turn back to Gaza and the self-help projects attempted there in the 1950s and '60s.

Self-help in Gaza

I have already noted that CARE provided education kits to schools. It also supplied carpentry kits, recreation kits, midwifery kits, shoemaker kits, training equipment for nurses, dental equipment, pumps for both drinking water and irrigation, and generators and other equipment to improve electricity in the Strip.[37] A 1959 request for support for agricultural hand-tool kits for an agricultural training center described the variety of factors that produced the need: "Apart from shortages of funds, which is endemic in these parts anyway, the schools were cleaned out by the Israelis when they moved out of Gaza. It's an uphill battle that is fought here against the forces of nature (the population is constantly swelling) and of nations." The proposal further noted that "the Agricultural Training School [ATS] was hit very hard. It reopened just six months ago after moving UNEF [United Nations Emergency Force] troops from the premises. This CARE representative was personally impressed by the Egyptian and Palestinian staff who operate the mission."[38] The proposal was approved, and fifty kits were provided to the ATS and other schools across the Strip.

Although this project appears to have been a success, the more complicated trajectories of both the water-pump and electricity project highlight some of the difficulties of doing development in Gaza. The water-pump project originated with a request from the director of the municipal and rural affairs department of the Egyptian administration in 1958. Describing conditions in Gaza City, the director related how before 1948 the water needs of the forty thousand-person population of the city were supplied by three pumping stations that operated ten hours a day.[39] After 1948, "the increase in population due to the influx of refugees and to a great number of them living in the town itself or spending the day there, has necessitated the addition of a new set and the doubling of the working hours of the pumps....With no stand-by sets, repairs to the machines is [sic] practically impossible and often a set comes to a standstill due to overwork and the water supply is cut from some quarters of the city."[40] The director noted that a new well had been dug, and what was needed to make it operational was a pump. This initial request was granted and ultimately the project was expanded to provide twenty-five pumps for irrigation water, too. The municipal pump project was deemed a success, provisioning the entire city with water and eliminating the need for private pumps to get water into rooftop tanks. As the concluding report on the project summed it up in 1961: "The best proof of the successfully completed project is that there is no discussion in the town anymore of a perennial water shortage. The memory of this shortage is fading from the citizens of Gaza."[41]

The irrigation pump project, however, could not be termed an unqualified success. There were problems from the outset in both implementation and communication. In 1962 CARE's Egypt director reported that "well over half of the very expensive 25 water pumps and diesel engines totaling over $90,000 sent to Gaza about a year ago are still lying unused."[42] A comprehensive account of the project in 1965 indicated that ultimately fourteen pumps were used for irrigation, seven were used to supply drinking water to rural areas and a refugee camp, and five or six were "subjected to scavenging." The report described both the successes and failures of the project. In the plus column the fourteen pumps used in irrigation had extended the growing time in areas that had previously depended on rain and had permitted the reclamation of sand dunes for agriculture. While the limited use of pumps for agriculture meant that the project had only realized 65 percent of its agricultural potential, the pumps supplying drinking water accounted for 35 percent of the rural water supply and "fifty thousand people depend on the CARE units for their only source of drinking water."[43] The report did object to the use of a pump for a refugee camp, not because it was frivolous, but because "I am not of the opinion that CARE should underwrite UNRWA responsibilities."[44] In 1965 the project could be called a qualified success, but by 1968 (on the other side of the 1967 war and the occupation of Gaza by Israel), few of the pumps remained in use. Of twelve pumps surveyed in September, only two were operational, and one of these was the original pump supplied to the municipality. The others had either broken down (and spare parts were very difficult to get), been neglected, or had been looted during the war. So this project, like many others, foundered in the face of the history of Gaza: both the wars that punctuated that history and the pressure of living in the unresolved aftermaths of such wars.

Unlike the water pump project, whose end result was the degradation of the pumps, CARE's electricity project succeeded in one sense—in that the equipment was deployed and lighting improved across the Strip—but failed in another—in that the hoped for outcomes of this upgrade were not achieved. When the governor general of the Gaza Strip asked for assistance in improving the electrical system, CARE representatives responded enthusiastically, seeing it as a "project which will be a *real* need contribution—more than that—a solution to many other needs."[45] The governor general identified five benefits of the project: lighting refugee camps and streets; improving water pumps in camps; improving industrial factories; making it easier for students to study; and improving irrigation pumps.[46] When CARE took on the project it focused on the industrial benefits as the most significant impact. In each of its reports on implementation this benefit was highlighted. The expectation was that there would be a quick development of light industries, including "a canning industry for oranges, grapes and fish, marmalade industry, refrigeration industry for fish."[47] In 1965, however, CARE concluded that "all equipment is working and the program is completed. The ultimate purpose of supplying this equipment was to encourage light industry (no pun intended) on Gaza, but thus far there have been no new developments. It has simply contributed to the consumption of electricity on the Strip."[48] Quite likely, it was experiences such as this that led to the conclusion, also in 1965, that "it is quite apparent, or should be by this time, that the Strip is dependent upon assistance. The frustrating part is that this assistance cannot be used in a way which leads to economic improvement and ultimately to self sufficiency because of the absence of economic potential."[49] Gaza, that is, could receive development assistance but could not be developed.

CARE's very careful thought about the different nodes in the aid circuit focused on donors, providers, recipients, and technologies. Much harder to really bring into project development, though not for lack of acknowledgment of its importance, were the broader conditions within which the work had to take place. A 1959 report on CARE's work in Gaza highlights this dynamic. Unlike the somewhat dejected assessment from 1965 quoted above, the 1959 report was quite upbeat: "After 11 years of economic torpor, the Gaza Strip is slowly beginning to grow and develop. Optimism, which is reflected all over the Strip, is a dominant sentiment in the area. New orange groves are being planted and equipped with expensive irrigation pumps."[50] And yet, even here, lurking problems were identified. The report acknowledged that the possibility for development and investment in the Strip was largely dependent on the security provided by the presence of UN peacekeepers along the border, without which "in 24 hours [Gaza] could even cease to exist as Arab territory with Arab inhabitants." Political factors were clearly recognized as factors that might impinge on success development, but there was no clear way to consider them as intrinsic to planning itself.

Even though it took another eight years, with the June 1967 Israeli occupation, for Gaza to cease to be governed as "Arab territory" (though it continued to have Arab inhabitants), by 1966 CARE was forced to acknowledge the severe limits on development imposed by the conditions of Gaza itself:

> Providing self-help has not been the main service of CARE in Gaza [which rather has been rations delivery]....Much has been done in the past decade, and a great deal needs to be done to bring the residents and refugees into even a token sharing of the benefits of modern times. The physical and political limitations on the people and the community make it most difficult for them to advance their economy....CARE will do its best to feed the needy and to lend a helping hand where the need is greatest.[51]

As the trajectories of the water and lighting projects made clear, in Gaza, self-help came to look very much like relief. Rather than commenting further on this particular report, which ended with a wish for "a better year with more hope for the people of Gaza" (and which came a little more than a year before conditions in Gaza were dramatically transformed by the Israeli occupation), it may suffice to note that in spring 2010—in yet another year where one was reduced to hoping for something better for the people of Gaza—of twenty-eight current projects in the West Bank and Gaza listed on CARE's website, six were identified as "development" projects and twenty-one as "emergency relief."

CONCLUSION

While some humanitarian organizations seek to maintain sharp boundaries between relief and development, CARE sees its responsibilities as lying in both domains. In this essay I have explored the process through which CARE moved from its initial relief mode into a permanent organization with a more expansive agenda. Gaza provides a helpful site for exploring these changes. As the Palestinian refugee problem began to acquire a long-term status, both sorts of assistance were deemed necessary for this place. At the same time, Gaza highlights some of the tremendous challenges in satisfactorily closing the aid circuit when aid is understood in this broader way. The mechanisms that CARE developed to try to ensure successful projects were imperfectly transferable to Gaza. As I have described, a key factor for CARE was a determination about the local population and government's capacity to utilize self-help assistance. Both Gazans and the Egyptian administration were judged highly in this regard and were complimented for their energy and skills. Nonetheless, many of the projects that were meant to help transform the Strip ended up looking more like relief projects by the time they reached their conclusion.

Although the reports and materials I described earlier emphasized the importance of finding the "right" recipients (the victims not the indolent) and preparing them properly to receive assistance, Gaza highlights the extent to which political conditions posed a problem for self-help. Gaza in the 1950s and '60s was not a place whose problems could be solved through development, the cultivation of further expertise, better understanding of the nature of "the gift" on the part of recipients, or more dedicated effort on the part of local bodies. Each of these requirements for successful programming existed. What was really needed for Gaza—and what is still needed now—was a political resolution to the already long-standing "refugee problem," the displacement and dispossession of the bulk of the Palestinian people.

CARE's experience in Gaza tells us something, not just about the challenges of this particular space, but about the dynamics of humanitarian action more generally. In the humanitarian circuit, assistance travels through networks of donors, providers, and recipients. The various forms such assistance takes further shape relations across this network—defining subjects in particular ways and demanding particular sorts of accounting and evaluation. Although the careful attention to "results and not receipts" that is a characteristic not only of development, but increasingly of relief as well, cannot guarantee such results, it does ensure that each of the participants in the circuit is closely described, observed, and attended to. Humanitarianism may not always be able to reach its target, but there is no doubt that it shapes its subjects.

Notes

1. CARE Archives, New York Public Library (hereafter CARE), Box 839, Discursive Reports, Egypt 1955–83, "Gaza Strip," n.d.

2. An internally produced history of the early years of the organization described the moment: "Relief work had for years been considered an almost exclusive province of religious denominations. The upheavals of the 1930's had led to the formation of a number of nonreligious agencies interested in specific areas and in political refugees, thus widening the field considerably" (CARE, Box 1, Charles Bromstein's *History of Care*, 1952, p. 18).

3. *History of Care*, p. 43.

4. *History of Care*, pp. 43–44.

5. Bromstein's history further indicates: "CARE's Board and staff are quite proud of the fact that the organization operates on business lines and uses every feasible modern innovation. Each aspect has been the subject of constant study, resulting in the application of machinery and procedures consonant with the most recent developments in the field, and frequently marking new and creative departures. The result of this effort is seen in the highly efficient organization capable of rapid expansion and contraction to meet seasonal needs, yet always functioning expertly and at comparatively low cost" (*History of CARE*, p. 306).

6. *History of CARE*, p. 45.

7. *History of CARE*, p. 203.

8. CARE, Box 6, Committee on the Future of CARE, 1948–51, letters dated December 13, 1949, and February 26, 1951.

9. CARE, Box 6, Committee on the Future of CARE, June 1951–56, Letter from Paul French to Members of the Future of CARE Committee, October 17, 1951.

10. CARE, Box 504, Program Department—training materials, 1965.

11. CARE, Box 504, Draft "Programs for Refugees and Displaced Peoples through CARE," October 1959.

12. CARE, Box 6, CARE Reorganization, September 1955–June 1956, Memo from Bernard Kerbel to Richard Reuter, September 2, 1955.

13. CARE, Box 6, Committee on the Future of CARE, 1948–51, Letter from Arthur Ringland to Paul French, February 26, 1951.

14. CARE, Box 6, Committee on the Future of CARE, 1951–56, Letter from Paul French to Members of the Future of CARE Committee, January 8, 1953.

15. CARE, Box 504, Program Department—training materials, 1965.

16. CARE, Box 504, Program Department, Résumé of Goals, Principles, and Guidelines of CARE Programming, n.d.

17. CARE, Box 291, #32–61, Refugee Camps UNRWA, Letter from Franklin Irving to Louis Hunter, January 31, 1961.

18. CARE, Box 291, #32–61, Program Proposal, February 27, 1961.

19. CARE, Box 291, #32–64, Orange Trees Production, Letter from Frank Goffio to Mrs. W. E. Wrather, October 13, 1964.

20. CARE, Box 281, #35–61, Dental Clinic for UNRWA,Letter from Lions to CARE, April 4, 1966.

21. CARE, Box 839, Discursive Reports, Egypt 1955–83, "The Gaza Strip," n.d.

22. CARE, Box 839, Discursive Reports, Egypt 1955–83, "CARE Activities in Egypt 1957–58."

23. CARE, Box 504, Draft "Programs for Refugees and Displaced Peoples through CARE," October 1959.

24. CARE, Box 504, Draft "Programs for Refugees and Displaced Persons through CARE," Letter from CARE Director to Bureau of Security Consular Affairs, US State Department, October 28, 1959.

25. CARE, Box 504, Draft "Programs for Refugees and Displaced Persons through CARE," Letter from CARE Director to Bureau of Security Consular Affairs, US State Department, October 28, 1959.

26. CARE, Box 504, Self-Help Programming, "CARE's Use of Tools in Self-Help Programs," n.d.

27. CARE, Box 504, Self-Help Programming, "CARE's Use of Tools in Self-Help Programs," n.d.

28. CARE, Box 504, Program Department, Résumé of Goals, Principles, and Guidelines of CARE Programming, n.d.

29. Though, it must be noted that somehow in the years since, it does seem to have become possible to talk about the West Bank and Gaza in these classic terms of economic development, terms that seem ridiculous in the face of the realities on the ground.

30. CARE, Box 839, Discursive Reports, Egypt 1955–83, "Self-Help Gaza," n.d.

31. CARE, Box 839, Discursive Reports—Egypt, 1955–83, "Gaza Strip," n.d.

32. CARE, Box 291, #13–58, Program Proposals, February 27, 1958.

33. CARE, Box 291, #22–58, Program Proposal, September 23, 1958.

34. CARE, Box 504, Booklet: CARE Equipment for Self-Help.

35. CARE, Box 504, CARE: Self-help Programming, "Summary of Ken Schneider's Report on Giving for Growth," n.d.

36. CARE, Box 504, Program Department—training materials.

37. The organization also turned down a number of proposals, including those for an egg incubator for a poultry project and a bulldozer for land leveling to increase farming capacity, when it felt the projects were too expensive, more properly provided by another party, and/or not likely to have success (CARE, Box 291 #12–37 and #11–57).

38. CARE, Box 291, #28–59, Program Proposal, March 11, 1959.

39. For more on water services during the British Mandate see Feldman 2008b.

40. CARE, Box 291, #26B–59, Report from Director of Municipal and Rural Affairs Department, October 31, 1958.

41. CARE, Box 291, #26A–59, "Progress Report: CARE Pump and Engine for Gaza Drinking Water," August 15, 1961.

42. CARE, Box 291, #26A–59, letter from CARE, Egypt, to CARE, New York, March 15, 1962.

43. CARE, Box 291, #26A–59, Evaluation Report, September 18, 1965.

44. These sorts of tussles over responsibility and jurisdiction were endemic. For more on this issue, particularly in relation to UNRWA and the Egyptian administration, see Feldman 2008a. Another pump was used to provide water for beach cabins for administration officials. CARE objected strongly to this but suggested the situation could be rectified by providing water to a nearby farmer. Whether this happened is not recorded.

45. CARE, Box 291, #26–59, Note from CARE Chief of Mission, Egypt, n.d.

46. CARE, Box 291, #26–59, Report on the Benefits of Changing the Present Electrical Voltage from Low to High Tension, February 2, 1959.

47. CARE, Box 291, #26–59, Program Proposal, September 21, 1961.

48. CARE, Box 291, #26–59, Notes from Conference, May 19, 1965.

49. CARE, Box 839, Discursive Report, June 1965.

50. CARE, Box 839, Discursive Reports, Egypt 1955–83, "Gaza Strip," n.d.

51. CARE, Box 839, Gaza Sub-Office Discursive Report, January 1966.

10

Humanitarianism and Its Discontents

Mariella Pandolfi

PROLOGUE

"Humanitarianism," John Tirman concisely reminds us, "has roots in war" (2003). This troubling kinship has become all too conspicuous over the past two decades with the emergence of a gray zone among conflicts, humanitarian aid, development, and security. Militaries metamorphose into armies of peace and/or humanitarian aid.[1] Multilateral institutions, with shifting mandates, manage crises with an urgency akin to that of war, present themselves as building enduring institutions and launching programs of "good governance" and "best practices," while in fact carrying out day-to-day policing and applying Band-Aids. NGOs, whether local or international, practice a parallel diplomacy, constantly remodeling and redefining their methods and objectives under pressure from donors, who in turn have their own changing priorities. This opacity, exacerbated and excused by an urgent need to intervene to save victims, perpetuates itself through a perennial state of exception, masked by the appearance of efficiency, which has grown with the recent militarization of humanitarian intervention and its reliance on the logistical infrastructures of national and international armed forces.

Like the fog of war, which obscures any higher purpose behind the immediate imperative to kill or be killed, the haze of humanitarianism hides the implications of its actions behind the immediate moral camouflage of saving lives. The purpose of the complex apparatus of humanitarian intervention is not to implement the long-term agenda of economic development; it is not the promotion of democracy; it is not advocacy for human rights. Its purpose is to provide an immediate response as dictated by the emergency imaginary with its emphasis on apparently sudden, unpredictable, and short-term explosions of suffering. "Emergency" is a way of grasping problematic events, a way of imagining them that emphasizes their apparent unpredictability, abnormality, and brevity and that carries with it the corollary that a response—intervention—is necessary. For some, intervention only consists of care—paradigmatically food, medicine, and shelter. Others add the duty to bear witness, an action short of a political response yet more than simply ignoring or refusing to judge the evils that occasion emergency. For still others, an international emergency both can and should be managed. One should use the best practices, methods, and technologies to alleviate as much suffering as possible.

In principle, this type of ambitious managerial response to emergency focuses on restoring order by alleviating as many threats as possible (see Duffield 2006, 2007). On the global scene, Bosnia, Kosovo, and Albania, where I have done fieldwork for over ten years, became emblematic steps toward the realization of contradictory apparatuses of humanitarian war, postconflict humanitarianism, and militarized pacification/democratization. These multiple scenes were, and still are, the post–Cold War political laboratories where paradigmatic forms of intervention take shape and become standardized, customized, and reusable.

SCENES OF WAR AT THE BORDER

The NATO bombardment of Pristina, of the outskirts of Belgrade, and of Podgorica began on March 24, 1999, a little after 8:00 p.m.[2] Only four days after the beginning of the war, at least sixty thousand refugees from Kosovo had found their way to Albania. On April 4, the Pentagon decided to send twenty-four Apache helicopters and two thousand soldiers to Albania, while at the same time starting an airlift for shipping humanitarian aid to the Kosovo refugees in Albania and Macedonia. During this same period, a few NATO countries had already declared that they were ready to "temporarily" provide for at least one hundred thousand refugees. On April 6, according to data provided by the United Nations High Commissioner for Refugees (UNHCR), 430,000 refugees had already left Kosovo or had massed at its borders. On April 7, Albania authorized the presence of

NATO forces in the country and, according to the UNHCR, the number of refugees from Kosovo had risen to 460,000.

On April 11, the NATO Council approved the "Allied Harbor"[3] operational military plan, which provided for the deployment of NATO troops to Albania in support of humanitarian assistance to refugees. On April 15, there were about 116,000 refugees from Kosovo in Macedonia. On April 16, another 50,000 refugees moved through the "corridors of terror" toward Albania to make it 320,000 refugees in that country, while the number of refugees in Macedonia hovered at around 122,000 with 75,000 more in Montenegro. According to the UNHCR, however, there were still about four hundred thousand to five hundred thousand individuals of Albanian origin in Kosovo. On April 17, the UN high commissioner for human rights, Mary Robinson, talked about "increasingly alarming" acts of violence and atrocities in Kosovo while, according to NATO, eighteen villages had been set ablaze with more than two hundred residential areas considered "seriously damaged" in the course of the preceding three weeks. On April 18, the number of refugees from Kosovo had risen to 711,000 according to the UNHCR, including the 170,000 who had fled before the intervention by NATO.

In the following days another 24,000 refugees from Kosovo entered Albania and Macedonia, bringing the total number of refugees to 735,000. On April 25, most of the Apache helicopters sent by the Pentagon arrived in Albania. Two days later, about a month after the war had begun, the UNHCR stated that there were 590,000 refugees in Kosovo's neighboring countries. In Macedonia the camps were full to the brim, while another two thousand refugees had entered Albania by way of the Morini border crossing. The bombardments and atrocities continued for the whole month of May. On June 8 the bombing campaign halted in anticipation of a peace treaty to be signed. Finally, on June 11, with the entry of contingents from the various countries belonging to the Alliance into Kosovo, the war was officially over. That same year, the International Criminal Tribunal accused Milosevic of crimes against humanity. He died in 2006, before the end of his trial.

The foregoing litany is a basic chronology of the three months of war in Kosovo. Related data can be found on the numerous websites narrating the stories of the war: NATO bombardments, escape from Kosovo, refugees in bordering countries, humanitarian organizations deployed in urgent interventions, the sending of NATO troops for humanitarian support, and so forth. Other statistics and information can also be found on NATO websites, those of the multinational forces in Albania (AFOR) and Kosovo (KFOR), and webpages of many military and humanitarian missions.[4] In the context of the gradual dismemberment of the Yugoslav federation that had begun in the early 1990s, the violence in these territories became the focus of the images on television and the front pages of newspapers. The end of the Cold War had led to an implosion and a decade of wars (Croatia, Bosnia, Kosovo) in the very heart of Europe, as the media tried to narrate these events through images of endless massacres, ethnic and religious hatred, and the powerlessness of Western diplomacy.

In this complex postbipolar scenario, the case of Kosovo stands both as an extreme example of crisis management and a paradigmatic case of the contemporary aporias related to humanitarian interventions, one of which was already encapsulated in the curious finding put forth by the Independent International Commission on Kosovo in 2000:[5]

> Such a conclusion is related to the controversial idea that a "right" of humanitarian intervention is not consistent with the UN charter if conceived as a legal text, but that it may, depending on context, nevertheless, reflect the spirit of the Charter as it relates to the overall protection of people against gross abuse. [2000:186]

"Illegal, yet legitimate" typically characterizes the ambivalent but idealized self-description NATO put forth to legitimize its Janus-faced operations: on the one hand, bombing Serbia and the Kosovo border almost simultaneously and, on the other, creating its first ad hoc military mission in Albania —Operation Allied Harbour—assigned to perform humanitarian aid for the massive influx of refugees.

A new scenario is therefore taking shape in the territories affected by crises, where the mandates of the military are rearticulated, humanitarian roles are professionalized, and both coincide in a new form of management justified on the same ethical plane. The victim to be saved, the wounded body to be tended to, the terrorist or torturer to be hunted, the military arsenals of the enemy to be destroyed now all require a single and identical ethical figure, imposed on the many protagonists in the field. Today, ideological complicity and shared propaganda are increasingly apparent within the space created by the blurred boundaries of humanitarian activity and military apparatuses.

Militarized tutelage, still present today in Bosnia, Kosovo, and ever more present in Albania, and economic tutelage by means of the special programs devised by the European Union (EU) or the various international agencies concerned with development and humanitarian affairs mobilize an increasingly wide array of sectors and protagonists. Calling upon development aid, military management of humanitarian assistance, humanitarian aid protected by the military, democracy training for judges organized by the local offices of UN agencies, plans for new constitutions, central banks, free market enablers of all sorts (politicians, businessmen), the development of a European bureaucracy, and so forth—these numerous participants all labor to prepare some of the Balkan states for an expected, yet quite remote, integration into Europe. Today, this massive and compulsive assemblage of contradictory practices has profound sociopolitical ramifications that simply cannot be overlooked and brushed aside in the name of an ideological pragmatics of saving the victims.

EMBEDDED

In April 1999, I needed to reach Tirana (Albania), and the only authorized means of transportation for entering territories that bordered the conflict area were either military planes or the charter flights of the World Food Program (WFP). The protection and authorization of NATO allowed this opening in the local air space to operate a continuous humanitarian bridge within these areas.

A few months before the conflict began, I had agreed to work in Albania as an expert for a UN program based out of Vienna. The war's outbreak had changed my research project, but it had made a stay in Albania during the months of April and May 1999 all the more necessary. For several weeks I attempted to find means to reach the area bordering the conflict, in the country that more than any other had welcomed hundreds of thousands of refugees fleeing Kosovo, but dilatory bureaucratic procedures had considerably slowed down that process. Nonetheless, this first encounter with what would become the major focus of my research certainly made a lasting impression.

The fact that each passenger who boarded these flights was required to sign a document in which she or he renounced any civil or criminal claims against the UN or the military bureaucracies should the airplane become involved in a crash or "collateral damage" was a blatant indication of other paradoxes to come. An employee made sure everyone accessing the airplane complied with these procedures, repeatedly counting the number of passengers and ensuring that the necessary statements were signed before each flight to Albania or Macedonia. The inexorable banality of bureaucratic technicalities seemed ambivalent to say the least: as people were dying or escaping death only a few hundred kilometers away, UN standardized procedures plodded on with a confused, slow steadiness likely to baffle even the most understanding among us.

Military and diplomatic personnel, journalists, and men and women who worked for international organizations in the most diverse hierarchical positions were all part of the sociocultural melting pot of authorized travelers bound for war zones and their borders. Baby boomers usually occupied higher-end jobs, like project managers, while the younger participants, between twenty-five and thirty-five years old, worked for organizations like CARE, Save the Children, or Oxfam. Carrying little backpacks and speaking English with the most diverse accents, these adventurers exchanged stories about their involvement in other war zones while waiting to embark on the next available charter. I recall one young recruit declaring that he had "done" Bosnia, was "doing" Albania, and "would do" Kosovo as soon as the bombardments ceased, while another emphasized that he had "done" Somalia and Rwanda instead.

During those days of proximity and shared life with the world of the military and humanitarian aid, I could easily decipher how a sense of belonging was constantly reinforced by sharing such idioms through these hyperactive yet fleeting networks. A specific humanitarian vocabulary of mixed languages (heavily infused with English phrases and acronyms) created an atmosphere imbued with pragmatism and the need to act now. At the same time an ever-growing culture of exceptionality stemmed from the circulating mandates and "terms of reference"—or ToR as they were called[6]—identifying individual projects and the specific experts who would be chosen to take part in them.

For a limited time, I likewise circulated in that world of international organizations and, like all the others, had participated in the apparatus that authorized one to move in the highly coveted spaces of "limited access." With badge in hand, I too had been accredited and gained a privileged "access" into the abstract and parallel dimension of intervention.

To be accredited means that in addition to rights claimed through citizenship—the right to cross a border with your passport, for example—an additional right has been granted to you by the badge of the international organization (civilian or military) for which you are working. This right is indispensable for moving around areas of conflicts and catastrophes. To be accredited also means that, from that moment on, you have the ability to move through the chessboard of world crises. One of the elected happy few, you are now part of a deterritorialized managerial space, tied to missions, projects, and investigations to be completed. You are now part of a planetary temporality of emergency that benefits from a series of norms that abstract you from your original social belonging—and which considerably increase your bargaining power with respect to local communities in the places you will be "doing."

That badge with your photograph, and the acronym of the international organization you belong to, becomes your new identity. It also serves as the key for opening the doors to your involvement in places where war, conflict, soldiers of peace, barbed wire, and checkpoints profoundly modify and regulate people caught within these clearly delimited spaces.

This phenomenon was highlighted on numerous occasions in the facilitated procedures at different airports for the embedded civilians—most notably at the Tirana (Albania) or Skopje (Macedonia) airports. At the Tirana airport, for example, a priority gate had been created for those who were in possession of a document or badge that identified them as members of the international community. Run by policemen or UN soldiers, the "border" between Macedonia and Kosovo was all the more illustrative of these dynamics. Since it remained a "strategic" point even after the end of the war—up until the airport in Pristina was reopened—it was highly securitized and the wait to enter a liberated Kosovo could last an entire day. Yet, what was all the more telling was the implicit hierarchical disposition elaborated through privileged corridors for all those involved with military logistics and their necessary supplies. During the long wait, the progressive militarization of the territory could also be measured by focusing on these privileged corridors through which one could easily notice the heightened circulation of military women and men and matériel.

Hours were spent waiting as confusion grew with the changing priorities imposed by UN soldiers. A confusion that gave rise to bottlenecks, tensions, and to a temporality that, while parallel to that of the efficiency of emergency, led instead to a general sense of resignation. Already manifest in the contradictions of bombing in order to liberate or democratize, the face of "tutelage" was now made abundantly clear. On the one hand, military and civilian personnel passed through the priority corridors whose access was limited to those with the necessary badges, legitimized by the state of emergency and exception. On the other, refugees returning to Kosovo a few weeks after the end of the war were blocked, subjected to checks, lined up indefinitely in another corridor. The soldiers of peace followed procedures that continually reminded one how a "liberated" territory, which seemed so close, could seamlessly become so unreachable.

SCENES OF COMPASSION

The theater of war stages two acts simultaneously. Both tend to unfold side by side and yet, somehow, constantly merge through media coverage. The first is the tragedy of those who are fleeing: the victims of the war who will have to confront these extreme experiences for the rest of their existence.[7] The second act shows us those who bear witness or provide aid to the victims, those who wish to expose the executioners and who claim to narrate and describe the experiences of a silenced other, offering testimony of the horrors of the world while remaining "neutral."

This humanitarian actor precariously walks a tightrope between empathetic witnessing, indignation, the ethics of intervention, and the ideals of neutrality linked to his or her profession. She or he joins the ranks of what one could call a mobile oligarchy (see Pandolfi 2000), playing a well-defined role in the political, military, and humanitarian strategies of any intervention. This engagement in emergency, through the civil, military, and religious international community, is the necessary seal of approval enabling him or her to become a legitimate narrator of the crises, the catastrophes, the genocides, and the massacres.

Memory, bearing witness, interviews, and so forth—all these accompany official events that have been granted space and legitimacy in the media. In addition to the accounts of those who gather the basic war bulletins, with the number of refugees or other figures related to humanitarian assistance, there are numerous websites that still preserve memories and firsthand accounts of war. After a few years, these come to resemble old pictures in a family album sent from the front lines. Doubts, snapshots of daily life in the camps, ambient confusion, and uplifting experiences all illustrate a will to memory that becomes a part of the nebulous bureaucratic apparatus. In the poetic recognition of a woman responsible for the project called "For a New Image of Albanian Women" who visited a refugee camp in Tirana:

> This memory is nothing but a brief flash, an image almost stolen, expressed with the fear of being regarded as an intruder who went to "watch" with no other interpretive tools than a great sense of respect for a situation whose dimensions I knew I could not be fully aware of.[8]

A priest in Lushnje favored a terse, descriptive account of the extreme situation:

> The city is about to explode with refugees. We already have over 3,000, but we are awaiting many more. A refugee camp with 1,000 people is being assembled, but the conditions are sub-human.

A journalist preferred to comment on the complexities of the new wars:

> We came to Albania to see how a country at war lives, a modern war composed of remote bombardments and refugees used as weapons, a Twenty-First century war without ground troops and with ultra-sophisticated technologies, but on a stage on which the worst of the past century is on display: deeply-rooted hatreds, nationalisms, communisms, ethnic cleansings, concentration camps and deportations. We have gathered fragments of truth and shreds of life, a composite puzzle made of actions and reactions, as complex and distorted as these damned Balkans are.

And an enthusiastic young volunteer stressed the importance of the bonds formed on the fields:

> It was 1999 and we were given the opportunity to help thousands of families from Kosovo, who had been torn from their houses and their land because of a war. It was a situation I thought I would never face, but I felt I needed to go to do something really useful, and do it in person, with my own resources. We were a large group of volunteers from the most diverse organizations, and immediately a bond formed. Once we received instructions on location on how to behave so as not to create problems, we left for the camp that would keep us busy 12 hours a day for the next 2 weeks, the Shjak refugee camp. These were the 12 most beautiful days of my life, and I thank the associations and the people who allowed me to live them.

The volunteers and other protagonists of the humanitarian experience bear witness to innumerable forms of suffering that the language of international organizations pigeonholes under the rubric of "humanitarian catastrophe." The bureaucratic language does not take into account those small fragments of humanity that we all perceive and recognize and that, for reasons tied to the technology of humanitarian intervention, are transformed into numbers and needs in emergency situations. These repeated effects of desubjectification produced by the technocratic and militarized apparatus help explain why some of the witnesses need to tell a more personal story and relate intimate experiences. Yet, this spectacular proliferation of the testimonial of suffering takes us back through the centuries to Augustinian perplexities.

In his *Confessions*, Saint Augustine reflected on the ambivalent nature of pity, marked by the enjoyment of the feeling of sorrow:

> How is it that a man wants to be made sad by the sight of tragic sufferings that he could not bear in his own person? Yet the spectator does want to feel sorrow, and it is actually his feeling of sorrow that he enjoys. Surely this is the most wretched lunacy? For the more a man feels such sufferings in himself, the more he is moved by the sight of them on stage. Now when a man suffers himself, it is called misery; when he suffers in the suffering of another, it is called pity. [Augustine 1943:397–398]

The publicity of the media, of firsthand accounts, of urgency, of interviews, of TV images have all become an intricate part of the apparatus itself, which makes this peculiar contemporary and highly media-oriented form of "suffering in the suffering of others" unavoidably more deceptive than it is intended to be. This industrious pity needs to be contrasted to other tentative forms of subjectification one finds in the camps to truly grasp what seems like, after the fact, the inherently voyeuristic, even pornographic, dimension to such proliferating narrations. These continuously serve to establish an abstracted distance between an "us" (the spectators) and a "them" (the victims); on a similar topic, see Boltanski 1999. In other words, these continuously render the lived experiences of the extreme (the other's misery) in the form of an acceptable, consensual, and legitimate shared pity.

In the hangar of one of the two welcome camps in Tirana, small tents and salvaged fabrics attempted to create a sort of virtual intimacy in which refugees could hide belongings and photographs. Paradoxically, this attempted space of recovery of one's history and dignity, by collecting and organizing one's personal belongings, was accompanied by a desire to communicate and exhibit the uniqueness of one's history. Although these individuals had become one of the numbers in another humanitarian catastrophe, they attempted to reestablish themselves as subjects. So even while surrounded by the comings and goings of strangers who were measuring their suffering in terms that seemed reduced to those of accountants, everyone needed to open the tent, to show the wedding photograph, to attempt to tell their individual stories, stories that differed from a situation they now shared with others because of religion, ethnicity, or the arbitrariness of events.

Yet how can one succeed in recalling those small acts, those gestures with which each of those refugees sought to maintain his or her own uniqueness and emerge from the cloud of "humanitarian catastrophe"? I have often asked myself this question, having also been part of that international circuit that went to "see," "visit," and "talk" with the "refugees." How can each description, narration, or action take into account the extreme experience of war?

In moving closer to that minimalist familiar territory—the land of small acts—recovered after dangers and discomforts, I felt I was once again desecrating an intimacy that had been violated by the violence experienced. And yet, in the gestures of those who had found refuge far away from that hell, there was no trace of a refusal to talk or to express oneself. On the contrary, it was striking to see how eagerly women, especially, would come out of their isolation and attempt to communicate once strangers in uniform approached with cameras, TV cameras, or ID badges.

Military and civilian personnel kept moving around because of the urgency and the pressure of accomplishing their tasks. The politicians and representatives who belonged to the institutions of the countries who were responsible for the "humanitarian war" moved even more rapidly through the indistinct multitude labeled "humanitarian catastrophe," shaking hands and caressing confused faces. The refugees slowly raised small, careful gestures around this extreme experience, in an attempt to endow their lives with any form of continuity they could find.

ETERNAL EMERGENCY

The end of the war in June of 1999 had created continuous movement between Albania and Kosovo, but only in one direction: NGOs, military personnel, and meddlers looking for some trick to take advantage of postwar business opportunities caught wind of the need to move from one place to the other. In a short period of time Pristina (in Kosovo) "stole" not only experts in humanitarian projects, but also the flow of money invested in the emergency, which had passed through Tirana (in Albania) during the three months of the war and then quickly moved elsewhere. Structures that had been erected to provide for Albanian-speaking refugees during the winter months of 2000 in Albania were no longer necessary and so were left poorly cared for or abandoned. The emergency had already moved elsewhere, leaving behind a social space in complete suspended animation.

For years returning to Kosovo has been like returning to a waiting area in any transit site: the apparent normalcy of the international presence, the local government, life in the cafés and restaurants, of statues that reinvent memory, all meshed with an ambient nervousness emanating from frustrations tied to this perpetual limbo. A decade after the end of the war, the normalcy of waiting and the cohabitation of ancient and new fears seem to have been internalized in daily social life, especially in the capital, Pristina.

The reports and the commissions, whether in Europe or New York, prepared in order to define and plan the destiny of a region, multiplied in the course of that decade, up to the unilateral declaration of independence of February 17, 2008. While the youths' lifestyles in the streets of the "new Pristina" do not seem to have been affected, the impasse over the future of Kosovo, and the contradictory reactions with respect to recognition within the international community itself, the tensions generated by sharing power among the institutions of a newly created state, and the multiplication of international forms of juridical-administrative tutelage, have continued to feed an energy produced by rage and the impossibility to act, an energy that looks for new "enemy" figures to target.[9]

The pairing of westernization and democracy, which was supposed to lead to freedoms for individuals and markets, increasingly appears like a lost illusion, or perhaps one that was never really pursued. In fact, in these laboratories of "postnational democracy," only a happy few are able to frequent summer schools, journalism courses, and the other activities aimed at "internationalizing" the area. In Pristina, the red and black Albanian flag has been put aside, replaced by Kosovo's new flag, whose colors and tonalities are reassuring to the international community. Both the stars and the blue background speak of a desire to be an integral part of Europe: of a respect for minorities and pacified ethnic tensions. It does not matter much that an atmosphere of militarization, certainly more discreet than during the previous decade, leaves one with a sense of how fragile the normalization of the area remains. Europe sends jurists and policemen, signaling that aid and recognition are only possible through the acceptance of forms of institutional security tutelage. International bureaucracy becomes an integral part, and even perhaps the main player, in the "construction" of the independent state.

Legally and politically the state of emergency becomes a state of exception,[10] where the rights of a sovereign state are gradually confused with the protean international legal and military forms of tutelage, with the organization of an economic system that is defined as free from the paralyzing economies of real socialism. Democracy and markets, humanitarianism and development, the priority mandate to save the bodies of the victims, and controlling the rights of individuals (victims) as a form of security necessary to peace in the area all contribute to the establishment of a paradigmatic form of therapeutic domination.[11]

SCENES OF MIGRANT SOVEREIGNTY

The territories of the war, of the conflicts, of reconstruction, of exported democracy are the stage on which a constellation of "international" actors play their parts. In other words, these military or civilian actors, technicians or businessmen, bureaucrats or diplomats, experts or young volunteers, and journalists are all "embedded" and identified as the "international community."[12] Very different from one another, but all joined in the common project of the need to intervene, they represent a mobile and exportable oligarchy, which tends to act with the same procedural approach in every crisis. Acting from within an expanding opacity, this oligarchy installs itself as a mobile "sovereignty" and operates according to a logic that, reinterpreting Agamben 1998, we could define as "extra-legal." Even though they are supported by mandates from the General Assembly, the Security Council, or the authoritative support of donors who want to "implement" rights, democracy, and health and development systems in areas that are considered at risk for catastrophe or in which catastrophes have already occurred, the management, control, and occupation practices of a specific territory or space are endowed with real powers[13] that result in "sovereign" forms of behavior. Therefore, in this context, the definition of sovereignty describes a form of authority that is both political and moral (Fassin 2010a).

Aid to development and, to an even greater degree, humanitarian intervention are both immersed today in a logic of militarization and in the ambiguous ethics of humanitarian conflicts or the ensuing operations for peace maintenance and continue to proliferate within these terms. Within this ever-present logic of war, humanitarian intervention has been abstracted into a "natural" necessity starting in the 1990s. If the 1980s and 1990s were the decades of humanitarian heroism, of a vision focused on engagement and non-neutrality with respect to the evils of the world, the years following the Kosovo war are those in which people began to ask themselves about the effects of the humanitarian apparatus, contaminated by the ambiguous role militarization has come to play in it. Rony Brauman (Brauman 2002), one of the protagonists of the golden age of Médecins Sans Frontières, attributes the dangerous drift of humanitarianism to the dangerous drift of the right, or duty, to interfere at the end of the 1990s. Others, like J. C. Rufin, have developed a critique that is internal to the "perverse" mechanisms that have invaded many humanitarian competences in areas in which one has engaged in the right to make war (for humanitarian reasons) or where humanitarian engagement has served as a cover for "illegitimate" wars. Rufin reminds us: "For humanitarian actors, the worst that could happen would be if one day human rights and those who defend them would emerge as one of the West's faces, and, more precisely, the one that supports arms trafficking and masks the West's other interests" (1999:423, my translation).

The margins within which one might be able to negotiate for a human-itarian intervention that is "free" of the political pressures of various forms of militarization appear increasingly uncertain and ambiguous. Defenders of such intervention seem forced to retreat to the terrain of technocratic professionalism and rely solely on depoliticized resources.

SELF-CRITICAL SELF-JUSTIFICATION

In recent years, however, numerous actors and protagonists of the era of "humanitarian" intervention have felt compelled to participate in debates in which the limits and distortions of many missions and projects have been revealed, criticized, and even condemned. During the late 1990s, probably due to the various wars in the former Yugoslavia, as a result of the traumatic effect of the interventions and noninterventions, or of the delayed interventions in Rwanda and Bosnia, the appeal of self-criticism grew with renewed vigor. France especially has been the stage of official repudiations, heated discussions, and the exchange of criticisms between various humanitarian actors (Rufin, Brauman) even though these debates have not led to any incisive process of reform. Voices of military "dissidents" have now been added to those of these "civilian" actors, revealing one of the most controversial aspects of the world of humanitarian intervention: the strict interdependence or, even better, dependence of the humanitarian side on the military apparatus. Some military men who performed key roles in peacekeeping operations (for example, General Romeo Dallaire in Rwanda and General Fabio Mini, former head of KFOR, Kosovo Force), have since dissociated themselves from their experiences and are now explicitly critical of them, albeit from somewhat different positions.

Both local and international leadership have become targets of sharp criticism, as the confused theater of operations—which allows for "petty tac-tics and stratagems that only seem functional to someone who is capable of crowing victory and then immediately departing" (Mini 2003:248)— is revealed for the world to see. The "Kosovo" model, for instance, has revealed dangerous vulnerabilities in the transition period, manipulated on the one hand by the rhetoric of stabilization and on the other by the latest and most dangerous rhetoric of the "gangster state." As Mini reminds us:

> The UN could learn the lesson, from Kosovo more than from
> any other crisis, that it is not able, in terms of both structure and
> culture, to handle either low-medium intensity crises or the
> aftermath of crises in complex realities efficiently, even if they
> are relatively small in size. [2003:248]

The key problem with these rapid and media-intensive military and humanitarian interventions is the ideological veil that accompanies liberation, which covers up the ambiguous and indefinite duration of the hydra-headed intervention. On the one hand programs are camouflaged in such a manner as to hide the fact that operations are of unlimited duration or that they use humanitarian needs as a justification for military presence. On the other hand these same forms of camouflage also allow one to abandon these occupied/liberated territories at any point, invoking arbitrary justifications once the geopolitical balance of power shifts.

The paradox that surfaces in many territories subjected to military or humanitarian interventions is that an encapsulated international military presence (NATO/UN) continues to hold the fort, while those NGOs and international organizations that are capable of affecting the development and stabilization of the area gradually withdraw after the emergency is over and move to other more "urgent" locations. Behind phrases like solidarity, democracy, and restoration of rights one can discern a paralyzed society, caught between welfare bureaucracies and authoritarian forms of tutelage. Certainly, in all of this frozen landscape, there are still spots that absorb all the potential of the machinery of international assistance and also manage to transform the contradictions of international tutelage into a relatively efficient device. The various voices that have been critical of humanitarian interventions, coming from a variety of backgrounds and invoking different logics, should not be forgotten. They have a legitimacy of their own, even if it may not be exhaustive. All of these voices address areas of the humanitarian universe and simultaneously help us reflect on more inclusive scenarios that question the relationship between globalization, the media, and local governmental institutions. In other words, while the humanitarian universe has undergone profound changes, the external rules of the economy, politics, and postbipolar equilibrium have also transformed the logics according to which militantism and humanitarian rhetoric had found their autonomous space and increasing legitimacy as the privileged interlocutors of local governments, donor governments, and UN agencies. This new and difficult balancing act of humanitarian intervention is tied to the often confusing superimposition of a transnational juridical system onto those systems that exist at the local level.

The self-critiques that have arisen within the humanitarian galaxy can be grouped into three main lines of inquiry. The first is internal to the actors themselves. One begins by questioning the behaviors and moral dilemmas of the humanitarian actors and discovers a disconcerting world of fragility, vague ideologies, and ruthless cynicism. Interesting examples in this vein are the books by Jordi Raich (2004) and Jean-Sélim Kanaan (2002); we must also mention Amina Yala's (2005) work, which reveals the multifaceted profile of the humanitarian expert and the contradictions between tales of suffering and evenings passed in the hotels or little villas for "the internationals," which one of the protagonists dubbed "Club Med under the bombs." The second line of criticism makes note of internal dysfunctions within individual NGOs, the contradictions between the need for media support, professional financial management, and the growing tendency to professionalize participants. Finally, the third, more carefully articulated line of criticism questions the ideological thrust that, by way of the right versus duty debates, allowed the gradual legitimization and increasing political autonomy of humanitarian interventions. In a published interview Rony Brauman (2002) courageously developed the idea that reflections on humanitarian issues should be inscribed in a new moral and political logic, dissociating them from greater or lesser self-congratulatory victories. Frozen in politically complex situations and endowed with significant budgets, NGOs are gradually transformed into logistical mechanisms whose legitimacy goes hand in hand with the "technically correct."

It is instructive that NGOs are themselves calling into question the legitimacy of their well-intentioned actions. Such self-criticism once again demonstrates the nonindifference of the global bureaucracy and coincides with a retreat from responsibility through "technical correctness." This self-criticism also points to the particular mode of legitimation that characterizes the political authority of migrant oligarchies.

To eternalize the state of exception, even once the emergency has passed, means creating an opaque and permanent area situated between the logic of peace and that of war, between the temporality of emergency in which one intervenes to sustain the victim and the temporality of the long term, during which intervention often gives rise to an inversion of roles, from victims to enemies. The victims (whose existence legitimized the use of weapons and humanitarian intervention) can, in fact, become potential enemies in the course of the processes of "stabilization" and justify a military logic and the use of arms in the postconflict period, even in the long term, in order to intervene in areas (refugee camps, for instance) that are gradually cataloged as potential terrorist locations.

It is within this sort of regime that one has to agree with Michel Agier (2003) when he points to a number of new elements that have emerged in the current makeup of the humanitarian apparatus. The first element we could define as the violence tied to wars that can alternatively be fast and efficient, or else be endless. Agier and Bouchet-Saulnier see such forms of warfare entering ever more deeply into the lives of civilian populations, who have become hostages to a situation where there is an increasing confusion between the urban areas of life and the locales of war (Agier 2008:22). The second element is that of an apparatus of care that seeks complete control of the victim: the desire to help in survival and the desire to control interact within the humanitarian universe at war. The bodies that need to be nourished or saved not only demand a capillary control of each body, but also a precise control of each territory in the form of access. The third element is the rigorous separation of the victim's space (the refugee camps) from the space of the mobile oligarchies (the green zones). Humanitarian logic tends to privilege those spaces that have been constructed for the refugees at the margins, both spatially and temporally, of the daily life of the postconflict period.

The apparatus of war and the apparatus of rescue are strongly dependent on contemporary views of crisis management and make a "critical turn" in anthropological work necessary. We are faced with a rhetoric that constructs war as a marginal and natural phenomenon, a hazard along the route, and not a permanent political strategy, and that highlights episodes of humanitarian action or aid to development once the territory has been made "safe."

THE ETHNOGRAPHY OF DISORIENTATION

In 1996 when I planned and then began my research project in Albania and Kosovo, the war in Bosnia was over, sealed through the Dayton Accords signed in 1995.[14] At this point, Bosnia-Herzegovina had only one capital (Sarajevo) for a single state composed of two distinct entities: the Srpska Republic and the Bosnia-Herzegovina Federation. Yet, three flags were frequently hoisted, since the territory was also subject to the tutelage of the international community through the Office of the High Representative (OHR) as well as the United Nations Mission in Bosnia and Herzegovina (UNMIBH).

Violence in Kosovo was increasing daily, and the tragic and implosive nationalism of the former Yugoslav Federation and the "laboratory" of the international peace mission in Bosnia led many to predict that Kosovo (and partially Albania) would encounter a similar fate in the near future. These continuous social and political upheavals already revealed the "extreme" forms of violence that would come to frame my research. An unforeseen path, since I had not taken the impact of the direct experience of war into account at the outset of the project, nor the need to understand how the entire international military and civilian apparatus was being deployed to manage the daily lives of people whether they were fleeing the war or returning from the war through voluntary or forced repatriation. This apparatus was clearly displayed on the ground behind all those military and civilian acronyms that one could find in the region incarnated through peace and security maintenance missions and the generalized actions of militarized humanitarian intervention.

Above all, I had not considered what an arduous, not to say impossible, task the elaboration of an analytical framework that could aptly encapsulate this scenario of the extreme would be. It became apparent that the turbulent spectacle could not be clearly discerned by the majority of the protagonists simply embedded in the ongoing processes and the comfort of their surrounding clichés: saving lives, doing something, helping the needy, and so forth. An intuitive uneasiness needed better formulation in other terms and with a different vocabulary.

This began, I must note, on a very personal level. I had been quickly interpolated by the theater of war, of "liberation," and of the postconflict situation, which suddenly reactivated long forgotten and fragmented memories. Those scenes of military matériel and uniforms, of soldiers and barbed wire fences, of checkpoints and "safe zones" brought me several decades back to my childhood in the aftermath of the Second World War in Italy. I unexpectedly remembered related aspects of life in Naples, partially militarized many years after the end of the war. There, the port was under military control, fences limited access to different areas, and warships belonging to the most important NATO base in the Mediterranean were docked and displayed for all to see.[15] In my hometown, the Sixth Fleet was a particular testament of the pervasive and dramatic legacy of the Second World War decades after its conclusion. The Forrestal aircraft carrier itself had become an integral part of the city's skyline in early 1959 and stayed there until the 1980s.[16]

These childhood images at the end of the fifties were inevitably intertwined with memories of the ambiguous narratives that also characterized Italy between 1943 and 1945. These were directly shaped by the collapse of Fascism, the legacy of civil war, the occupation of Anglo-American liberation forces, and the Marshall Plan. In other words, the imaginary of my generation had an intimate familiarity with the contradictions and dissonances of a defeated and liberated country that had to be rebuilt from rubble. When, in the late 1990s, I found myself face-to-face with violence, political collapse, civil wars, military occupation, reconstruction, and stabilization plans in the Balkan postcommunist territories, my childhood memories forcefully interacted with the task of interpreting what was going on before my eyes.

It never occurred to me that I had spent my childhood and my youth in a city that for decades had also been the largest NATO base in the Mediterranean. It was not until I saw the spotless-white uniforms in Albania and the camouflage uniforms in Kosovo that I remembered the MPs patrolling Naples's waterfront during my childhood. The wonder with which my fellow citizens would contemplate the towering Forrestal, anchored in Naples in the 1960s, seemed to reverberate in the curiosity with which Albanians were staring at Apache helicopters hovering over Tirana in the 1990s.

There, in front of my eyes, the oxymoron of a war of liberation had materialized again and revealed itself in a whole new context. Fragments from my past suddenly resurfaced: not only such images, but also specific memories, long forgotten voices and bits of conversations from childhood unexpectedly came back to me. Those reemerging elements of memory expressed ambivalence toward the "Allies," a feeling of gratitude for what they had done as "liberators," freeing us from Fascism and Nazism, combined with the resentment for their arrogant and violent behavior as "occupiers."

This uneasiness should not be considered as a simple rhetorical device used in order to explain a personal intellectual journey, justifying my own interests through memories of my childhood. It needs to be theorized. Putting oneself in play in a situation should not be a consolatory practice based on an indulgent reflexivity or a moral pragmatic of compassion (which, as we have seen, can become tantamount to an endorsement of the bureaucratic procedure through its excess: the poignant testimony of spectators). It legitimizes neither my presence, nor the order of things. Instead it should help underscore the moral tenor of depoliticized exception that enables contradictions to be consistently bypassed and suspended. In an attempt to transfer those characteristics one associates with physical disorientation to the intellectual, epistemological, and ethical level, I have come to define my own ethnographic approach as the "ethnography of disorientation."

The experience of living others' wars, others' suffering and violence, the frantic activity that uses either aid or violence to conceal the inexpressible, the implementation of technical apparatuses that allow one to suppress one's own emotions while acting, a perverse and almost ashamed "excitement" in spatially sharing the area where fighting and violence is occurring, of being in a place that, when reported by the media, becomes a planetary space where it is legitimate to narrate life and death—these are the paths that lead to the necessity of an ethnography of disorientation where the knot of urgency, utilitarianism, and compassion must constantly be unfastened. How can one define the limits of what can be said and determine who will say it? The ethnography of disorientation attempts to disentangle the order of discourses and disarticulate the "logics" that accompany the materiality of war. The logic of war; the logic of events; the statistics relating to deaths, military actions, bombs, refugees, humanitarian aid; the logic of human rights rhetoric, of the human beings to be protected are symmetrical to the logic of indignation, the logic of horror, the logic of interference, of emergency, and of the sense of guilt.

The ethnography of disorientation constitutes an ethical scene whose claim is to focus on the necessary dramatic rupture between ethics and publicity, between the narrative of suffering and the necessity of saving lives, between authenticity and engagement as social fact, between compassion as catharsis and the market of pity.

The ethnography of disorientation has to remove itself from the exemplarity of both the bureaucrats of war and those of peace and humanitarian aid; it has to withdraw from the technocratic language imposed by the experts' reports, but also from the empathy of those who bear witness and witness suffering (Nordstrom 2004). The ethnography of disorientation must also be able to remove itself from the emphasis on human rights as an essentialist, naturalized, and depoliticized project, which, as Spivak (2004) and Žižek (2005) pitilessly remind us, so many have fallen for. The ethnography of disorientation must renounce a style in which the ideology of indignation and *j'accuse* can become all too comforting for spectators fantasizing about being actors. Disorientation is a product of excess, of the obscenity of what one sees and of which we even involuntarily become accomplices, calling forth an avant-garde anthropology of spectacular suffering.[17]

Notes

1. For a more detailed account of the gray zone see Pandolfi 2006.

2. The details comprised in this section were originally published in French in an article for the journal *Anthropologie et Sociétés* (Pandolfi 2008a).

3. With reference to the deployment of NATO forces in Albania, http://www.globalsecurity.org states that on April 13, 1999, NATO approved Operation Allied Harbour (which became operative on April 16) in support of the humanitarian efforts being organized in order to take care of the new flow of refugees that resulted from the expulsion of the population of ethnic Albanian origin from Kosovo by the Serbs.

4. See, for example, http://www.nato.int/KFOR/ and http://www.jfcnaples.nato.int.

5. This report (Independent International Commission on Kosovo 2000), in which countries like Sweden, South Africa, Canada, and France took part, attempts to answer a number of very important questions, which are all in some fashion connected

to the legal issues of the legitimacy of the intervention and its limits: the relation between security and human rights, between domestic crises and international strategies for peace and security, or, in essence, the very problematic line of demarcation between what is legal and what is legitimate.

6. The ToR, or *terms of reference*, is how the task to be performed is presented: usually via a document midway between a schematic and bureaucratic description of what has to be done and a more technical plan dealing with where and how one intends to proceed. It is an extremely important document, more than a simple contract, since it becomes the first step on the path toward the normalization of experts. One needs to think, plan, and operate not only in a manner that follows contractual obligations, but that above all follows procedures that are already part of the routine in the program or project the expert has been called to participate in.

7. These are the individuals looking at these painful and traumatic experiences, trying to reassemble the fragments of their shattered lives, allowing the future transmission of memories, and enabling them, step by step, to transform the exception into the ordinary. For a detailed look at violence and ordinary life see Veena Das 2007.

8. The website belongs to the Medea association: http://medea.provincia.venezia.it/.

9. For more details see Pandolfi 2010.

10. At its etymological root, the state of exception refers to an ex-ception, that is, a "taking from without," and has a topological structure in which we can recognize the aporia of intervention. In this gray zone between might and right, the exception is brought to bear through very concrete governmental mechanisms in a double process in which force acquires legitimacy: on the one hand, we see the post hoc legalization of nonlegal procedures, that is, the introduction into legality of that which is extralegal; on the other hand, we observe the effort to preserve the integrity of the law despite its being confronted by a reality not in line with the conditions of applicability foreseen by the legal norm. In other words, the notion of the state of exception allows us to address two questions at the junction of law and violence today: How can the extralegal participate in a legal process? How, in the face of the legally unforeseen realities of life, can the law be suspended in order to guarantee its own preservation? This double process thus brings into being a link between life (the unforeseen, arbitrary force) and law in which life is written into the law or, as Agamben writes, "abandoned to law" (1998:90). Of course, Agamben furthers here the reflection of both Walter Benjamin and Carl Schmitt.

11. As McFalls states: "Paradoxically, and in contrast to legal-rational authority, the apparently disembodied norms of therapeutic authority focus precisely on the human body itself because of this mode of domination's extra-ordinary temporal

quality. Intervening in rupture with established practices, therapeutic domination not only depersonalizes but decontextualizes social relationships. Without any reference to culture or history, therapeutic domination reduces social agents to human bodies. Thus, unlike charismatic, traditional or even legal-rational authority, no particular conception of the good life, but only the minimal but absolute value of life itself, can inform therapeutic domination" (2010:323). From a different perspective Pupavac (2005) describes this victimization-salvation cycle as a new global therapeutic order where emotional norms of donor states and an emphasis on individual vulnerability articulate in new strategic ways a bureaucratic process of good governance and new cultural sensibilities.

12. On the importance of these emergent discourse and practices for the international community, see Calhoun 2004. On its politics of survival, see Abélès 2006.

13. On these emergent forms of power, see Pandolfi 2003, 2008b; Redfield 2005, 2008c; and Fassin 2006, 2007c. On some of the religious undercurrents working in specific programs see Bornstein 2006a.

14. Resolution 1088 sanctioned the transition from IFOR, the Implementation Force, to SFOR, the Stabilisation Force. IFOR's task was to implement peace (Operation Joint Endeavor) using a NATO contingent of about 60,000 soldiers, whereas SFOR's task was one of stabilization and peace maintenance, first with Operation Joint Guard from December 21, 1996, to June 19, 1998, and then with Operation Joint Forge from June 20, 1998, to December 2, 2004; the overall contingent used in these efforts went from the approximately 32,000 soldiers at the beginning of the mission to the approximately 12,000 soldiers of 2002 and finally to the 7,000 soldiers of 2004. As of December 2, 2004, SFOR was replaced by the EUFOR (European Union Force) Althea mission, which currently has approximately two thousand soldiers deployed.

15. These are the same docks used today for naval traffic associated with tourism and trade.

16. The Forrestal is a US aircraft carrier built in 1955, capable of carrying up to seventy aircraft loaded on its landing deck by means of forty huge lifts.

17. John Leavitt, Laurence Mcfalls, and Phillip Rousseau deserve special gratitude for their sustained and generous attention to this paper.

Afterword

Humanitarianism and the Scale of Disaster

"All the aid in the world won't be enough."

—*Red Cross spokesperson in Haiti¹*

As this volume neared completion, a massive earthquake struck the city of Port-au-Prince in Haiti. Among aid professionals such an event was neither unprecedented nor completely unanticipated—their publications had devoted pages to earthquakes in Iran, Pakistan, and China in preceding years, and attentive readers were well aware of the devastating risk tremors posed for any poorly constructed urban center. But the shock of Haiti struck a wider public, reverberating through the media and inspiring a passionate outpouring that recalled those following Hurricane Katrina and the Indian Ocean tsunami. It likewise echoed the Lisbon cataclysm of 1755, when Voltaire dismissed divine retribution as a possible cause and Rousseau stressed the human origins of such a "natural" disaster (see the introduction to this volume). While cameras broadcast horrendous images of suffering, organizations rushed to respond, and donations quickly mounted. All signs suggested this would become another doleful landmark in the chronicle of humanitarian affairs, a reference point for subsequent moments of disaster.

In closing we briefly turn to the contemporary Haitian rupture, both to reflect back on the strands of our collective project, recognizing the influence of two additional participants, and to gesture forward from its loose ends. This latest "ethical scene" of humanitarianism (as Lawrence Cohen phrased it during the SAR seminar) proved particularly intense in the United States. Due to Haiti's geographic proximity and its long history as a host for aid projects, it was familiar ground for many American religious charities as well as secular organizations alike. The fact that the country featured one of the densest concentrations of NGOs on the planet also starkly implicated the concerns of immediate relief with questions of future development (Feldman, this volume). Traces of the nation's tortured history—including its lengthy record as a site of international intervention—likewise surfaced amid media commentary. Haiti appeared a land of epic suffering, and ethical publics quickly coalesced around the spectacle of need, however much the precise moral lesson drawn from its agony might range from political denunciations of neoliberal economic policies to evangelist Pat Robertson's distinctly anti-Voltairean suggestion of a pact with the devil. Many faces and forms were familiar from earlier humanitarian crises, if somewhat accelerated by new technologies and the wide scale of enthusiasm. Past presidents of the United States led a blue-ribbon charity campaign, and music stars, young and old, rapidly produced benefit concerts and recordings. The specter of the recently deceased Michael Jackson even put in an appearance through a remake of "We Are the World" that circulated widely on YouTube and in Haiti itself. Church, civic, and school groups held their own modest fund-raisers for a constellation of projects, and solicitations to donate appeared at innumerable retail locations, along with opportunities to express non-monetary sympathy by, for example, camping in a cardboard box or sending letters of support. An international exhibition of giving was on prominent display. So too was the figure of the orphan (Bornstein, this volume), particularly once a maladroit effort by American missionaries to "rescue" a group of Haitian children by removing them from kin and country became a news story of its own. Even as offers of assistance poured in, a few select bodies trickled out. In the dramatic reaffirmation of the value of citizenship typical to emergency contexts, a means of evacuation quickly materialized for foreign nationals from wealthier countries. At the same time a handful of seriously injured Haitians received medical evacuation to the United States under the exceptional legal provision of "humanitarian parole"—a small echo of France's provision for illness in asylum (Ticktin, this volume).

For all that the earthquake might, on the surface, appear a natural disaster and not a war, the militarized edge of humanitarianism also quickly emerged. In the relative absence of a viable Haitian state and the disarray of the United Nations mission (its leadership impaired by the event, along with government buildings and much of the city's minimal infrastructure), international media reports breathlessly anticipated an eruption of looting and violence. Although remarkably little evidence of this Hobbesian theme appeared, it intermingled with stereotyped portrayals of Haiti as a cauldron of poverty and violence and helped legitimate a strong preemptive military operation by the United States. Taking control of the airport, American forces strove to produce a form of order by exerting temporary sovereignty. The results produced some specific controversy and questionable priorities: Médicins Sans Frontières for example, complained loudly about the diversion of a plane carrying half of its inflatable field hospital to the neighboring Dominican Republic, even while flights carrying celebrities mysteriously slipped into Port-au-Prince.[2] More generally, the rapid transplantation of security discourses and apparatus served to reinforce the naturalness of a militarized humanitarian response to disaster. Given the scale of Haiti's basic needs, the logic appeared compelling at a logistical level, categorically rather than strategically neutral (Redfield, this volume). But the practice itself also replicated divisions and inequalities, producing social barriers marked by uniforms and badges and keeping supplies on the tarmac even as massed crowds throughout the city waited in vain for assistance. An observer familiar with Kosovo's "gray zone" outlined by Pandolfi (this volume) might find similar shadows under the bright Caribbean sun.

The US military, of course, was hardly alone. Countries across the political spectrum sent specialized units and material, from Cuban doctors to an Israeli hospital, with their efforts achieving varied degrees of visibility and legitimacy in the eyes of the American media (Benthall, this volume). Many major international organizations had a preexisting presence on the ground, and these regrouped, reinforced, and reoriented their missions, while sending out new urgent funding appeals. The drama also inspired a wave of benevolent technical as well as financial responses by people far removed from the scene: the production of satellite maps of the city, efforts to facilitate search and rescue as well as donations through the use of cell phones (transaction fees waived by banks), experiments with telemedicine, and deployment of ingenious prefabricated solutions for shelter and medical care.[3] There is little reason to doubt the goodwill expressed by the protagonists of most of these ventures, any more than those involved in donating more intimate goods. Like the loving production of stuffed animals by Finnish volunteers Liisa Malkki described to us in our SAR seminar, these gestures expressed a surplus of genuine affect and moral commitment. Often the proffered objects and therapies spoke beyond the present to an implied future for the potential beneficiaries, a happier world of reconstituted, self-sustaining subjects (Hyde, this volume). At the same time they stood in stark contrast with the raw lack visible on the ground: collapsed buildings and absent infrastructure, bodies in the street, a dearth of basic supplies, and a crush of people with untreated wounds waiting in medical facilities. The press of broken bodies reportedly overwhelmed even veteran surgeons, as they desperately performed amputations. Amid the chaos of the streets, media cameras repeatedly cast international workers in primary heroic roles, often at the expense of Haitian colleagues on the ground.

What then might anthropology contribute to an understanding of humanitarianism in such a context? We would repeat key observations about the structural tensions of international aid that result in competition between organizations (Stirrat 2006) and emphasize the fact that the scale of disaster exceeds relief efforts (De Waal 1997). Even the greatest harvests of private fund-raising, after all, have only yielded a few billion dollars, and the larger promised donations of states and intrastate agencies do not always materialize (see the introduction to this volume). Beyond the philanthropy on the part of donors elsewhere, then, we would highlight the far less publicized or enumerated acts of care undertaken by Haitians—the vernacular world of neighbors, relatives, and passersby that plays a central role in responding to disaster, as it does in everyday life. With bare hands and minimal tools Haitians rescued far more of their own than any of the specialized teams with their elaborate equipment.[4] We would further recognize the deeper strains of violence running through this world and the stark inequities that frame them (Farmer 2003; Rylko-Bauer, Whiteford, and Farmer 2009), while hoping for future forms of assistance that integrate local vision (see, for example, in a rural context, Smith 2001). The presence of many practicing anthropologists in the larger aid world recalls that the discipline discovered both passion and ambivalence through participatory action within projects as well as through critical reflection about them. In contrast to the complex of institutions invested in the "emergency imaginary" that authorizes much international aid (Calhoun 2004), however, we suggest that anthropological analysis is unlikely to generate normative programs and mobile models ready for rapid transplantation. Nor is it likely to produce critiques dismissing all concern for suffering in clean categorical terms of political denunciation. Instrumental prescription and polemic both favor timeliness and certainty. Anthropology's legacy, in contrast, recognizes the messy mass of lived experience, the "friction" of specific action that attends to the movement of people, ideas, and things (Tsing 2005). Its classic strength therefore lies in unsettling, in reintroducing what was never quite left behind. The situated details of saving lives and giving gifts offer an always incomplete (and sometimes discomforting) picture. But as Englund (this volume) insists, real collaboration must confront the prospect of incommensurability and argument, even around such basic matters as life and death. Thus we can hardly offer a conclusion to the greater aporia of humanitarian action (Fassin, this volume). As engaged and critical observers, however, we can suggest continued attention to its loose ends and their significance in actual practice. Both devils and angels, as it were, reside in the details.

In turn, anthropology would recognize a key domain of contemporary moral discourse and affect, one that infuses higher education as well as international affairs (Abélès 2010; Fassin and Pandolfi 2010; Rabinow et al. 2008:41–42). The speed and scale of humanitarianism, moreover, mobilize the figure of the human in ways that exceed anthropology's temporal norms and trouble its critical tradition. As Lawrence Cohen observed, in dialogue with this volume, humanitarian concern for the suffering other locates itself precisely at "the juncture of present-oriented exception and future-oriented prognostication." Its claims thus rise beyond the everyday, demanding reaction and inspiring prophecy. By emphasizing the urgent and immediate relief of suffering, humanitarianism locates the future amid a mobile present. For its practitioners and consumers, crisis intervention is not a temporary engagement; they move on to the next emergency, along with the ominously inspiring dream of good intentions. To interrogate humanitarianism thus risks touching the untouchable, challenging the values of any analyst who cares for situated human life (Fassin, this volume). We suggest that it is precisely when facing disaster, however, that the slower work of attending to detail and recognizing patterns proves critical. Only then can the specificities of events like the Haitian earthquake grow distinct from the moral and affectual frames that now define them.

Notes

1. Comment on National Public Radio, January 14, 2010, as reported by one of the volume's reviewers.

2. See, for example, MSF Press Release of January 17, 2010, "Doctors Without Borders Cargo Plane with Full Hospital and Staff Blocked from Landing in Port-au-Prince." More detail on the controversy appears in a *New York Times* blog update (http://thelede.blogs.nytimes.com/2010/01/21/updates-on-the-crisis-in-haiti/) and a post entitled "How to Set Up a Plug-and-Play Hospital: Doctors Without Borders" (http://www.boingboing.net/2010/01/21/haiti-howto-set-up-a.html).

3. For example, see stories in the *New York Times* on telemedicine (Milt

Fereudenheim, "In Haiti, Practicing Medicine from Afar," February 9, 2010), the work of Ushahidi (Anand Giridharadas, "Africa's Gift to Silicon Valley: How to Track a Crisis," March 12, 2010) and Containers to Clinics (Henry Fountain, "Managing Disasters with Small Steps," January 19, 2010), and a profile of ShelterBox in *Time* magazine ("How Shelterbox Helps Haiti Earthquake Victims," February 15, 2010). At an event in Charlottesville, Virginia, one of the editors received a personalpresentation of one housing solution from a shuttle driver (see http://www.dignifieddisasterhousing.org/). The larger point is that the earthquake galvanized a remarkable array of exceptional actions, intermingling civic ingenuity with corporate charity.

4. For an illustrative account by an anthropologist see Laura Wagner, "Haiti: A Survivor's Story" (*Salon*, February 1, 2010, http://www.salon.com/news/haiti/index.html?story=/mwt/feature/2010/02/01/haiti_trapped_under_the_rubble).

References

Aall, Pamela, Daniel Miltenberger, and Thomas Weiss
2000   Guide to IGOs, NGOs and the Military in Peace and Relief Operations. Washington: United States Institute of Peace Press.

Abélès, Marc
2006   Politique de la survie. Paris: Flammarion.
2010   The Politics of Survival. Durham: Duke University Press.

Abu-Lughod, Lila
1993   Writing Women's Worlds: Bedouin Stories. Berkeley: University of California Press.

Adams, Vincanne, and Stacey Leigh Pigg
2005   Sex in Development: Science, Sexuality and Morality in Global Perspective. Durham: Duke University Press.

Agamben, Giorgio
1998   Homo Sacer: Sovereign Power and Bare Life. Daniel Heller-Roazen, trans. Stanford: Stanford University Press.
2005   State of Exception. Chicago: University of Chicago Press.

Agier, Michel
2002   Aux bords du monde, les réfugiés. Paris: Flammarion.
2003   La main gauche de l'empire, Ordre et désordres de l'humanitaire. Multitudes 11: http://multitudes.samizdat.net/La-main-gauche-de-l-Empire, accessed July 5, 2010.
2008   On the Margins of the World. The Refugee Experience Today. Cambridge: Polity Press.

Agier, Michel, and Françoise Bouchet-Saulnier
2004   Humanitarian Spaces: Spaces of Exception. *In* In the Shadow of "Just Wars": Violence, Politics and Humanitarian Action. Fabrice Weissman, ed. Pp. 297–313. Ithaca: Cornell University Press.

Allahyari, Rebecca
2000   Visions of Charity: Volunteer Workers and Moral Community. Berkeley: University of California Press.

REFERENCES

Allen, Tim, and David Styan
2000   A Right to Interfere? Bernard Kouchner and the New Humanitarianism. Journal of International Development 12:825–842.

Amin, Samir
1976   Unequal Development: An Essay on the Social Formations of Peripheral Capitalism. New York: Monthly Review Press.

Anderson, Leona
1997   Generosity among Saints, Generosity among Kings: Situating Philanthropy in South Asia. *In* Philanthropy and Cultural Context: Western Philanthropy in South, East, and Southeast Asia in the 20th Century. S. Hewa and P. Hove, eds. Pp. 185–202. Lanham: University Press of America.

Appadurai, Arjun
2002   Deep Democracy: Urban Governmentality and the Horizon of Politics. Public Culture 12(1):21–47.

Apparao, Hansa
1997   International Adoption of Children: The Indian Scene. International Journal of Behavioral Development 20(1):3–16.

Archer, David, and Sarah Cottingham
1996   The REFLECT Mother Manual—A New Approach to Literacy. London: ActionAid.

Arendt, Hannah
1963   On Revolution. New York: Viking Press.
1998   The Human Condition. 2nd edition. Chicago: University of Chicago
[1958]   Press.

Arnove, Robert F., ed.
1980   Philanthropy and Cultural Imperialism: The Foundations at Home and Abroad. Boston: G. K. Hall.

Asad, Talal
2003   Formations of the Secular: Christianity, Islam, Modernity. Stanford: Stanford University Press.

Augustine
1943   Confessions, Book III. Francis J. Sheed, trans. Pp. 397–398. New York: Sheed & Ward.

Baeck, Louis
1991   The Economic Thought of Classical Islam. Diogenes 154:99–115.

Baitenmann, Helga
1990   NGOs and the Afghan war: The Politicisation of Humanitarian Aid. Third World Quarterly 12(1):62–85.

Bano, Masooda
2007   Contesting Ideologies and Struggle for Authority: State-Madrasa Engagement in Pakistan. Birmingham: University of Birmingham Religions and Development Programme, Working Paper 14. http://www.rad.bham.ac

.uk/files/resourcesmodule/@random454f80f60b3f4/1211531042_working_
paper_14___for_web.pdf, accessed June 26, 2010.

Barboza, David

2008   Chinese Growth Begins to Lose Steam. International Herald Tribune,
        November 7:13.

Barnett, Michael

2002   Eyewitness to a Genocide: The United Nations and Rwanda. Ithaca: Cornell
        University Press.

2005   Humanitarianism Transformed. Perspectives on Politics 3(4):723–740.

Barnett, Michael, and Thomas G. Weiss, eds.

2008   Humanitarianism in Question: Politics, Power, Ethics. Ithaca: Cornell
        University Press.

Bartlett, Nick

2006   Independent Report on Drug Treatment in China.

Bass, Gary

2008   Freedom's Battle: The Origins of Humanitarian Intervention. New York:
        Knopf.

Bataille, Georges

1989   The Accursed Share. Vol. 1. New York: Zone Books.

Bauman, Zygmunt

2004   Wasted Lives: Modernity and Its Outcasts. Cambridge: Polity Press.

Bauslaugh, Robert

1991   The Concept of Neutrality in Classical Greece. Berkeley: University of
        California Press.

Bender, Thomas, ed.

1992   The Antislavery Debate. Berkeley: University of California Press.

Benediktsson, Karl, and Linley R. Kamtengeni

2004   Support for the National Adult Literacy Programme, Monkey Bay,
        2001–2004: External Evaluation. Reykjavík: Icelandic International
        Development Agency.

Benthall, Jonathan

1997   The Red Cross and Red Crescent Movement and Islamic Societies, with
        Special Reference to Jordan. British Journal of Middle Eastern Studies
        24(2):157–177.

1999   Financial Worship: The Quranic Injunction to Almsgiving. Journal of the
        Royal Anthropological Institute 5(1):27.

2006   Islamic Aid in a North Malian Enclave. Anthropology Today 22(4):19–21.

2008a   The Palestinian Zakat Committees, 1993–2007 and Their Contested
        Interpretations. Geneva: Graduate School of International and Development
        Studies, Program for the Study of International Organization(s).
        http://graduateinstitute.ch/webdav/site/iheid/shared/iheid/514/08-07-22
        _OP%202008-1_Palestinian%20ZC.pdf, accessed June 26, 2010.

2008b   Returning to Religion: Why a Secular Age Is Haunted by Faith. London: I.B.Tauris.

2010   Disasters, Relief and the Media. New edition. Wantage: Sean Kingston.

Benthall, Jonathan, and Jérôme Bellion-Jourdan

2009   The Charitable Crescent: Politics of Aid in the Muslim World. London:
[2003]   I.B.Tauris.

Bharadwaj, Aditya

2003   Why Adoption Is Not an Option in India: The Visibility of Infertility, the Secrecy of Donor Insemination, and Other Cultural Complexities. Social Science & Medicine 56:1867–1880.

Bharat, Shalini

1993   Child Adoption Trends and Emerging Issues: A Study of Adoption Agencies. Bombay: Tata Institute of Social Sciences.

Biehl, João Guilherme

2001   Vita: Life in a Zone of Social Abandonment. Social Text 19(3):131–149.

2006   Vita: Life in a Zone of Social Abandonment. Los Angeles and Berkeley: University of California Press.

2007   Will to Live: Aids Therapies and the Politics of Survival. In-formation. Paul Rabinow, series ed. Princeton: Princeton University Press.

Bigo, Didier

2002   Security and Immigration: Toward a Critique of the Governmentality of Unease. Alternatives: Global, Local, Political 27:63–92.

Blackburn, Robin

1997   The Making of New World Slavery: From the Baroque to the Modern, 1492–1800. London: Verso.

Boli, John, and George Thomas

1999   Constructing World Culture: International Nongovernmental Organizations since 1875. Stanford: Stanford University Press.

Boltanski, Luc

1999   Distant Suffering: Morality, Media and Politics. Cambridge: Cambridge
[1993]   University Press.

Bonjour, Edgar

1946   Swiss Neutrality: Its History and Meaning. London: George Allen and Unwin.

Bornstein, Erica

2001   Child Sponsorship, Evangelism, and Belonging in the Work of World Vision Zimbabwe. American Ethnologist 28(3):595–622.

2005   The Spirit of Development: Protestant NGOs, Morality, and Economics in
[2003]   Zimbabwe. Palo Alto: Stanford University Press.

2006a   No Return: A Brief Typology of Philanthropy and the Sacred in New Delhi. *In* The Practice of Altruism: Caring and Religion in Global Perspective.

Ruben Habito and Keishin Inaba, eds. Pp. 165–179. Cambridge: Cambridge Scholars Press.

2006b   Charitable Choice: L'humanitarisme et les Politiques de la Foi. Vacarme 34:189–193.

2007a   Faith, Liberty, and the Individual in Humanitarian Assistance. *In* Nongovernmental Politics. Michel Feher, Gaëlle Krikorian, and Yates McKee, eds. Pp. 658–667. New York: Zone Books/MIT Press.

2007b   Harmonic Dissonance: Reflections on Dwelling in the Field. Ethnos 72(4):483–508.

2009   The Impulse of Philanthropy. Cultural Anthropology 24(4):622–651.

Borofsky, Robert
2005   Yanomami: The Fierce Controversy and What We Can Learn From It. Berkeley: University of California Press.

Bouchet-Saulnier, Françoise
2002   The Practical Guide to Humanitarian Law. Lanham: Rowman and Littlefield.

Bouchet-Saulnier, Françoise, and Fabien Dubuet
2007   Legal or Humanitarian Testimony? History of MSF's Interactions with Investigations and Judicial Proceedings. Paris: MSF CRASH.

Bourdieu, Pierre
1977   Outline of a Theory of Practice. Richard Nice, trans. Cambridge, London, New York, and Melbourne: Cambridge University Press.

Bourgois, Philippe
1995   In Search of Respect: Selling Crack in El Barrio. New York and Cambridge: Cambridge University Press.

2000   Disciplining Addictions: The Biopolitics of Methadone and Heroin in the United States. Culture, Medicine, and Psychiatry 24(2):165–195.

Bourgois, Philippe, and Jeff Schonberg
2009   Righteous Dopefiend. California Series in Public Anthropology. Berkeley: University of California Press.

Bowie, Fiona, and European Association of Social Anthropologists (EASA)
2004   Cross-cultural Approaches to Adoption. London and New York: Routledge.

Bowie, Fiona, Deborah Kirkwood, and Shirley Ardener
1993   Women and Missions Past and Present: Anthropological and Historical Perceptions. Providence and Oxford: Berg Press.

Bradol, Jean-Hervé
2001   Motions Debated at the 30th General Assembly of Médecins Sans Frontières. Messages 116 (July–August):2.

2003   L'ordre international cannibale et l'action humanitaire. *In* A l'ombre des guerres justes. Fabrice Weissman, ed. Pp. 13–32. Paris: Flammarion.

2004   The Sacrificial International Order and Humanitarian Action. *In* The Shadow of "Just Wars": Violence, Politics, and Humanitarian Action. F. Weissman, ed. Pp. 1–22. Ithaca: Cornell University Press.

REFERENCES

Brauman, Rony

1993 L'action humanitaire. Paris: Flammarion.

2002 L'humanitaire, le dilemme. Entretien avec Philippe Petit. Paris: Les Editions
[1996] Textuel.

Breckenridge, Carol A., and Candace Vogler

2001 The Critical Limits of Embodiment: Disability's Criticism. Public Culture
13(3):349–357.

Brenneis, Donald

1999 New Lexicon, Old Language: Negotiating the "Global" at the National
Science Foundation. *In* Critical Anthropology Now: Unexpected Contexts,
Shifting Constituencies. George E. Marcus, ed. Pp. 123–146. Santa Fe:
School of American Research Press.

Bricmont, Jean

2005 Impérialisme humanitaire: droits de l'homme, droit d'ingérence, droit du
plus fort? Brussels: Aden.

Briggs, Charles, and Clara Mantini-Briggs

2003 Stories in the Time of Cholera: Racial Profiling during a Medical
Nightmare. Berkeley: University of California Press.

Buerhig, Edward

1971 The UN and the Palestinian Refugees: A Study in Nonterritorial
Administration. Bloomington: Indiana University Press.

Butt, Leslie

2002 The Suffering Stranger: Medical Anthropology and International Morality.
Medical Anthropology 21:1–24.

Calhoun Craig

2004 A World of Emergencies: Fear, Intervention, and the Limits of
Cosmopolitan Order. Canadian Review of Sociology and Anthropology
41(4):373–395.

2008 The Imperative to Reduce Suffering: Charity, Progress and Emergencies in
the Field of Humanitarian Action. *In* Humanitarianism in Question: Power,
Politics, Ethics. Michael Barnett and Thomas G. Weiss, eds. Pp. 73–97.
Ithaca: Cornell University Press.

2010 The Idea of Emergency: Humanitarian Action and Global (Dis)Order. *In*
Contemporary States of Emergency: The Politics of Military and
Humanitarian Intervention. Didier Fassin and Mariella Pandolfi, eds. New
York: Zone Books.

Campbell, Wallace

1990 The History of CARE: A Personal Account. New York: Praeger.

Cannell, Fenella

2006 Introduction. *In* The Anthropology of Christianity. Fenella Cannell, ed. Pp.
1–50. Durham: Duke University Press.

Caplan, Pat

1997   African Voices, African Lives: Personal Narratives from a Swahili Village. New York: Routledge.

Carsten, Janet

2000   Cultures of Relatedness: New Approaches to the Study of Kinship. Cambridge and New York: Cambridge University Press.

2004   After Kinship. Cambridge and New York: Cambridge University Press.

Cartwright, Lisa

2004   "Emergencies of Survival": Moral Spectatorship and the "New Vision of the Child" in Postwar Child Psychoanalysis. Journal of Visual Culture 3(1):35–49.

2005   Images of "Waiting Children": Spectatorship and Pity in the Representation of the Global Social Orphan in the 1990s. *In* Cultures of Transnational Adoption. T. A. Volkman, ed. Pp. 185–212. Durham and London: Duke University Press.

Chambers, Robert

1994   The Origins and Practice of Participatory Rural Appraisal. World Development 22:953–969.

1997   Whose Reality Counts: Putting the Last First. London: Intermediate Technology Publications.

China Daily

2009   China's Drug Users Grow at Lower Pace, October 24, 2009. http://www.chinadaily.com.cn/china/2009-10/24/content-8843345.htm, accessed January 24, 2010.

Chu, Tianxin, and Judith Levy

2005   Injection Drug Use and HIV/AIDS Transmission in China. Cell Research 15(11–12):865–869.

Clifford, James, and George E. Marcus, eds.

1986   Writing Culture: The Poetics and Politics of Ethnography. Berkeley: University of California Press.

Cohen, Lawrence

1999   Where It Hurts: Indian Material for an Ethics of Organ Transplantation. Special issue, "Bioethics and Beyond," Daedalus 128(4):135–166.

2001   The Other Kidney: Biopolitics beyond Recognition. Body & Society 7(2–3):9–21.

2004a   Operability: Surgery at the Margin of the State. *In* Anthropology in the Margins of the State. Veena Das and Deborah Poole, eds. Pp. 165–190. Santa Fe: School of American Research Press.

2004b   Operability, Bioavailability, and Exception. *In* Global Assemblages: Technology, Politics and Ethics as Anthropological Problems. Aihwa Ong and Stephen Collier, eds. Pp. 79–90. Malden: Blackwell.

Cohen, Roberta

2005   Developing an International System for Internally Displaced Persons. International Studies Perspectives 7:87–101.

2006   Developing an International System for Internally Displaced Persons. International Studies Perspectives 7:87–101.

Collier, Stephen J., and Andrew Lakoff
2005   On Regimes of Living. *In* Global Assemblages: Technology, Politics, and Ethics as Anthropological Problems. Aihwa Ong and Stephen J. Collier, eds. Pp. 22–39. Malden: Blackwell.

Collins, James
1995   Literacy and Literacies. Annual Review of Anthropology 24:75–93.

Comaroff, John, and Jean Comaroff
1997   Of Revelation and Revolution, vol. 1: The Dialectics of Modernity on a South African Frontier. Chicago: University of Chicago Press.

Comaroff, John, and Jean Comaroff, eds.
1999   Civil Society and the Political Imagination in Africa: Critical Perspectives. Chicago: University of Chicago Press.
2006   Law and Disorder in the Postcolony. Chicago: University of Chicago Press.

Cooke, Bill, and Uma Kothari, eds.
2001   Participation: The New Tyranny? London: Zed Books.

Cordier, Bruno De
2009   The Third Pillar: Islamic Development and Relief Organizations and the Humanitarian Frontline—A Field Analysis. Doctoral thesis, Faculty of Political and Social Sciences, Ghent University.

Coutin, Susan Bibler
1993   The Culture of Protest: Religious Activism and the U.S. Sanctuary Movement. Boulder: Westview Press.
2003   Cultural Logics of Belonging and Movement: Transnationalism, Naturalization, and U.S. Immigration Politics. American Ethnologist 30(4):508–526.

Cox, J. Charles
1911   The Sanctuaries and Sanctuary Seekers of Medieval England. London: George Allen and Sons.

Crane, Johanna, Kathleen Quirk, and Ariane van der Straten
2002   "Come Back When You're Dying": The Commodification of AIDS among California's Urban Poor. Social Science and Medicine 55(7):1115–1127.

Crombé, Xavier
2007   Humanitarian Action in Situations of Occupation. Paris: MSF CRASH.

Cruikshank, Barbara
1999   The Will to Empower: Democratic Citizens and Other Subjects. Ithaca: Cornell University Press.

Cunningham, Hilary
1999   The Ethnography of Transnational Social Activism: Understanding the Global as Local Practice. American Ethnologist 26:583–604.

D'Souza, Frances
1985   Anthropology and Disasters: A Roundup after Six Years. Anthropology Today 1(1):18–19.

Dachy, Eric
2001   Médecins Sans Frontières and Military Humanitarianism. Special publication newsletter. Contact MSF-Belgium (November–December).

Das, Veena
1995   National Honour and Practical Kinship: Of Unwanted Women and Children. *In* Critical Events: An Anthropological Perspective on Contem-porary India. Veena Das. Pp. 55–83. Oxford: Oxford University Press.
2007   Life and Words: Violence and the Descent into the Ordinary. Berkeley:
[2006] University of California Press.

Das, Veena, Arthur Kleinman, Margaret Lock, Mamphele Ramphele, and Pamela Reynolds, eds.
2000   Violence and Subjectivity. Berkeley: University of California Press.
2001   Remaking a World: Violence, Social Suffering, and Recovery. Berkeley: University of California Press.

Das, Veena, and Deborah Poole, eds.
2004   Anthropology in the Margins of the State. Santa Fe: School of American Research Press.

Dauvin, Pascal, and Johanna Siméant
2002   Le travail humanitaire: Les acteurs des ONG, du siege au terrain. Paris: Presses de Sciences Po.

Davis, Mike
2001   Late Victorian Holocausts: El Niño Famines and the Making of the Third World. London: Verso.
2004a   The Urbanization of Empire: Megacities and the Laws of Chaos. Social Text 22(4):9–15.
2004b   Planet of Slums: Urban Involution and the Informal Proletariat. New Left Review 26:5–34.

De Genova, Nicholas
2007   The Production of Culprits: From Deportability to Detainability in the Aftermath of "Homeland Security." Citizenship Studies 11(5):421–448.

De Torrente, Nicolas
1995   L'action de MSF dans la crise rwandaise: Un histoire critique. Avril–Décembre 1994. MSF report.

De Waal, Alex
1989   Famine That Kills: Darfur, Sudan. Oxford: Oxford University Press.
1997   Famine Crimes: Politics and the Disaster Relief Industry in Africa. Oxford: James Currey.

DeChaine, D. Robert

2002   Humanitarian Space and the Social Imaginary: Médecins Sans
         Frontières/Doctors Without Borders and the Rhetoric of Global
         Community. Journal of Communication Inquiry 26(4):354–369.

Delvaux, Denise

2005   The Politics of Humanitarian Organizations: Neutrality and Solidarity, the
         Case of the ICRC and MSF during the 1994 Rwandan Genocide. Master's
         thesis, Department of Political Studies and International Studies, Rhodes
         University. http://eprints.ru.ac.za/146/, accessed August 6, 2010.

Derrida, Jacques

1992   Given Time: I. Counterfeit Money. Peggy Kamuf, trans. Chicago and
         London: University of Chicago Press.

Dezalay, Yves, and Bryant Garth

1998   Droits de l'homme et philanthropique hégemonique. Actes de la Recherche
         en Sciences Sociales 121(121–122):23–41.

Diwan, Paras

2000   Law of Adoption, Minority, Guardianship, and Custody. Delhi: Universal
         Law.

Donini, Antonio

2004   Principles, Politics, and Pragmatism in the International Response to the
         Afghan Crisis. *In* Nation-Building Unraveled? Aid, Peace and Justice in
         Afghanistan. Antonio Donini, Norah Niland, and Karin Wermester, eds. Pp.
         117–142. Bloomfield: Kumarian Press.

Donini, Antonio, Larissa Fast, Greg Hansen, Simon Harris, Larry Minear,
Tasneem Mowjee, and Andrew Wilder

2008   The State of the Humanitarian Enterprise. Humanitarian Agenda 2015:
         Final Report. Tufts University, Feinstein International Center.
         https://wikis.uit.tufts.edu/confluence/download/attachments/14553671/H
         A2015+Final+Report.pdf?version=1, accessed August 6, 2010.

Dorow, Sara K.

2006   Transnational Adoption: A Cultural Economy of Race, Gender, and Kinship.
         New York: New York University Press.

DuBois, Page

1991   Torture and Truth. New York: Routledge.

Duffield, Mark R.

2001   Global Governance and the New Wars: The Merging of Development and
         Security. London: Zed Books.

2006   Securing Humans in a Dangerous World. International Politics 41:1–23.

2007   Development, Security and Unending War: Governing the World of Peoples.
         Cambridge: Polity Press.

Dunant, Henry

1986   A Memory of Solferino. Geneva: International Committee of the Red Cross.
[1862]

Durkheim, Emile
1995　The Elementary Forms of Religious Life. Karen Fields, trans. New York:
[1912]　Free Press.

Dynes, Russell R.
2000　The Dialogue between Voltaire and Rousseau on the Lisbon Earthquake:
The Emergence of a Social Science View. International Journal of Mass
Emergencies and Disasters 18(1):97–115.

Ecks, Stefan
2008　Global Pharmaceutical Markets and Corporate Citizenship: The Case of
Novartis' Anti-cancer Drug Glivec. BioSocieties 3(2):165–181.

Elias, Norbert
1978　The Civilizing Process, vol 1: The History of Manners. New York: Pantheon.
[1939]

Elisha, Omri
2008　Moral Ambitions of Grace: The Paradox of Compassion and Accountability
in Evangelical Faith-Based Activism. Cultural Anthropology: Journal of the
Society for Cultural Anthropology 23(1):154–189.

Engle, Karen
2001　From Skepticism to Embrace: Human Rights and the American
Anthropological Association from 1947–1999. Human Rights Quarterly
23:536–559.

Englund, Harri
2004　Conflicts in Context: Political Violence and Anthropological Puzzles. *In*
Violence and Belonging: The Quest for Identity in Post-colonial Africa.
Vigdis Broch-Due, ed. Pp. 60–74. New York: Routledge.
2006　Prisoners of Freedom: Human Rights and the African Poor. Berkeley:
University of California Press.

Evans-Pritchard, E. E.
1965　Theories of Primitive Religion. Oxford: Clarendon Press.

Fadlalla, Amal Hassan
2008　The Neoliberalization of Compassion: Darfur and the Mediation of
American Faith, Fear, and Terror. *In* New Landscapes of Inequality:
Neoliberalism and the Erosion of Democracy in America. Janes Collins,
Micaela di Leonardo, and Brett Williams, eds. Pp. 209–228. Santa Fe: School
for Advanced Research Press.

Fardon, Richard
1990　Localizing Strategies: The Regionalization of Ethnographic Accounts. *In*
Localizing Strategies: Regional Traditions of Ethnographic Writing. Richard
Fardon, ed. Pp. 1–35. Washington: Smithsonian Institution Press.

Farmer, Paul
2003　Pathologies of Power: Health, Human Rights, and the New War on the Poor.
Berkeley: University of California Press.

Fassin, Didier

2001a   The Biopolitics of Otherness: Undocumented Foreigners and Racial Discrimination in French Public Debate. Anthropology Today 17(1):3–7.

2001b   Une double peine: La condition sociales des immigrés malades du sida. L'Homme 2(160):137–162.

2004   La cause des victimes. Theme issue, "L'Humanitaire," Les Temps Modernes 59(627):73–91.

2006   L'humanitaire contre l'état, tout contre. Vacarme 34:15–19.

2007a   Humanitarianism as a Politics of Life. Public Culture 19(3):499–520.

2007b   When Bodies Remember: Experiences and Politics of AIDS in South Africa. Berkeley: University of California Press.

2007c   Humanitarianism: A Nongovernmental Government. *In* Nongovernmental Politics. Michel Feher, with Gaëlle Krikorian and Yates McKee, eds. Pp. 149–160. New York: Zone Books.

2008a   The Humanitarian Politics of Testimony: Subjectification through Trauma in the Israeli-Palestinian Conflict. Cultural Anthropology 23(3):531–558.

2008b   Aids Orphans, Raped Babies, and Suffering Children: The Moral Construction of Childhood in Post-Apartheid South Africa. *In* Healing the World's Children: Interdisciplinary Perspectives on Health in the Twentieth Century. G. Weisz, ed. Pp. 111–124. Montreal: McGill-Queens University Press.

2010a   Heart of Humaneness. *In* Contemporary States of Emergency: The Politics of Military and Humanitarian Intervention. Didier Fassin and Mariella Pandolfi, eds. Pp. 317–333. New York: Zone Books.

2010b   Inequality of Lives, Hierarchies of Humanity: Moral Commitments and Ethical Dilemmas of Humanitarianism, *In* In the Name of Humanity: The Government of Threat and Care. Ilana Feldman and Miriam Ticktin, eds. Durham: Duke University Press.

Fassin, Didier, and Estelle D'Halluin

2005   The Truth from the Body: Medical Certificates as Ultimate Evidence for Asylum Seekers. American Anthropologist 107(4):597–608.

Fassin, Didier, and Mariella Pandolfi, eds.

2010   Contemporary States of Emergency: The Politics of Military and Humanitarian Interventions. New York: Zone Books.

Fassin, Didier, and Richard Rechtman

2009   The Empire of Trauma: An Inquiry in the Condition of Victimhood. Princeton: Princeton University Press.

Fassin, Didier, and Paula Vasquez

2005   Humanitarian Exception as the Rule: The Political Theology of the 1999 Tragedia in Venezuela. American Ethnologist 32(2–3):389–405.

Faubion, James

2003   Religion, Violence and the Vitalistic Economy. Anthropological Quarterly 76(1):71–85.

Feher, Michel
2000   Powerless by Design: The Age of the International Community. Durham: Duke University Press.

Feher, Michel, Gaëlle Krikorian, and Yates McKee, eds.
2007   Nongovernmental Politics. New York: Zone Books/MIT Press.

Feldman, Allen
2004   Memory Theatres, Virtual Witnessing, and the Trauma-Aesthetic. Biography 27(1):163–202.

Feldman, Ilana
2006   Home as a Refrain: Remembering and Living Displacement in Gaza. History and Memory 18(2):10–47.

2007a   Difficult Distinctions: Refugee Law, Humanitarian Practice, and Political Identification in Gaza. Cultural Anthropology 22(1):129–169.

2007b   The Quaker Way: Ethical Labor and Humanitarian Relief. American Ethnologist 34(4):689–705.

2008a   Mercy Trains and Ration Rolls: Between Government and Humanitarianism in Gaza. In Interpreting Welfare and Relief in the Middle East. Inger Marie Okkenhaug and Nefissa Naguib, eds. Pp. 175–194. Leiden: Brill Press.

2008b   Governing Gaza: Bureaucracy, Authority, and the Work of Rule (1917–1967). Durham: Duke University Press.

Feldman, Ilana, and Miriam Ticktin, eds.
2010   In the Name of Humanity: The Government of Threat and Care. Durham: Duke University Press.

Ferguson, James
1990   The Anti-Politics Machine: "Development," Depoliticization, and Bureaucratic Power in Lesotho. Cambridge and New York: Cambridge University Press.

1997   Anthropology and Its Evil Twin: Development in the Constitution of a Discipline. In International Development and the Social Sciences. Frederick Cooper and Randall Packard, eds. Pp. 150–175. Berkeley: University of California Press.

2002   Spatializing States: Toward an Ethnography of Neoliberal Governmentality. American Ethnologist 29:981–1002.

2006   Global Shadows: Africa in the Neoliberal World Order. Durham: Duke University Press.

Fisher, William F.
1997   Doing Good: The Politics and Antipolitics of NGO Practices. Annual Review of Anthropology 26:439–464.

Flint, Julie, and Alex de Waal
2005   Darfur: A Short History of a Long War. London: Zed Books.

Forsythe, David
2005   The Humanitarians: The International Committee of the Red Cross. Cambridge: Cambridge University Press.

REFERENCES

Foucault, Michel

1978   The History of Sexuality, vol. 1: An Introduction. New York: Vintage Books.

1986   The History of Sexuality, vol. 3: The Care of the Self. New York: Random House.

1988   Madness and Civilization: A History of Insanity in the Age of Reason. New York: Vintage Books.

2000   "Omnes et Singulatum": Toward a Critique of Political Reason. *In* The
[1979] Essential Works of Michel Foucault, 1954–1984, vol 3: Power. James Faubion, ed. Pp. 298–325. New York: New Press.

2003   Society Must Be Defended: Lectures at the Collège de France, 1975–1976. David Macey, trans. New York: Picador.

2007   Security, Territory, Population: Lectures at the Collège de France, 1977–1978. New York: Palgrave Macmillan [first French publication 2004].

2008   Le gouvernement de soi et des autres. Cours au Collège de France, 1982–1983. Paris: Hautes Etudes–Gallimard–Seuil.

Fox, Fiona

2001   New Humanitarianism. Does It Provide a Moral Banner for the 21st Century. Disasters 25(4):275–289.

Fox, Renée C.

1995   Medical Humanitarianism and Human Rights: Reflections on Doctors Without Borders and Doctors of the World. Social Science and Medicine 41(12):1607–1626.

Frank, Andre Gunder

1969   Latin America: Underdevelopment and Revolution. New York: Monthly Review Press.

Frank, Robert

1992   La neutralité: Évolution historique d'un concept. *In* Neutrality in History/La neutralité dans l'histoire: Proceedings of the Conference on the History of Neutrality, Commission of History of International Relations. Pp. 25–31. Helsinki: Finnish Historical Society.

Franklin, Sarah, and Margaret Lock, eds.

2003   Remaking Life and Death: Toward an Anthropology of the Biosciences. Santa Fe: School of American Research Press.

Franklin, Sarah, and Susan McKinnon

2001   Relative Values: Reconfiguring Kinship Studies. Durham: Duke University Press.

Franklin, Sarah, and Helena Ragoné

1997   Reproducing Reproduction: Kinship, Power, and Technological Innovation. Philadelphia: University of Pennsylvania Press.

Freire, Paolo

1970   Pedagogy of the Oppressed. New York: Herder and Herder.

Friedman, Jonathan
2007   Commentary on Jane Guyer. American Anthropologist 34(3):426–429.

Frisch, Ephraim
1924   An Historical Survey of Jewish Philanthropy: From the Earliest Times to the Nineteenth Century. New York: Macmillan.

Geertz, Clifford
1963   Agricultural Involution: Social Development and Economic Change in Two Indonesian Towns. Berkeley: University of California Press.
1973   Religion as a Cultural System. *In* The Interpretation of Cultures. Basic Books.

Godelier, Maurice
1999   The Enigma of the Gift. Chicago: University of Chicago Press.

Good, Anthony
2008   Cultural Evidence in Courts of Law. Special issue, "The Objects of Evidence: Anthropological Approaches to the Production of Knowledge," Journal of the Royal Anthropological Institute 14(s1):S47–S60.

Good, Mary-Jo DelVecchio, Sandra Teresa Hyde, Sarah Pinto, and Byron Good, eds.
2008   Postcolonial Disorders. Ethnographic Studies in Subjectivity Series. Berkeley: University of California Press.

Goodale, Mark
2007   Locating Rights, Envisioning Law between the Global and the Local. *In* The Practice of Human Rights: Tracking Law between the Global and the Local. Mark Goodale and Sally Engle Merry, eds. Pp. 1–38. Cambridge: Cambridge University Press.

Gordon, Neve
2008   Israel's Occupation. Berkeley: University of California Press.

Gott, Gil
2002   Imperial Humanitarianism: History of an Arrested Dialectic. *In* Moral Imperialism: A Critical Anthology. Berta Esperanza and Esperanza Hernández-Truyol, eds. Pp. 19–38. New York: New York University Press.

Green, Maia
2000   Participatory Development and the Appropriation of Agency in Southern Tanzania. Critique of Anthropology 20:67–89.

Greenhalgh, Susan
2005   Governing China's Population: From Leninist to Neoliberal Biopolitics. Palo Alto: Stanford University Press.

Gregory, C. A.
1982   Gifts and Commodities. London and New York: Academic Press.

Grignon, Claude, and Jean-Claude Passeron
1989   Le savant et le populaire: Misèrabilisme et populisme en sociologie et en littèrature. Paris: Éditions Seuil.

Gupta, Akhil, and James Ferguson
1997   Discipline and Practice: "The Field" as Site, Method, and Location in Anthropology. *In* Anthropological Locations: Boundaries and Grounds of a Field Science. Akhil Gupta and James Ferguson, eds. Pp. 1–46. Berkeley: University of California Press.

Gusterson, Hugh
2007   Anthropology and Militarism. Annual Review of Anthropology 36:155–175.

Gutman, Roy, and David Rieff, eds.
1999   Crimes of War: What the Public Should Know. New York: W. W. Norton.

Hale, Charles
2006   Activist Research v. Cultural Critique: Indigenous Land Rights and the Contradictions of Politically Engaged Anthropology. Cultural Anthropology 21(1):96–120.

Hanlon, Joseph
2000   An "Ambitious and Extensive Political Agenda": The Role of NGOs and the AID Industry. *In* Global Institutions and Local Empowerment: Competing Theoretical Perspectives. K. Stiles, ed. Pp. 132–145. New York: St. Martin's.

Hansen, Thomas Blom, and Finn Stepputat, eds.
2001   States of Imagination: Explorations of the Postcolonial State. Durham: Duke University Press.
2005   Sovereign Bodies: Citizens, Migrants and States in the Postcolonial World. Princeton: Princeton University Press.

Hardt, Michael, and Antonio Negri
2000   Empire. Cambridge: Harvard University Press.

Harroff-Tavel, Marion
2003   Does It Still Make Sense to Be Neutral? Humanitarian Exchange 25:1–4.

Haskell, Thomas
1995   Capitalism and the Origins of Humanitarian Sensibility. *In* The Antislavery Debate. Thomas Bender, ed. Pp. 107–160. Berkeley: University of California Press. *Also in* The American Historical Review 90(2):339–361 *and* 90(3):547–556 (1985).

Hathaway, James
1984   The Evolution of Refugee Status in International Law: 1920–1950. International and Comparative Law Quarterly 33(2):348–380.

Haug, Hans
1996   Neutrality as a Fundamental Principle of the Red Cross. International Review of the Red Cross 315:627–630.

Headrick, Rita
1994   Colonialism, Health and Illness in French Equatorial Africa, 1885–1935. Daniel Headrick, ed. Atlanta: African Studies Association Press.

Heath, Deborah, Rayna Rapp, and Karen-Sue Taussig
2007   Genetic Citizenship. *In* A Companion to the Anthropology of Politics. David Nugent and Joan Vincent, eds. Pp. 152–167. Malden: Blackwell.

Heim, Maria

2004   Theories of the Gift in South Asia: Hindu, Buddhist, and Jain Reflections on Dāna Religion in History, Society, and Culture. New York and London: Routledge.

Henderson, Patricia

2007   South African Aids Orphans: Examining Assumptions around Vulnerability from the Perspective of Rural Children and Youth. Childhood 13(3):303–327.

Hiatt, L. R.

1996   Prologue. *In* Arguments about Aborigines: Australia and the Evolution of Social Anthropology. Pp. 1–12. Cambridge: Cambridge University Press.

Hickey, Samuel, and Giles Mohan, eds.

2004   Participation—From Tyranny to Transformation?: Exploring New Approaches to Participation in Development. London: Zed Books.

Hinton, Alexander, ed.

2002   Genocide: Anthropological Reader. Malden: Blackwell.

Hitchens, Christopher

1995   The Missionary Position: Mother Teresa in Theory and Practice. London and New York: Verso.

Hochschild, Adam

2005   Bury the Chains: Prophets and Rebels in the Fight to Free an Empire's Slaves. Boston: Houghton Mifflin.

Hoffman, Beatrix

2006   Sympathy and Exclusion: Access to Health Care for Undocumented Immigrants in the United States. *In* A Death Retold: Jesica Santillan, the Bungled Transplant, and the Paradoxes of Medical Citizenship. Keith Wailoo, Julie Livingston, and Peter Garbaccia, eds. Pp. 237–254. Chapel Hill: University of North Carolina Press.

Hoffman, Danny

2005   Violent Events as Narrative Blocs: The Disarmament at Bo, Sierra Leone. Anthropological Quarterly 78(2):329–354.

Hoffman, Peter, and Thomas Weiss

2006   Sword and Salve: Confronting New Wars and Humanitarian Crises. Lanham: Rowman and Littlefield.

Hoffman, Susanna, and Anthony Oliver-Smith

2002   Catastrophe and Culture: The Anthropology of Disaster. Santa Fe: School of American Research Press.

Holmes, Douglas R., and George E. Marcus

2005   Cultures of Expertise and the Management of Globalization: Toward the Re-functioning of Ethnography. *In* Global Assemblages: Technology, Politics, and Ethics as Anthropological Problems. Aihwa Ong and Stephen J. Collier, eds. Pp. 235–252. Oxford: Blackwell.

Hopgood, Stephen
2008   Saying "No" to Walmart? Money and Morality in Professional Humanitarianism. *In* Humanitarianism in Question: Politics, Power, Ethics. Michael Barnett and Thomas G. Weiss, eds. Pp. 98–123. Ithaca: Cornell University Press.

Hours, Bernard
2000   L'idéologie humanitaire ou le spectacle de l'altérité perdue. Paris: L'Harmattan.

HPN (Humanitarian Practice Network)
2003   Editorial: Neutrality. Humanitarian Exchange Magazine 25:1.

Huang, Julia C.
2005   The Compassion Relief Diaspora. *In* Buddhist Missionaries in the Era of Globalization. Linda Learman, ed. Pp. 185–209. Honolulu: University of Hawaii Press.

Husseini, Jalal
2000   UNRWA and the Palestinian Nation-Building Process. Journal of Palestine Studies 29(2):51–64.

Hutchinson, John F.
1996   Champions of Charity: War and the Rise of the Red Cross. Boulder: Westview Press.

Hyde, Sandra Teresa
2007   Eating Spring Rice: The Cultural Politics of AIDS in Southwest China. Berkeley: University of California Press.
2008   Everyday AIDS Practices: Contestations of Borders and Infectious Disease in Southwest China. *In* Postcolonial Disorders. Mary-Jo DelVecchio Good, Sandra Teresa Hyde, Sarah Pinto, and Byron Good, eds. Pp. 189–217. Ethnographic Studies in Subjectivity Series. Berkeley: University of California Press.

Hyndman, Jennifer
2000   Managing Displacement: Refugees and the Politics of Humanitarianism. Minneapolis: University of Minnesota Press.

ICRC (International Committee of the Red Cross)
2000   Catalog. Geneva: International Red Cross and Red Crescent Museum.

Ignatieff, Michael
1984   The Needs of Strangers. New York: Viking.
1997   The Warrior's Honor: Ethnic War and the Modern Conscience. New York: Henry Holt.
1999   Human Rights. *In* Human Rights in Political Transitions: Gettysburg to Bosnia. Carla Hesse and Robert Post, eds. Pp. 313–324. New York: Zone Books.

INCITE! (Women of Color against Violence)
2007   The Revolution Will Not Be Funded: Beyond the Nonprofit Industrial Complex. Cambridge: South End Press.

Inda, Jonathan Xavier, and Renato Rosaldo
2001   Anthropology of Globalization: A Reader. Malden: Blackwell.

Independent International Commission on Kosovo
2000   The Kosovo Report: Conflict, International Response, Lessons Learned. New York: Oxford University Press.

Isaac, Ephraim
1993   Humanitarianism across Religions and Cultures. *In* Humanitarianism across Borders: Sustaining Civilians in Times of War. Thomas Weiss and Larry Minear, eds. Pp. 13–22. Boulder: Lynne Rienner.

Jackson, Stanley W.
2001   Presidential Address: The Wounded Healer. Bulletin of the History of Medicine 75:1–36.

James, Erica Caple
2004   The Political Economy of "Trauma" in Haiti in the Democratic Era of Insecurity. Culture, Medicine and Psychiatry 28(2):127–149.

Jean-Klein, Iris, and Annelise Riles
2005   Introducing Discipline: Anthropology and Human Rights Administrations. Political and Legal Anthropology Review 28(2):173–202.

Jordt, Ingrid
2007   Burma's Mass Lay Meditation Movement: Buddhism and the Cultural Construction of Power. Athens: Ohio University Press.

Kanaan, Jean-Sélim
2002   La guerre à l'indifférence. Paris: Robert Laffont.

Kaplan, Charles, and Eric Broekaert
2003   An Introduction to Research on the Social Impact of the Therapeutic Community for Addiction. International Journal of Social Welfare 12(3):204–210.

Kapoor, Rakesh, and Amit Kumar Sharma
2000   Religious Philanthropy and Organised Social Development Efforts in India. Occasional Papers, No. 3. New Delhi: Indian Centre for Philanthropy.

Kavanaugh, Sarah
2008   ORT, The Second World War and the Rehabilitation of Holocaust Survivors. London and Portland: Vallentine Mitchell.

Keck, Margaret E., and Kathryn Sikkink
1998   Activists beyond Borders: Advocacy Networks in International Politics. Ithaca: Cornell University Press.

Kennedy, David
2004   The Dark Side of Virtue: Reassessing International Humanitarianism. Princeton: Princeton University Press.

Kidder, Tracy
2003   Mountains beyond Mountains: The Quest of Dr. Paul Farmer, a Man Who Would Cure the World. New York: Random House.

Kim, Jim Yong, Joyce Millen, Alec Irwen, and John Gershman, eds.
2000   Dying for Growth: Global Inequality and the Health of the Poor. Monroe: Common Courage Press.

Kipnis, Andrew
2006   *Suzhi*: A Key Word Approach. China Quarterly 186:195–313.

Kleinman, Arthur, Veena Das, and Margaret Lock, eds.
1997   Social Suffering. Berkeley: University of California Press.

Knight, W. S. M.
1920   Neutrality and Neutralism in the Sixteenth Century—Liège. Journal of Comparative Legislation and International Law, Third Series 2(1):98–104.

Konrad, Monica
2005   Nameless Relations: Anonymity, Melanesia, and Reproductive Gift Exchange between British Ova Donors and Recipients. New York: Berghahn Books.

Lachenal, Guillaume, and Bertrand Taithe
2009   Une généalogie missionnaire et coloniale de l'humanitaire: Le cas Aujoulat au Cameroun, 1935–1973. Le Mouvement Social 227(April–June):45–63.

Laidlaw, James
1995   Riches and Renunciation: Religion, Economy, and Society among the Jains. Oxford: Clarendon.
2000   A Free Gift Makes No Friends (Anthropological Analysis of the "Pure" or "Free" Gift). Journal of the Royal Anthropological Institute 6(4):617.

Lakoff, Andrew
2007   Preparing for the Next Emergency. Public Culture 19(2):247–271.

Lakoff, Andrew, ed.
2010   Disaster and the Politics of Intervention. New York: Columbia University and SSRC.

Lalande, André
1993   Vocabulaire technique et critique de la philosophie. Paris: Presses
[1926] Universitaires de France.

Lambek, Michael
1998   Body and Mind in Mind, Body and Mind in Body: Some Anthropological Interventions in a Long Conversation. *In* Bodies and Persons: Comparative Perspectives from Africa and Melanesia. Michael Lambek and Andrew Strathern, eds. Pp. 103–123. Cambridge: Cambridge University Press.

Laqueur, Thomas
1987   Bodies, Details and the Humanitarian Narrative. *In* The New Cultural History. Lynn Hunt, ed. Pp. 176–204. Berkeley: University of California Press.
2009   Mourning, Pity, and the Work of Narrative. *In* Humanitarianism and Suffering: The Mobilization of Empathy. Richard Wilson and Richard Brown, eds. Pp. 31–57. Cambridge: Cambridge University Press.

las Casas, Bartolomé de
1992   A Short Account of the Destruction of the Indies. London: Penguin Classics.
[1552]

Lassiter, Luke Eric
2005a   Collaborative Ethnography and Public Anthropology. Current Anthropology 46:83–106.
2005b   The Chicago Guide to Collaborative Ethnography. Chicago: University of Chicago Press.

Latour, Bruno
1987   Science in Action: How to Follow Scientists and Engineers through Society. Cambridge: Harvard University Press.
2005   Reassembling the Social: An Introduction to Actor-Network Theory. Oxford: Oxford University Press.

Leebaw, Bronwyn
2007   The Politics of Impartial Activism: Humanitarianism and Human Rights. Perspectives on Politics 5(2):223–239.

Leopold, Mark
2005   Inside West Nile: Violence, History and Representation on an African Frontier. Santa Fe: School of American Research Press.

Letts, James W.
1996   Emic/Etic Distinctions. *In* Encyclopedia of Cultural Anthropology, Vol. 2. David Levinson and Melvin Ember, eds. Pp. 382–383. New York: Henry Holt.

Levine, Harry G.
1978   The Discovery of Addiction: Changing Conceptions of Habitual Drunkenness in America: Part 1. Journal of Studies on Alcohol 15:493–506.

Levitt, Matthew
2006   Hamas: Politics, Charity, and Terrorism in the Service of Jihad. New Haven: Yale University Press.

Li, Tania
2007   The Will to Improve: Governmentality, Development, and the Practice of Politics. Durham: Duke University Press.

Lindenberg, Marc, and Coralie Bryant
2001   Going Global: Transforming Relief and Development NGOs. Bloomfield: Kumarian.

Lindqvist, Sven
2000   A History of Bombing. New York: New Press.

Liogier, Raphaël
2007   L'ONG comme agent institutionnel optimal du champ religieux individuo-globalisé. *In* Les ONG confessionnelles: Religions et action internationale. Bruno Duriez, François Mabille, and Kathy Rousselet, eds. Pp. 263–276. Paris: L'Harmattan.

Lippert, Randy
2004   Sanctuary Practices, Rationalities, and Sovereignties. Alternatives 29(5):335–355.

Lischer, Sarah K.
2007   Military Intervention and the Humanitarian "Force Multiplier." Global Governance 13:99–118.

Lobo, Aloma, and Jayapriya Vasudevan
2002   The Penguin Guide to Adoption in India. New Delhi and New York: Penguin Books.

Lock, Margaret
2002   Twice Dead: Organ Transplants and the Reinvention of Death. Berkeley: University of California Press.

Lovell, Anne
2006   Addiction Markets. *In* Global Pharmaceuticals: Ethics, Markets, Practices. Adriana Petryna, Andrew Lakoff, and Arthur Kleinman, eds. Pp. 136–170. Durham: Duke University Press.

Lu, L., H. H. Jia, J. Y. Lu, H. B. Luo, X. P. Zhang, and Y. L. Ma et al.
2005   Analysis of HIV/AIDS Prevalence in Yunnan Province. AIDS/STD Prevention and Control 11(3):164, 172–174.

Lugard, Lord Fredrick
1965   The Dual Mandate in British Tropical Africa. London and New York:
[1926]   Routledge.

Lyons, Maryinez
1992   The Colonial Disease: A Social History of Sleeping Sickness in Northern Zaire, 1900–1940. Cambridge: Cambridge University Press.

Maalouf, Jean, ed.
2001   Mother Teresa Essential Writings, Modern Spiritual Masters Series. Maryknoll: Orbis Books.

Maharaj, Dnyaneshwar
1972   Gita the Mother. Manu Subedar, trans. Ludhiana: Kalyani.

Malinowska-Sempruch, Kasia, and Nick Bartlett
2006   Who Needs Protecting?: Rethinking HIV, Drugs and Security in the China Context. China and Eurasia Forum Quarterly 4(1):25–30.

Malkki, Liisa H.

1995   Purity and Exile: Violence, Memory, and National Cosmology among Hutu Refugees in Tanzania. Chicago and London: University of Chicago Press.

1996   Speechless Emissaries: Refugees, Humanitarianism, and Dehistoricization. Cultural Anthropology 11(3):377–404.

2007   Tradition and Improvisation in Ethnographic Field Research. *In* Improvising Theory: Process and Temporality in Ethnographic Fieldwork. Allaine Cerwonka and Liisa H. Malkki, authors. Pp. 162–187. Chicago: University of Chicago Press.

Mamdani, Mahmood

2001   When Victims Become Killers: Colonialism, Nativism, and the Genocide in Rwanda. Princeton: Princeton University Press.

Manjhi, Firoze, and Carl O'Coill

2002   The Missionary Position: NGOs and Development in Africa. International Affairs 78(3):567–583.

Manu

1991   The Laws of Manu. London and New York: Penguin.

Marcus, George

1995   Ethnography in/of the World System: The Emergence of Multi-Sited Ethnography. Annual Review of Anthropology 24:95–117.

Markowitz, Lisa

2001   Finding the Field: Notes on the Ethnography of NGOs. Human Organization. Human Organization 6(1):40–46.

Maurer, Bill

2003   Please Destabilize Ethnography Now: Against Anthropological Showbiz-as-Usual. Reviews in Anthropology 32:159–169.

Mauss, Marcel

1985   A Category of the Human Mind: The Notion of Person; the Notion of Self.

[1938]   *In* The Category of the Person: Anthropology, Philosophy, History. M. Carrithers, Steven Collins, Steven Lukes, eds. Pp. 1–25. Cambridge: Cambridge University Press. Original edition, 1938, Une catégorie de l'esprit humain: La notion de personne celle de "moi." Journal of the Royal Anthropological Institute 68.

1990   The Gift: Forms and Functions of Exchange in Archaic Societies. New York:

[1925]   W. W. Norton.

Mbembe, Achille

2001   On the Postcolony. Berkeley: University of California Press.

McCarthy, Kathleen D., ed.

1990   Lady Bountiful Revisited: Women, Philanthropy, and Power. New Brunswick and London: Rutgers University Press.

REFERENCES

McFalls, Laurence
2010   Benevolent Dictatorship: The Formal Logic of Humanitarian Government. *In* Contemporary States of Emergency: The Politics of Military and Humanitarian Interventions. Didier Fassin and Mariella Pandolfi, eds. Pp. 317–333. New York: Zone Books.

Meintjes, Helen, and Sonja Giese
2007   Spinning the Epidemic: The Making of Mythologies of Orphanhood in the Context of Aids. Childhood 13(3):407–430.

Merry, Sally Engle
2003   Human Rights Law and the Demonization of Culture (and Anthropology along the Way). Political and Legal Anthropology Review 26:55–76.
2005   Human Rights and Gender Violence: Translating International Law into Local Justice. Chicago: University of Chicago Press.

Meyerhoff, Barbara
1978   Number Our Days: A Triumph of Continuity and Culture among Jewish Old People in an Urban Ghetto. New York: Simon & Schuster.

Minear, Larry
1999   The Theory and Practice of Neutrality: Some Thoughts on the Tensions. International Review of the Red Cross 833:63–71.
2002   The Humanitarian Enterprise: Dilemmas and Discoveries. Bloomfield: Kumarian Press.

Mini, Fabio
2003   La guerra dopo la guerra. Soldati, burocrati e mercenari nell'epoca della pace virtuale. Turin: Einaudi.

Minn, Pierre
2007   Toward an Anthropology of Humanitarianism. Journal of Humanitarian Assistance. http://jha.ac/2007/08/, accessed June 10, 2010.

Mitchell, Timothy
2002   Rule of Experts: Egypt, Techno-Politics, Modernity. Berkeley: University of California Press.

Miyazaki, Hirokazu
2004   The Method of Hope: Anthropology, Philosophy, and Fijian Knowledge. Stanford: Stanford University Press.

Modell, Judith Schachter
1994   Kinship with Strangers: Adoption and Interpretations of Kinship in American Culture. Berkeley: University of California Press.
2002   A Sealed and Secret Kinship: The Culture of Policies and Practices in American Adoption. New York: Berghahn Books.

Montaigne, Michel de
1994   On Cannibals. *In* Essays. Pp. 105–118. London: Penguin Books.
[1580]

Moore, Henrietta L.

1996   The Changing Nature of Anthropological Knowledge: An Introduction. *In* The Future of Anthropological Knowledge. Henrietta L. Moore, ed. Pp. 1–15. New York: Routledge.

Moorehead, Caroline

1998   Dunant's Dream: War, Switzerland and the History of the Red Cross. New York: Carroll and Graf.

Morris, David

1996   A Gift from America: The First Fifty Years of CARE. Marietta: Longstreet Press.

Mosse, David

2005   Cultivating Development: An Ethnography of Aid Policy and Practice. London: Pluto Press.

MSF (Médecins Sans Frontières)

1999   The 1999 Nobel Lecture. Delivered by Dr James Orbinski, President of the MSF International Council, in Oslo, December 10.

2006   La Mancha Gazette. Geneva: MSF International.

2007   Manuel des acteurs de l'aide. Paris: Fondation Médecins Sans Frontières/CRASH.

MSF-H (Médecins Sans Frontières Holland)

2000   Final Report of Workshop on Humanitarian Principles. The Future of Humanitarianism: Back to the Basics or Political Engagement? Final Report of Workshop on Humanitarian Principles, Soesterberg, The Netherlands.

MSF (Médecins Sans Frontières) and MSF CRASH

2002   Dossier special: Guerre à la terreur. La Sélection du CRASH, 2: MSF Foundation/Centre de Recherche sur l'Action et les Savoirs Humanitaires.

Murdoch, Lydia

2006   Imagined Orphans: Poor Families, Child Welfare, and Contested Citizenship in London. New Brunswick: Rutgers University Press.

Nader, Laura

1972   Up the Anthropologist: Perspectives Gained from Studying Up. *In* Reinventing Anthropology. Dell Hymes, ed. Pp. 284–311. New York: Pantheon.

NALP (National Adult Literacy Programme)

1986   National Adult Literacy Policy. Lilongwe: National Adult Literacy Programme.

2005   Proposal on Malawi Mass Literacy Campaign (2006–2008). Lilongwe: National Adult Literacy Programme.

Neff, Stephen

2000   The Rights and Duties of Neutrals: A General History. Manchester: Manchester University Press.

Neusner, Jacob
1990   Tzedahak: Can Jewish Philanthropy Buy Jewish Survival? Brown Judaic
Studies, 205. Atlanta: Scholars Press.

Nevakivi, Jukka, ed.
1993   Neutrality in History/La neutralité dans l'histoire. Proceedings of the
Conference on the History of Neutrality, Commission of History of
International Relations. Pp. 9–12. Helsinki: Finnish Historical Society.

Nguyen, Vinh-Kim
2005   Anti-retroviral Globalism, Biopolitics and Therapeutic Citizenship. *In* Global
Assemblages: Technology, Politics, and Ethics as Anthropological Problems.
Aihwa Ong and Stephen Collier, eds. Pp. 124–144. Malden: Blackwell.

Nguyen, Vinh-Kim, and Karine Peschard
2003   Anthropology, Inequality and Disease: A Review. Annual Review of
Anthropology 32:447–474.

Nichols, Bruce J.
1988   The Uneasy Alliance: Religion, Refugee Work, and U.S. Foreign Policy. New
York and Oxford: Oxford University Press.

Nichols, Bruce, and Gil Loescher
1989   The Moral Nation: Humanitarianism and U.S. Foreign Policy Today. Notre
Dame: University of Notre Dame.

Nietzsche, Friedrich
1967   On the Genealogy of Morals. New York: Vintage Books.
[1887]

Nordmann, Charlotte
2006   Bourdieu/Rancière: La politique entre sociologie et philosophie. Paris:
Éditions Amsterdam.

Nordstrom, Carolyn
2004   Shadows of War: Violence, Power, and International Profiteering in the
Twenty-First Century. Berkeley: University of California Press.

Olivier de Sardan, Jean-Pierre
2005   Anthropology and Development: Understanding Contemporary Social
Change. London: Zed Books.

Ong, Aihwa, and Stephen J. Collier, eds.
2005   Global Assemblages: Technology, Politics, and Ethics as Anthropological
Problems. Malden: Blackwell.

Orbinski, James
2008   An Imperfect Offering: Humanitarian Action for the Twenty-First Century.
New York: Walker.

Pandolfi, Mariella
2000   L'industrie humanitaire: Une souveraineté mouvante et supracolonial.
Multitudes 3:97–105. Also as electronic document, http://multitudes.samizdat
.net/article.php3?id_article=182, accessed June 10, 2010.
2003   Contract of Mutual (in)Difference: Governance and the Humanitarian

Apparatus in Contemporary Albania and Kosovo. Indiana Journal of Global Legal Studies 10(1):369–381.

2006   La zone grise des guerres humanitaires. Special issue, "War and Peace/La guerre et la paix," Ellen Judd, ed. Anthropologica 48(1):43–58.

2007   Vivre la guerre des autres. Humanitaire Hors série 4:62–8.

2008a   Théâtre de guerres: Passions politiques et violences. Anthropologie et Sociétés 32(3):99–119.

2008b   Laboratory of Intervention: The Humanitarian Governance of the Postcommunist Balkan Territories. In Postcolonial Disorders. Mary-Jo Delvecchio Good, Sandra Hyde, Sarah Pinto, and Byron Good, eds. Pp. 157–186. Berkeley: University of California Press.

2010   From Paradox to Paradigm: The Permanent State of Emergency in the Balkans. In States of Contemporary Emergency: The Politics of Military and Humanitarian Interventions. Didier Fassin and Mariella Pandolfi, eds. Pp. 153–172. New York: Zone Books.

Parry, Jonathan

1986   The Gift, the Indian Gift and the "Indian Gift." Man (N.S.) 21:453–473.
[1985]

1989   On the Moral Perils of Exchange. In Money and the Morality of Exchange. J. Parry and M. Bloch, eds. Pp. 64–93. Cambridge and New York: Cambridge University Press.

1994   Death in Banaras. Lewis Henry Morgan Lectures. Cambridge and New York: Cambridge University Press.

Pendse, Sandeep

1995   Toil, Sweat, and the City. In Bombay: Metaphor for Modern India. Sujata Patel and Alice Thorner, eds. Pp. 3–25. Bombay: Oxford University Press.

Penslar, Derek J.

1998   The Origins of Modern Jewish Philanthropy. In Philanthropy in the World's Traditions. Warren F. Ilchman, Stanley N. Katz, and Edward L. Queen II, eds. Pp. 197–214. Bloomington and Indianapolis: Indiana University Press.

Petryna, Adriana

2002   Life Exposed: Biological Citizens after Chernobyl. In-Formation Series. Princeton: Princeton University Press.

Petryna, Adriana, Andrew Lakoff, and Arthur Kleinman, eds.

2006   Global Pharmaceuticals: Ethics, Markets, Practices. Durham: Duke University Press.

Plattner, Denise

1996   ICRC Neutrality and Neutrality in Humanitarian Assistance. International Review of the Red Cross 311:161–179. http://www.icrc.org.libproxy.lib.unc.edu/eng/resources/documents/misc/57jn2z.htm, accessed January 14, 2011.

Prashad, Vijay

1997   Mother Teresa as the Mirror of Bourgeois Guilt. Economic and Political Weekly 32 (44/45):2856–2858. http://www.jstor.org/stable/4406036, accessed June 10, 2010.

Pupavac, Vanessa

2001   Therapeutic Governance: Pyscho-Social Intervention and Trauma Risk
        Management. Disasters 25(4):358–372.

2004   International Therapeutic Peace and Justice in Bosnia. Social and Legal
        Studies 13(3):377–401.

2005   Human Security and the Rise of Global Therapeutic Governance. Conflict,
        Development and Security 5(2):161–182.

Qian, Hanzhu, Joseph E. Schumacher, Huey T. Chen, and Yuhua Ruan

2006   Injection Drug Use and HIV/AIDS in China: Review of Current Situation,
        Prevention and Policy Implications. Harm Reduction Journal 3(4):1–8.

Qian, Hanzhu, S. H. Vermund, and N. Wang

2005   Risk of HIV/AIDS in China: Subpopulations of Importance. Sexually
        Transmitted Infections 81:442–447.

Qureshi, Jawad Hussain

        Earthquake Jihad: The Role of Jihadis and Islamist Groups after the 2005
        Earthquake. Humanitarian Practice Network. London: Overseas
        Development Institute.

Rabinow, Paul

1996   Essays on the Anthropology of Reason. Princeton: Princeton University
        Press.

1999   French DNA: Trouble in Purgatory. Chicago: University of Chicago Press.

2003   Anthropos Today: Reflections on Modern Equipment. Princeton: Princeton
        University Press.

Rabinow, Paul, George E. Marcus, James D. Faubion, and Tobias Rees

2008   Designs for an Anthropology of the Contemporary. Durham: Duke
        University Press.

Ragoné, Helena

1994   Surrogate Motherhood: Conception in the Heart. Boulder: Westview Press.

Ragoné, Helena, and France Windance Twine

2000   Ideologies and Technologies of Motherhood: Race, Class, Sexuality,
        Nationalism. New York: Routledge.

Raheja, Gloria Goodwin

1988   The Poison in the Gift: Ritual, Prestation, and the Dominant Caste in a
        North Indian Village. Chicago and London: University of Chicago Press.

Raich, Jordi

2004   El espejismo humanitario. Rome: Debate.

Rancière, Jacques

2004   The Philosopher and His Poor. Durham: Duke University Press.

Ratcliffe, John

2007   Islamic Charities after Catastrophes: The Kashmir Earthquake and the
        Indian Ocean Tsunami. *In* Understanding Islamic Charities. Jon B. Alterman
        and Karin von Hippel, eds. Pp. 48–63. Washington: CSIS Press.

Ray, Gene

2004   Reading the Lisbon Earthquake: Adorno, Lyotard and the Contemporary Sublime. Yale Journal of Criticism 17(1):1–18.

Redeker, Robert

1996   L'humanitaire devant l'avenir. Critique de la non-anthropologie humanitaire. Les Temps Modernes 322–343.

Redfield, Peter

2005   Doctors, Borders and Life in Crisis. Cultural Anthropology 20(3):328–361.

2006   A Less Modest Witness: Collective Advocacy and Motivated Truth of a Medical Humanitarian Movement. American Ethnologist 33(1):3–26.

2008a   Sacrifice, Triage and Global Humanitarianism. In Humanitarianism in Question: Politics, Power, Ethics. Michael Barnett and Thomas G. Weiss, eds. Pp. 196–214. Ithaca: Cornell University Press.

2008b   Doctors Without Borders and the Moral Economy of Pharmaceuticals. In Human Rights in Crisis. A. Bullard, ed. Pp. 129–144. Aldershot: Ashgate Press.

2008c   Vital Mobility and the Humanitarian Kit. In Biosecurity Interventions: Global Health and Security in Question. A. Lakoff and S. Collier, eds. Pp. 147–171. New York: Columbia University Press.

Rieff, David

2002   A Bed for the Night: Humanitarianism in Crisis. New York: Simon & Schuster.

Riles, Annelise

2000   The Network Inside Out. Ann Arbor: University of Michigan Press.

2006   Anthropology, Human Rights, and Legal Knowledge: Culture in the Iron Cage. American Anthropologist 108(1):52–65.

Roitman, Janet

2005   Fiscal Disobedience: An Anthropology of Economic Regulation in Central Africa. Princeton: Princeton University Press.

Rose, Nikolas

1996   Inventing Ourselves: Psychology, Power, and Personhood. Cambridge: Cambridge University Press.

2001   The Politics of Life Itself. Theory, Culture and Society 18(6):1–30.

2007   The Politics of Life Itself: Biomedicine, Power and Subjectivity in the Twenty-First Century. In-Formation. Paul Rabinow, series ed. Princeton: Princeton University Press.

Rose, Nikolas, and Carlos Novas

2005   Biological Citizenship. In Global Assemblages: Technology, Politics, and Ethics as Anthropological Problems. Aihwa Ong and Stephen J. Collier, eds. Pp. 439–463. Malden: Blackwell.

Rosen, Lawrence

2008   Faith, Charity, and Terror. Contemporary Islam 2:139–145.

Rothstein, Robert
1966   Alignment, Nonalignment, and Small Powers, 1945–1965. International
        Organization 20(3):397–418.

Rufin, Jean-Christophe
1999   Pour l'humanitaire: Dépasser le sentiment d'échec. Le Débat 105:4–21.

Rylko-Bauer, Barbara, Linda Whiteford, and Paul Farmer, eds.
2009   Global Health in Times of Violence. Santa Fe: School for Advanced
        Research Press.

Saillant, Francine, ed.
2007   Entre-lieux de l'humanitaire. Anthropologie ét Sociétés 31(2):7–321.

Sampson, Steven
2003   "Trouble Spots": Projects, Bandits and State Formation. *In* Globalization, the
        State, and Violence. Jonathan Friedman, ed. Pp. 309–342. Walnut Creek:
        Alta Mira Press.

Schaeublin, Emanuel
2009   The West Bank Zakat Committees (1977–2009) in the Local Context. CCDP
        Working Paper 5. Geneva: Graduate Institute of International and
        Development Studies. http://www.charityandsecurity.org/system/files/
        CCDP_Working_Paper_5.pdf, accessed January 14, 2011.

Schatz, David, Chaim I. Waxman, Nathan J. Diament, eds.
1997   Tikkun Olam: Social Responsibility in Jewish Thought and Law. Northvale:
        Jason Aronson, Inc.

Scheper-Hughes, Nancy
2000   The Global Traffic in Human Organs. Current Anthropology
        41(2):191–224.

2002   Commodity Fetishism in Organs Trafficking. *In* Scheper-Hughes, Nancy, and
        Loic J. D. Wacquant. Commodifying Bodies. Pp. 31–62. London: Sage.

2005   The Last Commodity: Post-Human Ethics and the Global Traffic in "Fresh"
        Organs. *In* Global Assemblages: Technology, Politics and Ethics as
        Anthropological Problems. Aihwa Ong and Stephen Collier, eds. Pp.
        145–167. Malden: Blackwell.

Scheper-Hughes, Nancy, and Loic J. D. Wacquant
2002   Commodifying Bodies. London: Sage.

Schneider, David Murray
1980   American Kinship: A Cultural Account. Chicago: University of Chicago Press.

1984   A Critique of the Study of Kinship. Ann Arbor: University of Michigan Press.

Schrift, Alan, ed.
1997   The Logic of the Gift: Toward an Ethic of Generosity. New York: Routledge.

Scott, David
2004   Conscripts of Modernity: The Tragedy of Colonial Enlightenment. Durham:
        Duke University Press.

Sharma, Sanjay
2001   Famine, Philanthropy and the Colonial State: North India in the Early Nineteenth Century. Oxford and New York: Oxford University Press.

Shetty, Priya
2007   How Important Is Neutrality to Humanitarian Aid Agencies? Lancet 370(9585):377–378.

Siddiqui, Noor Jahan
1997   Adolescent Orphan Girls in Delhi: A Sociological Profile. New Delhi: Regency.

Sidel, Mark
2004   States, Markets, and the Nonprofit Sector in South Asia. Tulane Law Review 78(5):1611.

Sidel, Mark, and Iftekhar Zaman, eds.
2004   Philanthropy and Law in South Asia. Quezan City, Phillipines. Asia Pacific Philanthropy Consortium.

Singer, Amy
2008   Charity in Islamic Societies. Cambridge: Cambridge University Press.

Slim, Hugo
1998   Sharing a Universal Ethic: The Principle of Humanity in War. International Journal of Human Rights 2(4):28–48.

2000   Dissolving the Difference between Humanitarianism and Development: The Mixing of a Rights-based Solution. Development in Practice 10(3/4):491–494.

Slovic, Paul
2007   "If I Look at the Mass I Will Never Act": Psychic Numbing and Genocide. Judgment and Decision Making 2(2):79–95.

Smith, Adam
1982   The Theory of Moral Sentiments. D. D. Raphael and A. L. Macfie, eds. Indianapolis: Liberty Fund (original edition 1759).

Smith, Jennie M.
2001   When the Hands Are Many: Community Organization and Social Change in Rural Haiti. Ithaca: Cornell University Press.

Sontag, Susan
2003   Regarding the Pain of Others. New York: Picador, Farrar, Straus and Giroux.

Soussan, Judith
2008   MSF and Protection: Pending or Closed? Paris: MSF CRASH.

Soyez, Veerle, and Eric Broekaert
2005   Therapeutic Communities, Family Therapy, and Humanistic Psychology: History and Current Examples. Journal of Humanistic Psychology 45(3):302–332.

REFERENCES

Sperber, Dan
1985   On Anthropological Knowledge. Cambridge: Cambridge University Press.

Spivak, Gayatri Chakravorty
2004   Righting Wrongs. South Atlantic Quarterly 103(2/3):523–581.

Sridhar, Devi
2008   The Battle against Hunger: Choice, Circumstance, and the World Bank. Oxford: Oxford University Press.

Stadtmauer, Gary J., M.D., Elizabeth Singer M.D., and Eva Metalios M.D.
2010   An Analytical Approach to Clinical Forensic Evaluations of Asylum Seekers: The HealthRight International Human Rights Clinic. Journal of Forensic and Legal Medicine 17(1):41–45.

Steinberg, Kerri P.
2002   Contesting Identities in Jewish Philanthropy. *In* Diasporas in Exile: Varieties of Jewish Identity. Howard Wettstein, ed. Pp. 253–278. Berkeley: University of California Press.

Stephens, Sharon
1995   Children and the Politics of Culture. Princeton: Princeton University Press.

Stirrat, Jock
2006   Competitive Humanitarianism: Relief and the Tsunami in Sri Lanka. Anthropology Today 22(5):11–16.

Stockton, Nicholas
1998   In Defence of Humanitarianism. Disasters 22(4):352–360.

Stoler, Ann
2001   Colonial Aphasia and the Place of Race in France: The Politics of Comparison, 1951–2001: Transatlantic Perspectives on the Colonial Situation, Conference in Honor of George Balandier, April 27–28.

Strathern, Marilyn
1987   The Limits of Auto-anthropology. *In* Anthropology at Home. Anthony Jackson, ed. Pp. 16–35. London: Tavistock.
1988   The Gender of the Gift: Problems with Women and Problems with Society in Melanesia. Berkeley: University of California Press.
2004   Losing (Out on) Intellectual Resources. *In* Law, Anthropology, and the Constitution of the Social: Making Persons and Things. Alain Pottage and Martha Mundy, eds. Pp. 201–233. Cambridge: Cambridge University Press.
2006   A Community of Critics?: Thoughts on New Knowledge. Journal of the Royal Anthropological Institute 12:191–209.

Sullivan, Sheena, and Wu Zunyou
2007   Rapid Scale Up of Harm Reduction in China. International Journal of Drug Policy 18:118–128.

Sundar, Pushpa
1997   Charity for Social Change and Development: Essays on Indian Philanthropy.

Occasional Papers, No. 1. New Delhi: Indian Centre for Philanthropy.

2000   Beyond Business: From Merchant Charity to Corporate Citizenship. New Delhi: Tata McGraw-Hill.

Taithe, Bernard

2004   Reinventing (French) Universalism: Religion, Humanitarianism and the "French Doctors." Modern and Contemporary France 12(2):147–158.

Takkenberg, Lex

1998   The Status of Palestinian Refugees in International Law. Oxford: Clarendon Press.

Tanguy, Joelle

1999   The Médecins Sans Frontières Experience. *In* Framework for Survival: Health, Human Rights, and Humanitarian Assistance in Conflicts and Disasters. Kevin M. Cahill, ed. Pp. 226–244. New York: Routledge.

Tanguy, Joelle, and Fiona Terry

1999   Humanitarian Responsibility and Committed Action: Response to Principles, Politics and Humanitarian Action. Ethics and International Affairs 13(1):29–34.

Tate, Winifred

2007   Counting the Dead: The Culture and Politics of Human Rights Activism in Colombia. Berkeley: University of California Press.

Terrell, John, and Judith Modell

1994   Anthropology and Adoption. American Anthropologist 96(1):155–161.

Terry, Fiona

2001   The Principle of Neutrality: Is It Relevant to MSF? Les Cahiers de Messages 113:1–5.

2002   Condemned to Repeat? The Paradox of Humanitarian Action. Ithaca: Cornell University Press.

Terzani, Folco, producer

1990   Mother Teresa's First Love. Filmakers Library. New York.

Theidon, Kimberly

2007   Gender in Transition: Common Sense, Women, and War. Journal of Human Rights 6:453–478.

Ticktin, Miriam

2005   Policing and Humanitarianism in France: Immigration and the Turn to Law as State of Exception. Interventions: A Journal of Postcolonial Studies 7(3):347–368.

2006a   Where Ethics and Politics Meet: The Violence of Humanitarianism in France. American Ethnologist 33(1):33–49.

2006b   Medical Humanitarianism In and Beyond France: Breaking Down or Patrolling Borders? *In* Medicine at the Border: Disease, Globalization and Security, 1850 to the Present. A. Bashford, ed. Pp. 116–135. New York and Basingstoke: Palgrave Macmillan.

Tirman, John
2003   The New Humanitarianism. How Military Intervention Became the Norm. Boston Review, December 2003/January 2004. http://bostonreview.net/ BR28.6/tirman.html, accessed July 5, 2010.

Tizora, Amos
2004   The Birth and Evolution of REFLECT in Malawi. REFLECT Newsletter 1:1.

Tronto, Joan C.
1993   Moral Boundaries: A Political Argument for an Ethic of Care. New York: Routledge.

Tsing, Anna Lowenhaupt
2000   The Global Situation. Cultural Anthropology 15(3):327–360.
2005   Friction: An Ethnography of Global Connection. Princeton: Princeton University Press.

Tucker, Ruth A.
1988   Guardians of the Great Commission: The Story of Women in Modern Missions. Grand Rapids: Academie Books.

UNDP (United Nations Development Programme)
2001   Malawi Human Development Report 2001. Lilongwe: United Nations Development Programme.

UNICEF
2006   State of the World's Children 2006: Excluded and Invisible.
2007   State of the World's Children 2007: Women and Children: The Double Dividend of Gender Equality.
2008   State of the World's Children 2008: Child Survival.

United Nations Relief and Works Agency
1982   UNRWA: A Brief History, 1950–1982. Vienna: UNRWA.

Vail, Leroy, and Landeg White
1989   Tribalism in the Political History of Malawi. In The Creation of Tribalism in Southern Africa. Leroy Vail, ed. Pp. 151–192. Berkeley: University of California Press.

Vallaeys, Anne
2004   Médecins Sans Frontières: La biographie. Paris: Fayard.

Van der Veer, Peter
1994   Religious Nationalism: Hindus and Muslims in India. Berkeley: University of California Press.

Vaughn, Megan
1991   Curing Their Ills: Colonial Power and African Illness. Stanford: Stanford University Press.

Vernon, James
2007   Hunger: A Modern History. Cambridge: Harvard University Press.

Volkman, Toby Alice

2005   Cultures of Transnational Adoption. Durham: Duke University Press.

Wagner, Sarah

2008   To Know Where He Lies: DNA Technology and the Search for Srebrenica's Missing. Berkeley: University of California Press.

Waldby, Catherine

2000   The Visible Human Project: Informatic Bodies and Posthuman Medicine. London: Routledge.

Walzer, Michael

1977   Just and Unjust Wars: A Moral Argument with Historical Illustrations. New York: Basic Books.

1988   The Company of Critics: Social Criticism and Political Commitment in the Twentieth Century. New York: Basic Books.

Warrier, Maya

2003   Processes of Secularization in Contemporary India: Guru Faith in the Mata Amritanadamayi Mission. Modern Asian Studies 37(1):213–253.

2006   Modernity and Its Imbalances: Constructing Modern Selfhood in the Mata Amritanadamayi Mission. Religion 36:179–195.

Watanabe, Makiko

2004   Japan's Humanitarian Assistance. Humanitarian Exchange 26. http://www.odihpn.org/report.asp?id=2617, accessed June 10, 2010.

Watts, Jonathan

2008   Sex, Drugs, and HIV/AIDS in China. Lancet 371(January 12):103–104.

Weber, Max

1946a   Religious Rejections of the World and Their Directions. In From Max Weber: Essays in Sociology. H. H. Gerth and C. W. Mills, eds. Pp. 323–359. New York: Oxford University Press.

1946b   The Social Psychology of the World Religions. In From Max Weber: Essays in Sociology. H. H. Gerth and C. W. Mills, eds. Pp. 267–301. New York: Oxford University Press.

1993   The Sociology of Religion. Boston: Beacon Press.

Weiner, Annette B.

1992   Inalienable Possessions: The Paradox of Keeping-While-Giving. Berkeley and Los Angeles: University of California Press.

Weiss, Thomas

1999   Principles, Politics, and Humanitarian Action. Ethics and International Affairs 13:1–22.

Weiss, Thomas, and Cindy Collins

1996   Humanitarian Challenges and Intervention: World Politics and the Dilemmas of Help. Boulder: Westview Press.

REFERENCES

Weiss, Thomas, and Larry Minear, eds.
1993   Humanitarianism across Borders: Sustaining Civilians in Times of War. Boulder: Lynne Rienner.

Weissbrodt, David, and Nathaniel Nesbitt
2010   The Role of the United States Supreme Court in Interpreting and Developing Humanitarian Law. University of Minnesota Law School, Legal Studies Research Paper Series, Research Paper 10–31. http://papers.ssrn.com/sol3/papers.cfm?abstract_id=1615224, accessed January 14, 2011.

Weissman, Fabrice, ed.
2004   In the Shadow of "Just Wars": Violence, Politics, and Humanitarian Action. Ithaca: Médecins Sans Frontières/Cornell University Press.

Weitz, Eric
2008   From the Vienna to the Paris System: International Politics and the Entangled Histories of Human Rights, Forced Deportations and Civilizing Missions. American Historical Review 113(5):1313–1343.

Weston, Kath
1991   Families We Choose: Lesbians, Gays, Kinship. New York: Columbia University Press.

Wilson, Richard A.
1997   Representing Human Rights Violations: Social Contexts and Subjectivities. *In* Human Rights, Culture and Context: Anthropological Perspectives. Richard A. Wilson, ed. Pp. 134–160. London: Pluto Press.

Wilson, Richard, and Richard Brown, eds.
2008   Humanitarianism and Suffering: The Mobilization of Empathy. Cambridge: Cambridge University Press.

Wu, Zunyou, Wei Luo, Sheena G. Sullivan, Keming Rou, Peng Lin, Wei Liu, and Zhongqiang Ming
2007   Evaluation of a Needle Social Marketing Strategy to Control HIV among Injecting Drug Users in China. AIDS 21(suppl. 8):S115–S122.

Xiao, Yan, S. Kristensen, J. Sun, L. Lu, and S. H. Vermund
2007   Expansion of HIV/AIDS in China: Lessons from Yunnan Province. Social Science and Medicine 64(3):665–675.

Yala, Amina
2005   Volontaire en ONG: L'aventure ambiguë. Paris: ECLM (Éditions Charles Léopold Mayer).

Yan, Yunxiang
2003   Private Life Under Socialism: Love, Intimacy and Family in a Chinese Village 1949–1999. Palo Alto: Stanford University Press.

Yngvesson, Barbara
2002   Placing the "Gift Child" in Transnational Adoption. Law & Society Review 36(2):227–256.

2004 National Bodies and the Body of the Child: "Competing" Families through International Adoption. *In* Cross-Cultural Approaches to Adoption. F. Bowie, ed. Pp. 211–226. London and New York: Routledge.

Young, Allan
1995 The Harmony of Illusions: Inventing Post-Traumatic Stress Disorder. Princeton: Princeton University Press.

Zelizer, Viviana A. Rotman
1985 Pricing the Priceless Child: The Changing Social Value of Children. New York: Basic Books.

Zhang, Everett Yuehong
2007 The Birth of *Nanke* (Men's Medicine) in China. American Ethnologist 34(3):491–508.

Zhang, Li
2001 Strangers in the City: Reconfigurations of Space, Power, and Social Networks within China's Floating Population. Stanford: Stanford University Press.

Žižek, Slavoj
2005 Against Human Rights. New Left Review 34:115–131.

Zwitter, Andrej
2008 Humanitarian Action on the Battlefields of the Global War on Terror. Journal of Humanitarian Assistance. http://jha.ac/2008/10/25/humanitarian-action-on-the-battlefields-of-the-global-war-on-terror/, accessed June 26, 2010.

Index

School for Advanced Research Advanced Seminar Series

PUBLISHED BY SAR PRESS

Participants in the School for Advanced Research advanced seminar "Between Politics and Ethics: The Anthropology of Global Humanitarianism" co-chaired by Erica Bornstein and Peter Redfield, March 9–13, 2008. *Standing, from left:* Didier Fassin, Ilana Feldman, Lawrence Cohen, Miriam Ticktin, Jonathan Benthall, Peter Redfield, Erica Bornstein. *Seated, from left:* Mariella Pandolfi, Sandra Teresa Hyde. *Not pictured:* Harri Englund. Photograph by Jason S. Ordaz.